Managing at the Leading Edge

Managing at the Leading Edge is a joint initiative of Compass Partnership and the Centre for Civil Society at the London School of Economics. The Lead Sponsor was Zurich. The Supporting Sponsors were the Calouste Gulbenkian Foundation, the Paul Hamlyn Foundation and the Kings Fund.

Praise for Managing at the Leading Edge

'Mike Hudson takes a fresh and innovative look at nonprofit management, and comes up with fascinating results that are well-grounded in theory and relevant to practitioners. Looking at management practices and developments in the US through a UK lens, this book is a treasure trove of thought-provoking ideas and key insights.' *Helmut Anheier, Centennial Professor, London School of Economics and Professor, Public Policy School, UCLA*

'The focus on performance, leadership and governance make *Managing at the Leading Edge* essential reading for tomorrow's NGOs.' *Robert Napier, Chief Executive, World Wide Fund for Nature, UK*

'Mike Hudson is not afraid to draw appropriate lessons from the United States about building capacity, managing performance, creating alliances, funding and leadership, all crucial issues for the UK sector in the next ten years. This is a 'must read'.' *Stuart Etherington, Chief Executive, National Council for Voluntary Organisations*

'*Managing at the Leading Edge* is a terrific resource for all those who care about the performance of nonprofit organizations, from current nonprofit staff and board members to students who will be tomorrow's nonprofit leaders.' *Alan Abramson, Director, Nonprofit Sector and Philanthropy Program, The Aspen Institute*

'The voluntary sector can learn a great deal from inter-country comparisons. This book sets an example of the highest standards.' *Lord Joffe, Chair, The Giving Campaign*

'From building organizational capacity to creating strategic alliances, Hudson highlights numerous best practices among leading nonprofit organizations.' *John H. Graham IV, Chief Executive Officer, American Diabetes Association*

Compass Partnership

Compass Partnership is a management consultancy specialising in the management and development of independent non-profit-seeking organisations. Founded in 1982, Compass has worked with over 800 nonprofit clients and has built up a body of knowledge on management in this field and a tried and tested range of approaches to consultancy. Compass specialises in working in large organisations with complex problems, combining rigorous intellectual analysis with an understanding of how organisations work and how to achieve change.

Compass Partnership e-mail: demerson@compassnet.co.uk Tel: +44 (0)1628 478561

Website: www.compasspartnership.co.uk

The Centre for Civil Society at the London School of Economics seeks to improve understanding of the set of organisations located between the market, the state and household institutions that are variously referred to as non-governmental, voluntary, non-profit and third-sector organisations. These institutions are part of a wider civil society and form a social economy of private organisations serving public purposes.

The Centre's mission is to become the European academic centre of excellence for the study of civil society, social economy and philanthropy.

Website: www.lse.ac.uk

ZURICH

The Zurich Community Trust is a registered charity funded by profits and donations from Zurich's people. It provides an umbrella for all Zurich's community involvement in the UK. Its programmes create sustainable change through long-term funding and active involvement. Its Effective Charities Management Programme helps organisations in the voluntary sector to function more effectively.

Website: www.zurich.org.uk

MIKE HUDSON

Managing at the Leading Edge

NEW CHALLENGES

IN MANAGING

NONPROFIT

ORGANISATIONS

DSC

Published by
Directory of Social Change
24 Stephenson Way
London NW1 2DP
Tel. 08450 77 77 07; Fax 020 7391 4804
E-mail publications@dsc.org.uk
www.dsc.org.uk
from whom further copies and a full books catalogue are available.

Directory of Social Change is a Registered Charity no. 800517

First published 2003
Reprinted 2007

ISBN–10 1 903991 43 9
ISBN–13 978 1 903991 43 5

British Library Cataloguing in Publication Data
A catalogue record for this book is available from the British Library

Cover design by Keith Shaw
Edited by Rosie Clay
Text designed and typeset by GreenGate Publishing Services, Tonbridge
Printed and bound by Page Bros., Norwich

Directory of Social Change Northern Office:
Federation House, Hope Street, Liverpool L1 9BW
0151 708 0136

Contents

Acknowledgements

This book could not have been written without the support of many people and organisations. The research was made possible by the four funders, led by Zurich Community Trust and supported by the Calouste Gulbenkian Foundation, the Paul Hamlyn Foundation and the Kings Fund. I am most grateful for their financial support.

The project was overseen by a Steering Group of leading figures from the UK voluntary sector. Members are listed in Appendix 3. The Group was ably chaired by Richard Gutch, who ten years earlier had travelled to the US to look at practices in contracting nonprofit organisations to deliver public services. The Group met three times to scope the project, hear a mid-term report and consider the emerging findings. Members also commented on an early draft of this book and I am deeply grateful for their support of the project and the time they gave as members of the Steering Group.

The project could not have happened without the support and advice of Helmut Anheier, Centennial Professor at the London School of Economics and Director of the Center for Civil Society at the School of Public Policy and Social Research at UCLA. Helmut's contacts in the US, his willingness to help raise the funds and promote the project, and his academic oversight of the work, were all invaluable.

I am grateful for support from James Austin, Chair of the Initiative on Social Enterprise, and his colleagues at Harvard Business School. James willingly provided names of leading organisations and people to visit and began the 'snowball' that finally led me to the people who were interviewed for the research.

I am particularly grateful to the 65 people who were kind enough to give me time in their busy schedules for interviews, some of which lasted for more than two hours. Their names are listed in Appendix 2 and their contributions are the foundations of this book.

I am also grateful to the many authors whose work I have drawn upon to deepen my understanding the context and key developments in the management and governance of nonprofits in the US. They are all referred to in the text, but I would particularly like to acknowledge Christine Letts, David La Piana, Peter Hall, Lester Salamon, Paul Light,

James Austin, Jane Arsenault, Jed Emerson, Bill Ryan, Burt Nanus, Stephen Dobbs and Frances Hesselbein. I have drawn heavily on your work and I hope I have reflected its significance appropriately.

The draft of this book was reviewed by people on both sides of the Atlantic. From the US I am particularly grateful to Michael Edwards, Director of Governance and Civil Society at the Ford Foundation, Bill Ryan, independent consultant and Research Fellow at the Hauser Centre for Nonprofit Organizations, Char Mollison, Vice President Constituency Services at the Council on Foundations, Abby Snay, Executive Director of Jewish Vocational Services of San Francisco and Marilyn Wyatt, Director of Consulting and Training at BoardSource. Thank you for all your valuable comments.

From the UK I received valuable comments on the draft from members of the Steering Group, Su Sayer, Chief Executive of United Response, David Jones, Principal Grants Officer at the Kings Fund and Keith Smith, a colleague at Compass, who also provided great support and enthusiasm from the first glimmer of the idea to the final full stop in the book. I would also like to thank Mark Rosenman, Distinguished Public Service Professor of the Union Institute who flew over to the UK and provided valuable criticism at a seminar on the findings at the National Council for Voluntary Organisation's Annual Conference. Noel Muddiman, Chief Executive of Motability, and Mike Aaranson, Chief Executive of Save the Children, gave me interviews to provide comparisons with the US interviews.

I would also like to thank all my current and past colleagues at Compass Partnership who have contributed to and challenged my thinking. My current and past clients deserve particular thanks as they have given me the opportunity to work in this field and learn so much from practical experience.

There are a few people who deserve special thanks for their contributions. Chris Staples, Community Affairs Director at Zurich Financial Services, was a funder, a member of the Steering Group and a consistent supporter throughout the project. Melinda Letts was also on the Steering Group and went through the draft manuscript with a tooth-comb, greatly enhancing the logic and the language of the book. Sam Norrington, then my PA at Compass Partnership undertook the task of setting up the first 40 interviews to take place in a three-week period and arranging all the travel between those meetings.

One person who deserves a particular acknowledgement is Natalia Leshchenko, who whilst studying for her Doctorate at the LSE undertook all the early research that identified many of the interviewees. Many nights were spent telephoning and e-mailing to get their agreement to contribute to the project. She also researched and drafted material on the history of the nonprofit sectors in the US and the UK. I am deeply grateful for her never-ending commitment to this project.

Debbie Emerson set up the second trip to the US involving a further 25 interviews to be scheduled into a two-week period and, as with my last book, took responsibility for converting a mixture of typescript and handwritten notes into clean manuscript. I am as ever very grateful for her support.

Finally I am grateful to my wife, Diana, and our four children, Jennifer, Tim, Jessy Anne and Katherine, for putting up with me hiding in my garden office when I should have been being a husband and a father.

Notwithstanding all this support any mistakes and misjudgements in the book are solely my responsibility.

Mike Hudson
August 2003

Permissions

Grateful acknowledgement is made those mentioned below for permission to reprint the following previously published material:

Excerpts from *Forging Nonprofit Alliances* by Jane Arsenault, copyright © 1998 by The National Alliance for Nonprofit Management & Jossey-Bass Inc. Publishers: this material is used by permission of John Wiley & Sons Inc. Excerpts from *Leaders Who Make a Difference* by Burt Nanus and Stephen Dobbs, copyright © 1999 Jossey-Bass Inc. Publishers, Burt Nanus & Stephen Dobbs: this material is used by permission of John Wiley & Sons Inc. Excerpts from *Collaboration Challenge* by James Austin, copyright © 2000 by James E. Austin and The Peter F. Drucker Foundation for Nonprofit Management: this material is used by permission of John Wiley & Sons Inc. Excerpts from *Independent Sector/New Nonprofit Almanac and Desk Reference* by Murray Weitzman *et al.* at the Independent Sector, copyright © 2002 by Independent Sector: this material is used by permission of John Wiley & Sons Inc. Excerpts from Lester M. Salamon, *America's Nonprofit Sector – A Primer*, copyright © 1999 Lester M. Salamon, all rights reserved: printed with permission of the author. Excerpts from Lester M. Salamon *et al.*, *Global Civil Society: Dimensions of the Nonprofit Sector*, copyright © 1999, Lester M. Salamon: reprinted with permission of the author. *The Nonprofit Times Top 100 Organizations*, published in November 2002, downloaded from their website www.nptimes.com and reprinted with permission of Nonprofit Times. Excerpts from *The State of Nonprofit America* by Lester M. Salamon, copyright © 2002, Lester M. Salamon: reprinted with permission of The Brookings Institution Press. Excerpts from *The Capacity Building Challenge* by Paul Light and Elizabeth Hubbard, 2002: reprinted with permission from The Brookings Institution Press. Excerpts from *Echoes from the Field – Proven Capacity Building Principles for Nonprofits* by Allison Fine, Nancy Kopf and Colette Thayer, 2002: reprinted with permission from Innovation Network Inc. Excerpts from *Philanthropy Measures Up* reprinted by permission of the publishers, World Economic Forum, 2003. Excerpts from *Collaboration: What Makes it Work, 2nd Edition*, by Paul Mattessich, Marta Murray-Close and Barbara Monsey, copyright © 2001 Amherst H. Wilder Foundations: used with permission. For more information on Wilder Foundation publications, call 001-800-274-6024. Excerpts from *Raising the Value of Philanthropy* by Dennis Prager, 1999: reprinted with permission of the publishers, Grantmakers In Health. Excerpts from *Reflections on Five Years of Venture Philanthropy Implementation* by Melinda Tuan: reprinted with permission from the publishers, *Alliance Magazine*, Allavida, June 2002, www.allavida.org/alliance Excerpts from *Private Action, Public Benefit* by The Strategy Unit, published by The Cabinet Office, Crown Copyright, 2002. Excerpts from *The Nonprofit Governance Index* by BoardSource and Stanford University, a publication of BoardSource, formerly the National Center for Nonprofit Boards. For more information about BoardSource, call 001-800-883-6262 or visit www.boardsource.org BoardSource © 2000. Text may not be reproduced without written permission from BoardSource. Key Statistical Comparisons 2001 data downloaded from the website of Organisation for Economic Co-operation and Development (www.oecd.org), source: OECD Main Economics: Page 1 Population Statistics OECD copyright © 2003; page 1 Gross Domestic Product for OECD countries, copyright © OECD 2003; pages 1 and 3 Basic Structural Statistics, copyright © OECD 2003. Excerpts from *Women's World Banking: Catalytic Change Through Networks*, copyright © 1999 by the President and Fellows of Harvard College. Harvard Business School case 9-300-050 by J.E. Austin was written as a basis for class discussion rather than to illustrate either

About the author

Mike Hudson is the Director of Compass Partnership. He was the Administrative Director of Friends of the Earth during its formative years. Following this, Mike worked in the UK and US for a business strategy consultancy.

He has worked as a consultant to not-for-profit organisations for 20 years leading teams that bring about major change in complex organisations. His clients include the chairs and chief executives of a wide range of national and international organisations in the voluntary, housing, education, international aid and arts sectors.

His book, *Managing Without Profit: The Art of Managing Third Sector Organizations* (Penguin 1999 and Directory of Social Change 2002), is in its second edition, has been translated into two other languages and has sold over 15,000 copies. He is a Visiting Fellow at the London School of Economics.

About DSC

The Directory of Social Change (DSC) aims to help voluntary and community organisations become more effective. A charity ourselves, we are the leading provider of information and training for the voluntary sector.

We run more than 350 training courses each year as well as conferences, many of which run on an annual basis. We also publish an extensive range of guides, handbooks and CD-ROMs for the voluntary sector, covering subjects such as fundraising, management, communication, finance and law. Our trusts database is available on both a CD-ROM and a subscription website.

Charityfair, the annual three-day conference, events programme and exhibition, is organised by DSC and takes place each spring.

For details of all our activities, and to order publications and book courses, go to www.dsc.org.uk or call 020 7391 4800.

Glossary

This glossary has been written primarily for people outside the US. It describes frequently used terms in the US that are not so common elsewhere.

Capacity building Strengthening organisations by investing internally in their people, systems and technology, and externally in new ideas, services and relationships.

Chapter The branch of a national, regional or state level organisation.

Charitable and religious organisation An organisation that can receive tax-deductible contributions, is registered under section 501 (c) (3) of the Internal Revenue Service Tax Code but has limits on its lobbying activities.

Faith-based organisation An organisation whose origin is a church, congregation or other religious entity and that provides services to people in need. Under current law, if such organisations receive government grants or contracts, they cannot use those funds to proselytise to their service users and they must follow federal anti-discrimination laws in recruitment. Not to be confused with organisations with religious origins that provide services but do not proselytise.

Balanced scorecard A package of measures for reporting on organisations' health and performance.

High engagement philanthropy A funding relationship in which the funder provides a range of support to organisations and expects a high level of accountability for results from the organisation.

Human services A generic term covering a wide range of activities including social services and employment services.

Independent sector A term used to describe the nonprofit sector comprising several categories of tax-exempt organisations under US law, including charitable and religious organisations, associations, philanthropic foundations, and social welfare organisations. Not to be confused with Independent Sector, the umbrella organisation that represents some of these organisations.

Management service organisation An organisation that provides 'back office' services such as finance, human relations, information technology and facilities management for a number of nonprofit organisations.

Management support organisation An organisation that exists at city, state, regional or national levels to provide management and technical support to nonprofit organisations. It may be nonprofit or for-profit.

Nonprofit capital market The market created by suppliers of funds, such as foundations, government and individuals, and the recipients of funds.

Nonprofit organisation An organisation that is chartered under federal law, separate from government, non-profit distributing, self governing, voluntary and of public benefit.

Nonprofit sector The widest term defining the sector. The term covers independent sector organisations, cooperatives, social and fraternal organisations, business and professional associations, labour unions and political parties.

Outcome measurement Quantitative and qualitative measures of what organisations achieve.

Performance management The process of measuring and managing organisations' overall achievements, learning from experience and using the knowledge to inform strategic decisions.

Programme related investment Investment of a foundation's capital directly into nonprofit organisations and social enterprise usually as low-cost or no-cost loans for buildings or other capital investments and sometimes for programmes.

Scale deep Achieving greater impact in the local community by reaching more of the client population, finding new ways to serve them or extending current services to different client groups.

Scale up The replication of successful programmes to increase an organisation's impact and to achieve economies of scale.

Social return on investment A financial measure of the value to society of organisations that help under-privileged people. It is based on reduced use of public services and increased contributions to society through the payment of taxes (defined more fully on pages 81 and 82).

Social welfare organisation Strictly speaking the term defines a nonprofit organisation that cannot receive tax deductible contributions, is registered under section 501 (c) (4) of the Internal Revenue Service Tax Code, but does not have limits on its spending on lobbying activities. However, it is used more loosely to mean charitable organisations registered under 501 (c) (3) of the Tax Code that often provide social welfare.

Strategic alliance A significant, long-term relationship between organisations that share resources to achieve their missions more effectively. The term includes joint ventures, group structures, mergers and other relationships that are defined in Chapter 4.

Strategy map A chart setting out the key drivers required to deliver impact and the associated performance measures.

Technical assistance Management, functional, specialist and technical support provided to nonprofit organisations to enable them to achieve their missions more effectively.

Venture philanthropy A source of substantial, long-term funding and management support linked tightly to ambitious performance targets and rigorous accountability to the funders (explained in section 5.3).

Note

Throughout the book single quotation marks indicate quotations from published sources and double quotation marks indicate quotations from interviews with me, or in a few cases, with other interviewers.

Introduction

Nonprofit organisations in many parts of the developed world were transformed during the last quarter of the twentieth century. In the 1960s and 70s they were seen as disparate and unconnected organisations at the margins of health care, education, international development, medical research and other fields. Most were small, employed few staff and were run on a shoestring. Concepts of management were either not understood or positively shunned because they were seen as being relevant only to business.

Today, many countries see these organisations as the constituent parts of the 'third sector' – organisations that do not exist to make profits and are not part of the public sector. They are viewed by government, academics and the sector itself as being critical elements of civil society.

It is increasingly recognised that community, social, cultural and even economic development all depend on a diverse and healthy nonprofit sector. Community development is almost entirely based on nonprofit organisations such as clubs, churches, community centres and action groups. Social development is based on local and national networks of organisations for health, disability, social welfare and campaigning groups for almost every facet of human and animal life. Cultural development is heavily dependent on nonprofit arts organisations, and economic development is supported by nonprofit trade and professional associations and by business promotion organisations.

These organisations play a critically important role in the democratic process. They represent people's views to local and national governments on a wide range of issues. They reflect the diverse and fragmented nature of modern society and they provide some of the 'glue' that holds that society together.

They are also renowned as the instigators of new ideas and social innovations. Many of the great services that people in these countries now take for granted were incubated in nonprofit organisations before governments saw their value, and made them universally available.

Recognition of the crucial roles that the sector plays has led to greatly increased government and private funding which has in turn driven dramatic growth of the sector. Today these organisations deliver a huge range of essential services and they mobilise the great campaigns of our time. Increased income from donations, foundations, bequests and other sources has created organisations that now have significant resources at their disposal.

Management has been professionalised

Twenty to thirty years ago these organisations were often run by amateurs – people who believed in a cause and wanted to do something about it but who did not always have the necessary management expertise.

Today many of these organisations are managed by talented professionals, supported by a growing body of knowledge about the special characteristics of nonprofit organisations, and the skills required to manage these, as opposed to public and private concerns. The techniques of working with multiple stakeholders, of juggling diverse income streams into an ever wider range of activities and of responding to increased public scrutiny are now well understood by experienced nonprofit managers and board members.

Nonprofit organisations have been through enormous change already, but more change is undoubtedly on the horizon. The sector will grow even further over the coming years. Governments are likely to continue to contract out more services currently delivered by the public sector. Private income is predicted to grow as significant numbers of very wealthy people come to the end of their lives and want to benefit others through creating private foundations and bequests. Managers and board members now face a new set of questions about how to increase further the impact of their organisations and about how they should direct their own efforts.

There are demands that nonprofit organisations should report on the results they achieve, in addition to their activities and finances. There is pressure to discover which services really make a difference, to focus their activities and to 'scale up' so they achieve greater impact. There is pressure to form strategic alliances, with other nonprofit organisations and with the public and private sectors, to achieve ever more demanding objectives. There is an expectation that these organisations become more sustainable, rather than lurching from one challenge to the next. There is increased regulation, sometimes from bodies that have different and conflicting requirements. These are just a few of many challenges that managers are now facing.

Critical questions for the future

This is the context in which I set out to answer some critical questions about the future management and governance of nonprofit organisations in developed countries:

- What are the leading-edge approaches to managing nonprofit organisations?
- What should managers and board members be doing differently to enhance the performance of their organisations?
- How can the impact of the nonprofit sector be significantly increased?

To gain some new insights into these questions, I decided to visit the US. I chose America because it has the largest nonprofit sector in the world with over 1.2 million nonprofit organisations, attracting revenues of over \$486 billion.[1] It accounts for 6.7% of national income, compared to the government sector which contributes 13.3%.[1] It employs almost 11 million people, representing 7.1% of the workforce.[1] Such size enables it to support a significant research community at leading universities and a large infrastructure of intermediary or umbrella bodies.

I did not assume that ideas from the US were necessarily better than ideas from elsewhere. Indeed there are practices elsewhere in the world that would be of great interest to managers in the US. But I did suspect that chief executives, senior managers, consultants and academics could provide a rich source of new data on these questions.

The research

The research was based on 65 face-to-face interviews with chief executives and senior managers of nonprofit organisations, foundations and umbrella bodies, leading academics, and consultants who specialise in the sector. They were chosen through a process known in the academic world as 'snowballing' – identifying leading figures in the field and asking them for examples of well-managed organisations and of people who were saying and writing interesting things about management. In addition the project team approached organisations and individuals mentioned in the literature and reviewed lists such as the Arco '100 best nonprofits to work for', the *NonProfit Times*' list of the largest organisations and the Foundation Center's list of largest foundations. Over 100 books and reports were gathered and reviewed to supplement the data from the interviews.

I set out with a list of headings concerned with management, governance, leadership, mergers, teams and organisation learning. I did discuss these, but overwhelmingly the subjects that people talked about were capacity building, performance management, strategic alliances and the other topics that have become the chapters of this book.

It could be argued that selecting interviewees who are at the top of organisations or who advise those at the top, and combining these with the opinions and prejudices I bring from my own experience, led to the conclusions I wanted to find. To minimise these risks I interviewed academics as well as leaders and a sample of Americans reviewed the draft of this book.

A further doubt concerns the ways in which the approaches to management and governance set out in this book are experienced by people in the middle and at the front line of organisations. Perhaps they see them as management 'fads' that in practice contribute little to organisational effectiveness. No doubt some do, but the combination of the evidence from the interviews, the literature review, and monitoring the US nonprofit sector press (which can be highly critical), leads me to conclude that I have captured the essence of either what people think makes a difference or what has been demonstrated to work in practice. I believe the research has identified the ideas that can contribute most to the effectiveness of nonprofit organisations. These are the cutting-edge issues on which managers and board members can have greatest impact.

These topics are not new to managers and board members in the UK. All of them are being considered and acted upon in some parts of the sector. What is different is that the nonprofit sector in the US has the scale and the resources to invest significant funding in each of the areas reviewed, to research their impact more systematically and to spread good practices more quickly. As a result, even allowing for some significant cultural differences, there is much that managers, board members and policy makers in the UK and other countries can learn from their experiences.

The research was undertaken when the US economy was peaking, the stock market bubble had not completely burst and significant additional funds were flowing into the sector. As the book goes to print, there are growing concerns about funding and a recognition that in future there will far less money to invest in the ideas set out here. However, one of the enduring characteristics of the sector is its robustness in the face of external challenge. The most recent book on the sector characterises the history of the sector as 'a story of resilience'.[2] So whilst there may be a downturn in the short term, I suspect that when better times come, these same six issues will emerge as the topics that give managers and board members the greatest grip on the organisations for which they are responsible.

The book

This book is the result of the journey I undertook. The aim of the journey was to get an overview – a task that is often easier for an outsider – and to tease out some of the most interesting developments.

The book is a report of what I learned set in the context of the latest academic and practitioner literature. It is seen through the eyes of someone who has worked in, consulted to and studied the sector in the UK for over 20 years. It aims to inform and inspire people who wish to champion the sector and see it achieve even more over the coming years.

A number of my interviewees reminded me of the journey made by the French political scientist Alexis de Tocqueville in 1831. He spent nine months touring the country and on returning to France wrote *Democracy in America* – a treatise that is used in courses today and frequently referred to in the literature on nonprofits. Like me, de Tocqueville travelled to New York, Boston and Washington and we both had the benefit of seeing a country from outside, of being warmly welcomed by many people and of having time to reflect on what we learned.

The parallel ends there because my visit was shorter and more comfortable (he had to travel on horseback). He spent time in the Mid-west and the South and did not venture further west than Michigan whilst I had the pleasure of travelling to the West Coast. His book was an enduring review of democracy whilst mine focuses on one part of life in the US – the management and governance of nonprofit organisations.

The central propositions

It took the nonprofit sector in the developed world many years to accept notions of management and to begin to understand what is distinctive about managing nonprofits organisations. Business management experience provided a good source of ideas, but the approaches that worked for business did not always work for nonprofits. The sector is now developing its own understanding of the distinctive competencies required to create effective nonprofit organisations.

There is also a growing recognition amongst some organisations primarily concerned with service delivery that their current approaches will not resolve the more fundamental issues the nation faces. For example, food distribution may offer temporary assistance for hungry people but it will not solve the problem of people unable to feed themselves. Service organisations may focus their resources on deprived people, but that will not address the fundamental problem of growing disparities between the rich and the poor.

It is in this context that this book makes six central propositions. Nonprofit organisations need to:

1 **Strengthen their own capacity** – they need to invest much more heavily in their people, systems and infrastructure so that they have the organisational capacity to deliver greater impact. This is not about creating unnecessary administration and bureaucracy – it is about systematically building organisations that have the clout to make a sustainable difference to pressing social, economic and environmental problems.

2 **Manage performance** – they need to develop a clear understanding of what performance means, how it should be measured and then focus people and systems sharply on the desired results. Reporting on what an organisation does is no longer sufficient – it is the results that matter.

3 **Create strategic alliances** – they need to work with each other and with public and private sector organisations in long-term strategic alliances. Working in isolation is not an option – there is too much to be learned from other nonprofits and from private and public sector organisations.

4 **Exploit changing patterns of funding** – they need to understand the difference between capital and revenue funding, tap into a much wider range of sources of finance and structure their funding to use different types of finance to suit different circumstances.

5 **Be led with integrity** – leaders need to mobilise people around the mission, focus them on results, create small teams and invest in leadership and management development so everyone is motivated to achieve the organisation's objectives.

6 **Continuously strengthen their governance** – board members and managers need to establish crystal clarity over the board's role, structure the board around governance tasks, and monitor the

performance of the board and its members in an open and transparent way.

Together these propositions add up to a new agenda that is about paying much greater attention to outcomes and focusing the whole organisation on achieving them.

Application of the propositions

One of the most vital characteristics of the nonprofit sector in the US and other countries is its extraordinary diversity. There are organisations for almost every conceivable human activity. Some exist primarily to provide services and some were created to change the way people behave, the balance of power and our very conception of society and the environment in which we live.

It might be assumed that this book provides an agenda for service-delivering organisations rather than campaigning organisations. That is not the case. I spoke with organisations that exist to achieve social change as well as with those that deliver services and have a strong social change agenda. The propositions are applicable to both, though they are frequently much more difficult to implement in more politicised campaigning organisations that often have the widest agenda and the least resources.

The propositions in this book apply mainly to medium-sized and large organisations – those that employ 10 or more staff and those with an income of £1 million per annum or more. I recognise the importance of smaller organisations and that they form the majority in many countries. But appropriate approaches to managing and governing small organisations are very different from those required by larger organisations and my experience and interest is in the latter.

An overriding characteristic of the nonprofit sector throughout the world, as in the US, is the extraordinary variety of organisations. They all have different histories, stakeholders and sources of finance; they champion different causes and have different cultures. They are also full of contradictions and ambiguities. No two nonprofit organisations are quite the same.

Consequently approaches to management and governance that are appropriate for some may be entirely inappropriate for others. There are principles, but they do not always hold, and there is good practice, but it may not be right for some organisations. So whilst you, like me, may get excited by some of the ideas in this book, it comes with a health warning – take those parts that really fit the needs of your organisation today and leave the rest for others to use in different circumstances and at different times.

The audience

This book has been written for:

- managers and board members of nonprofit organisations
- funders who provide the resources
- fundraisers who seek the funding
- intermediary bodies that support the sector
- academics who study the sector
- consultants who assist the sector.

I wrote for readers from outside the US who wanted a glimpse into the country as well as for those in America who wanted an overview from an outsider.

Following the contextual opening chapter, the book is set out in the order in which managers and board members might think about strengthening their organisations. It will sometimes be logical to start by building organisation capacity and establishing systems for measuring performance. When the organisation is strong, they can consider creating strategic alliances and diversifying funding. They will then need stronger leadership at every level of the organisation and finally they will need to strengthen the arrangements for governance.

However, every organisation has to carry out its own assessment of its performance and determine which investments in organisation devel- opment will bring the greatest rewards. In practice the place to start will vary from organisation to organisation. Each chapter, therefore, has been written to stand on its own, so the book can be read in any order the reader wishes.

The book contains a mixture of quotations from my interviews and from the literature. Throughout this book, single quotation marks are used to identify quotations from books and reports and double quota- tions are used to identify what people said in interviews with me or, in a few cases, in other interviews.

I consider this first version of the book to be 'work in progress'. There is always more work to be done to understand what truly makes a differ- ence in management and governance. I would therefore warmly welcome challenges to what I found, further examples of successful implementation of the ideas presented and identification of concepts that I have overlooked. Please send your views to **Compass Partnership, Greenbanks, New Road, Bourne End, Bucks, SL8 5BZ, England** or to mhudson@compassnet.co.uk. I look forward to hearing from you and promise to reply.

References

1 Murray Weitzman *et al.* at Independent Sector, *The New Nonprofit Almanac and Desk Reference*, San Francisco, Jossey-Bass, 2002

2 Lester Salamon, *The State of Nonprofit America*, Washington, Brookings Institution Press, 2002

1 Setting the context

At the heart of this book is an agenda for the management and governance of nonprofit organisations in developed countries – an agenda aimed at helping organisations meet the challenges of the coming years.

In order to identify the key components of this blueprint, managers and board members need to find out what ideas and practices can contribute most to the effectiveness of nonprofit organisations. The US has the biggest nonprofit sector in the world. Its practices are not necessarily any better or worse than those of other developed countries, but the extent and breadth of the sector offers an incomparably rich source of data and experience.

Total income to the US nonprofit sector exceeds $486 billion, accounting for 6.7% of national income.[1] If the sector was a separate country its revenues would be greater than the total economic activity of most countries of the world including India, Australia, Canada, The Netherlands and Spain.[2]

The sector consists of 1.6 million formally constituted organisations, a number that is growing at over 5% per year, twice the rate of formation of business organisations. It employs over 11 million people and it benefits, in addition, from voluntary effort of almost 6 million full-time equivalent people. This represents just over 7% of the total US paid and voluntary workforce.[1]

Nonprofit organisations provide a huge range of services in health care, education, social services, culture, employment and training, housing, community development and emergency aid. They are responsible for:

- half the nation's hospitals
- one-third of its health clinics
- over a quarter of its nursing homes
- nearly half (46%) of its higher education institutions
- four-fifths (80%) of its individual and family service agencies
- 70% of it vocational rehabilitation services
- 30% of day care services
- over 90% of its orchestras and operas
- delivering over 70% of its foreign disaster assistance.

Source: Lester Salamon, *The State of Nonprofit America*[3]

Nonprofit organisations drive campaigns for social improvement, and have been responsible for creating many of the great movements for change. Campaigns against slavery and for women's suffrage, civil rights, environmental protection and gay rights have all been orchestrated through nonprofit organisations.

These organisations, 'give institutional expression to two seemingly contradictory principles that are both important parts of American national character; the principle of individualism – the notion that people should have freedom to act on matters that concern them – and the principle of solidarity – the notion that people have responsibilities not only to themselves, but also to their fellow human beings and to the communities of which they are part'.[3]

Giving is an essential part of the American character, and it is reflected in the $212 billion given annually by individuals, foundations and corporations.[4] People also give their time, with 110 million people (56% of the population over 18 years) volunteering an average of 3.5 hours per week.[1]

This commitment to nonprofit action derives in part from distrust of government involvement in the delivery of many services. There is a strong view that if people want action, then they must organise to make it happen. It is not that American people are against government in principle, it is that they believe government should only undertake those activities that it is uniquely positioned to carry out. This perspective is reflected in the fact that the business sector accounts for 80% of national income, the government sector just over 13% and the nonprofit sector almost 7%. It is more than half as big as government when assigned values for volunteers and unpaid family workers are included.[1]

This chapter

Chapter 1 sets the context for the book by:

- reviewing the roots of nonprofit activity in the US
- identifying key developments in the twentieth century
- analysing the size and shape of the sector today
- exploring the current policy issues.

The first two sections draw heavily on work by Peter Hall, a leading author on the history of the nonprofit sector.

1.1 The roots of nonprofit activity in the US

As America was once a British colony, the roots of nonprofit organisation can be traced back to the Elizabethan Statute of Charitable Uses Act of 1601. Up to the time of the War of Independence (1775–83), colonial legislatures did not have power to create corporations. The immense difficulty of creating formalised organisations meant that charitable activity was carried out primarily in the sphere of personal action rather than through organisations.

After the War, private corporations were formed to serve public purposes such as the creation of bridges, turnpikes and canals. These corporations were delegated powers by the state, but their existence was time limited and they were viewed more as stewards of public funds than organisations created to make profits. States' policies towards corporations differed, ranging from encouragement in New England to hostility in the South. There was much tension between the role private corporations and that of the state.

In the early years of the nineteenth century, views on the need for nonprofit corporations were divided. The 'federalists' believed in strong government and argued for the delegation of state power to groups of respectable individuals. The 'dissenters' remained steadfastly hostile to private nonprofit corporations.[5]

The federalist view began to prevail as churches, bible societies, lyceums and teachers' institutes all began to reach out for public support and a culture of organisation began to take hold. Development was strongly influenced by those who favoured the nonprofit role. 'Wherever an orphanage, a library, a college, a hospital, an academy or a professional society originated, it was almost invariably the work of a migrant New Englander with evangelical connections'.[6] However, it was not until 1844 that the Supreme Court placed private nonprofit corporations under federal law, a decision which began the process of creating a uniform set of regulations around nonprofit activity.

The growth of private business that wanted to operate on a national scale led to demands for a more educated workforce which in turn led business to fund nonprofit organisations, in particular colleges. Universities and colleges were funded by business and academic research centres were used to gather and interpret social information needed by for-profit companies. Gifts and bequests to Harvard University reached almost $6 million in the five years to 1890. Other fields also benefited, as business and individuals financed the growth of libraries, hospitals and professional organisations. Middle and lower classes also contributed to the burgeoning sector through the establishment of labour unions, mutual benefit societies, volunteer fire companies, building and loan associations and even cooperatively owned nonprofit businesses.[5]

The processes of industrialisation and urbanisation, and the economic liberalism of the nineteenth century facilitated and encouraged growth of philanthropic activity. Whilst this growth led to further debate about the relationship between the nonprofit sector and the state, nonprofit activity was unequivocally seen as an alternative to governmental welfare provision. 'Private non-profit corporations became the main form of social palliative, dislodging the competing idea that it should fall into the sphere of governmental competence'.[5]

The nineteenth century is referred to as the 'golden age of philanthropy', and it reflected social, cultural and economic conditions of that period. However, the concept of a distinct and separate nonprofit sector only emerged towards the end of the century.[7] Reformers started to rationalise organisations by creating 'united charities' which combined the resources of small organisations and state organisations known as charity commissions. This began a period of professionalisation and management improvement which led to the creation of today's nationwide organisations such as the Red Cross and United Way.

1.2 Key developments in the twentieth century

At the turn of the century Americans remained averse to government solutions to social and economic problems. Private solutions were voluntary, and their survival and success depended on how efficiently organisations were run, not on government legislation. These views were strengthened by the disreputable and uncontrollable nature of American politics that discouraged people from giving greater powers to government.[5]

Around the turn of the century wealthy Americans began creating a new type of philanthropic institution, the charitable foundation.[5] In 1889 the steel industry tycoon and generous philanthropist Andrew Carnegie wrote an influential essay entitled 'The Gospel of Wealth' which argued that philanthropy should orient itself not to the cure but to prevention of social problems. This led to the establishment of a new type of organisation known as an 'open-ended' foundation. The contributors provided money to a panel of experts who chose which projects to support. The first 'open-ended' foundation in the US was the Sage Foundation (1907) and it was followed by Rockefeller Foundation (1917).

The establishment of these foundations was controversial. There were fears that they might have undue influence on public policy and this made them very cautious in their funding decisions. It was left to a few, such as the Brookings Institution (1916) and the Twentieth Century Fund (1919) to address public policy issues directly.

The dominant model of social welfare during the first quarter of the twentieth century was known as 'welfare capitalism'. Starting in the 1880s, welfare capitalism aimed to encourage firms to work more efficiently and more equitably. It involved both the construction of company towns and investments in people to make them more productive and enable them to identify more closely with their employers. As a result, the role of nonprofit sector in social welfare provision was considerable and often greater than that of the government.

Until 1930, private sector welfare provision was also seen as the main means of thwarting socialism. The dominant paradigm was known as the 'associative state', developed under the influence of Herbert Hoover's book *American Individualism* published in 1922.[8] This model encouraged reliance on cooperative institutions.[5] An important feature of the model was National Recovery Administration – a system of agreements by which the government guaranteed stability to for-profit and nonprofit corporations in return for their work generating employment and delivering social services.

This 'private' alternative did not withstand the economic depression of 1929–33. As business became less able to provide social services, the government stepped in. The foundations of America's social welfare system were established in Roosevelt's 'New Deal'. The main programmes included the provision of old-age pensions, unemployment insurance and needs-tested cash assistance for elderly and disabled people and families with dependent children.

These welfare policies, with increased taxation of the rich on the one hand, and encouragement of charitable donations on the other, spawned a rapid increase in the number of foundations, from 239 in 1930 to 535 in 1939.[9] Private nonprofit organisations continued to perform a significant role due to the patchy nature of public provision, but in the general atmosphere of insecurity, nonprofits were not seen to be particularly innovative during this period.

The Second World War led to greater government involvement in the provision of social services. Before the War, the nonprofit and for-profit sectors provided basic social, cultural and welfare services with encouragement from government. After the War, the government assumed greater responsibility for the provision of social services, and it employed the non-profit sector to deliver them.

The 1960s were a period of significant expansion of federal programmes, including Medicare, the federal health insurance programme for the elderly, and Medicaid, the programme to finance health care for poor people. Support for research at universities and new social service and community development programmes also grew rapidly. However, because of Americans' ingrained hostility to centralised government, new services were delivered by a mixture of state and city governments and most notably by nonprofit organisations, reflecting the long-standing inter-relationships between government and nonprofit organisations stretching back to colonial times.[10] Moreover, even when states and cities received funding they often sub-contracted delivery to the nonprofit sector.

In the 1970s, the statutory-nonprofit relationship was scrutinised in a number of governmental and private reports including the Filer Commission report in 1973. They arrived at similar conclusions about the necessity of continued governmental support for the sector and expediency of tax incentives to encourage charitable giving.[11]

By the late 1970s, nonprofit organisations were delivering a larger share of government-financed human services than all levels of government combined, and income from government support grew to almost twice the income from private charitable donations. It seemed that a consensus was emerging on the value of statutory-nonprofit partnership.

This understanding was changed during the 1980s and early 1990s when the traditional conservative commitment to limiting the role of the state and minimising social spending had a huge impact on the nonprofit sector. The government's withdrawal from social service provision was presented during the Regan years as 'freeing the field', or creating opportunities for nonprofits. Further tax incentives for charitable giving were introduced.

As government spending on social service provision fell, so did nonprofits' income. It is estimated that the nonprofit sector (outside the health field)

Key dates in the history of the US nonprofit sector

Policy developments	Organisations established
1601 Statute of Charitable Uses Act	
1792 Virginia repeals Statute of Charitable Uses	
1835 De Tocqueville's *Democracy in America* published	
1844 Private nonprofit corporations placed under federal law	1881 American Red Cross
	1860 Boys and Girls Club of America
	1887 United Way Denver
1894 Tax exemptions for charitable organisations	1896 Volunteers of America
	1900 Cleveland Community Foundation
	1902 Goodwill Industries
	1907 The Sage Foundation
	1913 Rockefeller Foundation American Cancer Society
1917 Charitable tax deductions permitted for individuals	1916 Planned Parenthood Federation
	1924 American Heart Association New York Community Trust
	1926 Charles Stewart Mott Foundation
1936 Charitable tax deductions permitted for corporations	1937 Lilly Endowment
	1948 Annie E Casey Foundation
	1951 The Nature Conservancy
1965 Establishment of Medicare and Medicaid	1964 David and Lucile Packard Foundation
1969 Tax reform Act put foundations under federal oversight	1969 Public Broadcasting Service
1973 Filer Commission highlighted lack of knowledge of the sector	1976 Habitat for Humanity
	1979 America's Second Harvest
	1980 Independent Sector
	1996 California Endowment
2001 CARE Act proposed support for faith-based organisation	

lost $17 billion in governmental support between 1982 and 1985, with a reduction of up to 36% in federal support for social service organisations.[11]

In 1992 Bill Clinton was elected to the presidency and growth in some programmes resumed, particularly support for children and families and programmes to encourage poor people to become more self-sufficient. From 1989 to 1994, the expansion of eligibility for Medicaid and the widening of Medicare payments to include home health care contributed to a real increase of 39% in health spending. Income assistance spending increased and social service spending grew by 19% during this five-year period.[2]

Overall income to the independent sector grew by 17% in real terms from 1992 to 1998 (the most recent year for total income figures[1]) driven mainly by increased fee income for nursing home care and children's day care. Income from donations, for which more recent data is published, also showed an acceleration towards the end of the decade and registered a small decline in real terms in 2001.[4] Following the bursting of the stock market bubble and the slow-down in the US economy, it became clear that the boom years of the 1990s had come to an end and the sector was again facing a tougher period.

1.3 The size and shape of the sector today

Although inter-country comparisons are notoriously difficult, the nonprofit sector in the US is many times larger than its equivalent in all other countries of the world in terms of total revenues and number of employees. It is six times larger in revenue terms than any other country besides Japan and it employs around five times as many people as any other country.[12]

Country	Nonprofit cash revenues $bn	Country	Nonprofit cash revenues $bn
US	632	Argentina	15
Japan	287	Brazil	12
Germany	96	Israel	11
UK	82	Austria	7
Netherlands	61	Finland	6
France	58	Ireland	5
Australia	21	Czech Republic	1

Source: Lester Salamon and Wojciech Sokolowski, *Global Civil Society – Dimensions of the Nonprofit Sector*[12]

Although the US nonprofit sector has greater income than the nonprofit sectors of Japan, Germany, the UK, the Netherlands, France, Australia, Argentina and Brazil combined, it is not the largest in relative terms. Comparing the nonprofit sector's share of total paid employment, the US is only the fifth largest:

Nonprofit share of paid employment in different countries

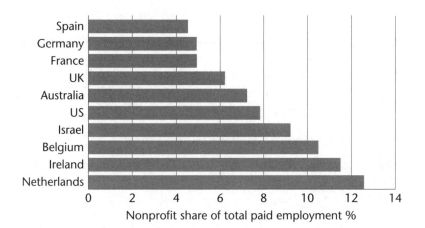

Nonprofit share of total paid employment %

Source: Lester Salamon and Wojciech Sokolowski, *Global Civil Society – Dimensions of the Nonprofit Sector*[12]

Nonprofit organisations in the US today are defined by a leading research authority[2] as having six characteristics. They are a collection of entities that are:

- **Organisations** – most commonly they are corporations chartered under state law. This excludes informal and temporary gatherings of people.
- **Private** – they are separate from government. Although they receive significant government funding, their boards are not dominated by government officials.
- **Non-profit distributing** – they may accumulate profits, but these must be re-invested in achieving the organisation's mission.
- **Self governing** – they have their own governance arrangements and are not controlled by outside entities.
- **Voluntary** – they involve volunteers on the board and often in delivering the organisation's work as well.
- **Of public benefit** – they serve some public purpose and contribute to the public good.

Types of nonprofit organisations

There is no single body of law regulating nonprofit organisations in the US. Instead, they are governed by a multitude of separate federal and state laws. The formation of nonprofit organisations has traditionally been seen as a right rather than a privilege bestowed by government. Whilst individuals can come together to create organisations, they need to pass a set of federal tax laws to be exempted from federal income taxes.

The US tax code differentiates 25 different classes of tax exempt organisations which can be divided into two broad categories – public-serving organisations that exist primarily to benefit the general public and member-serving organisations that exist primarily to benefit a defined group of people.

There are two categories of public-serving organisations:

- charitable and religious organisations defined in the Internal Revenue Code with the snappy title of '501(c) (3)s'
- social welfare organisations, known as '501(c) (4)s'.

Both categories must work for public benefit, rather than member benefit. The first category, charitable and religious organisations, is the only group that can receive tax deductible contributions from individuals and corporations, and there are restrictions on the legislative lobbying they can undertake. The second category, social welfare organisations, cannot receive tax deductible donations but can lobby for legislative changes.

These two categories are known as the independent sector and together they account for 6.1% of national income. The remaining 23 classes of tax-exempt organisations account for a further 0.6% of national income.

Distribution of national income by major sector 1998

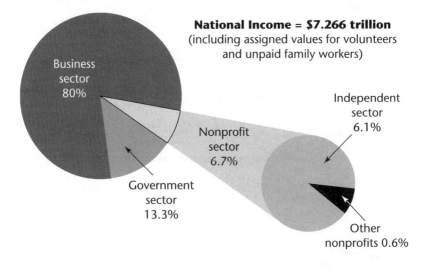

National Income = $7.266 trillion
(including assigned values for volunteers and unpaid family workers)

Business sector 80%

Independent sector 6.1%

Nonprofit sector 6.7%

Government sector 13.3%

Other nonprofits 0.6%

Source: Murray Weitzman *et al., The New Nonprofit Almanac and Desk Reference*[1]

Number of organisations

Calculating the number of nonprofit organisations is not easy in any country because there is no clear-cut boundary between 'formal' and 'informal' organisations. In the US organisations with revenues of less than $5,000 per year are not required to register with the Inland Revenue Service.

There are a total of 1.6 million formally constituted nonprofit organisa-tions in the US, including 734,000 charitable and religious organisations, 140,000 social welfare organisations and 400,000 other organisations.[1]

Over the 10 years to 1997, the latest year for which figures are available, the total number of independent sector organisations grew at an annual rate of 2.7% and within this sector, the number of charitable and reli-gious organisations grew even faster, at 5.1% per year.[1]

Anatomy of the nonprofit sector – estimates of the number of organisations

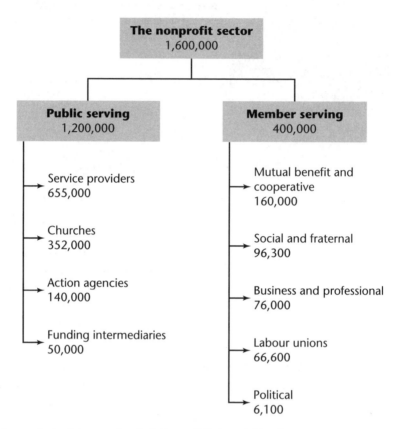

Source: Lester Salamon, *America's Nonprofit Sector – A Primer*[2]

Sources of income

In the US, release of statistical information on nonprofits tends to take several years. The following data comes from Independent Sector, the coalition of nonprofit organisations representing charitable groups across the country, and was the latest available at the time of writing.

Total revenues of the nonprofit sector were over $486 billion in 1998.[1] The majority of this consists of private payments for membership dues and services (38%) and government contracts and grants (31%). Only 20% came from private contributions and although these are growing in real terms, they are a declining percentage of total income.

Sources of independent sector revenue 1987 and 1997

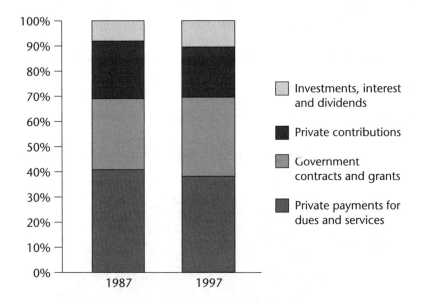

Source: Murray Weitzman *et al., The New Nonprofit Almanac and Desk Reference[1]*

The nonprofit sector is particularly large in comparison to the size of the government sector. In no other country of the world is the nonprofit sector half the size of the government sector. The nonprofit sector's share of national income was 6.7% in 1998, a figure that has grown consistently over the last 20 years.[1] This figure includes an imputed amount of the value for volunteer time, which represents approximately one-third of the independent sector's contribution to national income.

Distribution of national income

	1977	1998
Business sector	79%	80%
Government sector	15.4%	13.3%
Nonprofit sector	5.5%	6.7%

Source: Murray Weitzman *et al., The New Nonprofit Almanac and Desk Reference[1]*

Despite the sale of many nonprofit hospitals to the private sector, health services continue to dominate the sector, accounting for just under half its total income. Education and research account for a further 18% and religious organisations 11.5%. Together these three components of the sector account for over three-quarters of the nonprofit sector's revenues.[1]

Distribution of income by subsector 1987

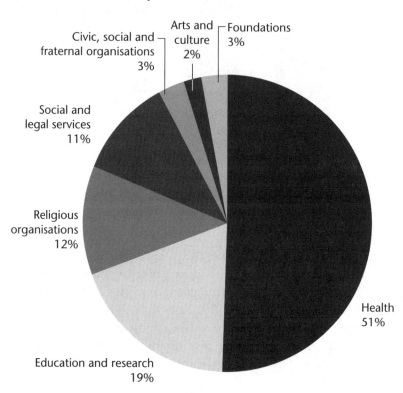

Source: Murray Weitzman *et al., The New Nonprofit Almanac and Desk Reference*[1]

The largest organisations are huge. The top 8 organisations all have an income of over $1 billion and the top 20 all have revenues exceeding $0.5 billion per annum. The top foundations are also huge, the largest giving away more than $1 billion a year and the largest 25 all making grants of more than $100 million a year.

The top 25 nonprofit organisations in the US 2001*

Name	Income $m in 2001	% of income from public support
Lutheran Services in America	7,655	23
The National Council of YMCAs	4,123	19
American Red Cross	2,712	24
Catholic Charities USA	2,621	15
United Jewish Communities	2,231	94
Goodwill Industries International	1,941	15
Salvation Army	1,915	74
Fidelity Investments Charitable Gift Fund	1,251	84
Boys & Girls Club of America	998	43
American Cancer Society, Inc	923	83
The Metropolitan Museum of Art	763	65
The Nature Conservancy	732	63
Boy Scouts of America	727	40
Habitat for Humanity International	690	61
Gifts In Kind International	681	99
Girl Scouts of the USA	680	20
Planned Parenthood Federation of America	661	29
America's Second Harvest	652	99
YWCA of the USA	646	25
Volunteers of America	592	14
Easter Seals	583	23
Public Broadcasting Service	537	48
World Vision	529	75
American Heart Association	503	81
Smithsonian Institution	499	31

Source: *The Nonprofit Times Top 100 Organizations*[13]

* This list includes organisations that raise at least 10% of their income from public sources. It excludes organisations that are more than 90% government funded.

The top 25 foundations by total giving 2001

Foundation	Total giving ($m)	Assets ($m)
Bill & Melinda Gates Foundation	1,147	32,751
The Ford Foundation	829	10,815
Lilly Endowment Inc	598	12,814
David and Lucile Packard Foundation	429	6,197
Annenberg Foundation	355	2,355
Robert Wood Johnson Foundation	271	9,045
Starr Foundation	245	4,781
W. K. Kellogg Foundation	201	5,530
Theodore and Vada Stanley Foundation	195	–
Pew Charitable Trusts	192	4,339
Andrew W. Mellon Foundation	182	4,136
Bristol-Meyers Squibb Patient Assistance Foundation	176	–
John D. and Catherine T. MacArthur Foundation	168	4,216
Annie E. Casey Foundation	153	2,592
California Endowment	148	3,366
Robert W. Woodruff Foundation	142	2,423
Open Society Institute	132	–
New York Community Trust	127	1,785
Rockefeller Foundation	127	3,211
Kresge Foundation	124	2,416
William and Flora Hewlett Foundation	120	6,081
Ford Motor Company Fund	113	–
Robert R. McCormick Tribune Foundation	112	1,600
Charles Stewart Mott Foundation	111	2,460
The Duke Endowment	105	2,489

Source: www.fdncenter.org

Paid and voluntary employment

The independent sector in the US employed almost 11 million people in 1998, a figure that has nearly doubled over the last 12 years. The sector also benefited from the full-time equivalent of 5.8 million volunteers. Together, these represent 7.1% of the total workforce. The nonprofit sector as a whole represents 9.3 % of paid employees.[1]

Employment is dominated by women, who account for almost 71% of employees. African Americans are better represented in the sector than in non-agricultural employment as a whole (14.4% compared to 11.3% of employees) and Hispanic people are less well represented (6.9% compared to 9.6% of employees).[1]

In 1998 an estimated 110 million Americans aged 18 and above volunteered for an average of 3.5 hours per week, the highest level of volunteer participation recorded by Independent Sector surveys. Just under 20 billion hours were spent volunteering, three-quarters in formal volunteering and one-quarter in informal volunteering. Formal voluntary work was mainly for religion (36% of all volunteer hours), youth development, education and human services.[1]

Volunteering is more predominant amongst:

- women (61%)
- people aged 35–54 years
- households in the $40,000+ per annum income bracket
- college graduates, part-time workers and married people.

Seventy per cent of volunteer time was spent in the independent sector, 16% in the government sector, 10% in the for-profit sector and 3% with other nonprofits.

Types of organisation that benefit from private funding

Religious organisations are by far the largest beneficiary of philanthropy, receiving 44% of private giving. The proportion of funding given to religious organisations has varied between 40% and 50% over the last 30 years with no overall trend up or down. Organisations concerned with education are the second largest beneficiary, receiving 14% of private giving, followed by health and human service organisations.

Distribution of private contributions 1998

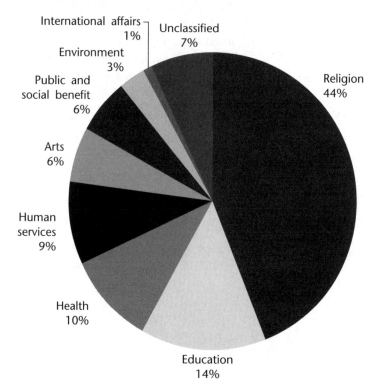

Source: Center on Philanthropy – Indiana University, *Giving USA 1999*[14]

1.4 **The current policy issues**

A number of policy issues influence the context in which managers and board members have to operate. They include:

- debate over the role of the sector
- demands for greater accountability
- questions over tax exemptions
- pressure for further commercialisation
- argument over the role of faith-based organisations
- pressures for foundations to increase payout rates
- growing competition from for-profit organisations.

Issue 1: Debate over the role of the sector

There is a vibrant debate in the US about the roles that different kinds of nonprofit organisations should play in civil society. People who take the 'citizen action' perspective believe that greater social justice comes from grass roots organisations that enable people to campaign for their causes and provide services that fit with the culture, religion and circumstances of their local communities. They argue that development should be from the 'bottom up' and driven by a desire to empower and strengthen marginalised groups. They stress the importance of the representative functions of nonprofits and value representation in the ways organisations are managed and governed. They believe that diversity is a great strength of the sector and that nonprofits should network with each other, share good practice and come together as movements rather than organisations.

People who take the 'managerial perspective' believe that the sector needs fewer, stronger organisations that can command the resources required to have a significant impact on the great social issues that the nation faces. They see significant wastage of resources in duplicating the governance and central management infrastructure of a large number of small organisations. They believe that small organisations tend to give managers and staff jobs that far exceed the scale of the resources at their disposal and as a result they are often stressed and 'burn out' in a short period of time. They argue that effectiveness could be increased by larger organisations that define more realistic jobs, provide staff with appropriate training and support, and hold them to account for their performance in more effective ways.

Issue 2: Demands for greater accountability

Since the early 1990s there have been growing demands for greater accountability of nonprofit organisations. A series of scandals rocked public confidence in the sector. In 1995 William Aramony, President of United Way of America, was convicted of defrauding the organisation of $1 million. In the same year, the Foundation for New Era Philanthropy, which attracted investments of over $41 million, was discovered to be an elaborate ruse which collapsed into bankruptcy.

More recently, debate over the use of funds raised by the American Red Cross following the destruction of the World Trade Centre on September 11th 2001 has again raised questions about accountability.

In parallel questions have been raised about donors' rights and their need for information to hold organisations to account. The Guidestar website has made nonprofit organisations' '990' tax forms easily accessible and ever-increasing scrutiny by a growing number of watchdog groups has led to greater interest in organisations' fundraising and administrative cost ratios.

The debate is now moving on to question accountability not just for expenditure but also for outcomes, and moves are afoot to enable organisations to record voluntarily information about their outcomes on the web.

Issue 3: Questions over tax exemptions and taxes on nonprofits

Tax exemptions are an important incentive to charitable giving and there is evidence that more money is donated to nonprofits when tax exemptions are increased. Among the provisions of the proposed CARE Act are further tax incentives for charitable giving, most notably an increase in the charitable deduction allowed for people who do not submit itemised tax returns to $400 per annum. This measure is intended to encourage giving by low and middle-income people and is expected to cover some 86 million individuals. This incentive is planned for only two years. The CARE Act also proposes that the limit for charitable deductions for corporations also be raised.

There are moves to increase taxes on nonprofit organisations, in particular various states are proposing to impose property taxes on nonprofits. In some cities nonprofit organisations are the largest employers after the state itself. Facing a funding crisis, some authorities see this as a potential source of new revenues. Furthermore, as competition between for-profits and nonprofits grows, some for-profits are calling for a level playing field, without hidden subsidies for nonprofits.

Issue 4: Pressure for further commercialisation

Over the last 20 years, nonprofit organisations have earned a growing proportion of their income from fees paid directly by users or indirectly by government. This trend has been driven partly by changes in government policies that have reduced payments to providers for delivering services, and replaced them with vouchers for users to purchase services. In addition nonprofits have found a variety of ways to sell their services directly to customers. Consequently fee income has grown faster than all other sources of income.

There is no evidence of this trend changing, so nonprofits are likely to become more commercialised over the coming years.

Changing structure of nonprofit revenue 1977–97

Revenue source	Percentage change 1977–97	Share of total revenue		Share of revenue growth 1977–97
		1977 %	1997 %	%
Fees and charges	145	46	47	47
Government	195	27	33	37
Philanthropy	90	27	20	16
Totals	144	100	100	100

Source: Lester Salamon: *The State of Nonprofit America*[3]

Pressure for commercial income is also leading organisations to establish a wide range of business activities whose primary aim is to raise funds and that are sometimes unrelated to their mission. This has led to some concerns about 'mission drift' and questions about whether such activities are distracting organisations from their primary purpose.

Issue 5: Argument over the role of faith-based organisations

In 1996 charitable choice legislation established new relationships between government funders and faith-based providers of social services. It required government not to discriminate against faith-based providers and the providers in turn not to require service users to engage in religious activities. The legislation aimed to create a level playing field between secular and faith-based organisations, to ensure that funds went to the most effective providers and to leverage the resources of faith-based organisations.

When President Bush Jnr was elected he proposed to expand the role of faith-based organisations to allow them to promote spiritual activities and to require service users to opt out of programmes with religious content if they did not wish to participate in them. He also proposed in the CARE Act to allow these organisations to discriminate on the basis of religious affiliation when hiring staff to provide services funded by federal grants.

The most controversial part of the CARE Act is the provision for equal treatment of secular and faith-based social service providers. Faith-based organisations would not be required to:

- remove religious art or symbols
- alter or remove religious provisions in their charters
- alter or remove religious qualifications for members of their governing boards.

The initiative has raised much debate. On the one hand it is argued that these organisations are close to the community, have appropriate values and command comparatively high public trust. On the other hand, they can lack the management capacity and accountability required to deliver consistently high quality services. A recent review concluded, 'Legislators and the public should make no assumptions about the innate ability of faith-based organisations to plan, develop, implement and evaluate social services'.[15]

At the time of writing the CARE Act is stalled in Congress, though a scaled back version may provide a way forward.[16]

Issue 6: Pressures for foundations to increase payout rates

Foundations are required by the 1969 Tax Reform Act to distribute a proportion of their net assets each year to stop them accumulating funds by paying out less than they are earning on their investments. The current minimum payment rate is 5%, a figure set by Congress in 1981. Most foundations see the 5% figure as a maximum as well as a minimum, but there are growing pressures to increase this payout ratio.

Research by McKinsey used the principle of discounted cash flow to demonstrate that the current payout rate results in fund distribution that is worth less than the value of the tax benefits that foundations receive. 'Today's low distribution rates amount to an implicit decision to hold back funds in the expectation that worthier causes will appear in the future. But many current social needs are already overwhelming. Numerous foundations and endowed nonprofit institutions ought to spend their wealth sooner rather than later.'[17] They argue for a minimum payout ratio of at least 7%.

The distinguished commentator Pablo Eisenberg argued in the *Chronicle of Philanthropy*[18] that 'it is in the interests of all nonprofit groups to support an increase in the payout rate to 6% and require that all of that be distributed in the form of grants'. At present administrative costs can be included in the 5% ratio.

Issue 7: Growing competition from for-profits

The creation of markets for the provision of social services has attracted for-profit organisations into the field and many have grown successfully because of their ability to raise capital, their management and marketing skills and their willingness to invest in technology. 'Between 1977 and 1992 forprofit firms captured 80% of the growth in day care centres, and in home health and clinic care for-profit firms captured close to 90% of the growth of facilities.'[2]

Greater competition is anticipated in future. Interestingly, there is some evidence that nonprofits have greater capacity to survive the ups and downs of markets which are driven primarily by government decisions on fee reimbursement levels. 'Nonprofits can hold their own only where they have well established institutions, where they can secure capital, where they manage to identify a meaningful market niche and a distinctive product, and where individual consumers or those paying on their behalf value the special qualities that nonprofits bring to the field.'[3]

Taken together, these issues present the sector with a massive new agenda – far larger than the policy changes facing equivalent business organisations. However, an enduring feature of the sector is its resilience and its ability to adapt to changing circumstances. Few doubt that it will emerge stronger and more effective because at the very core of the sector is a set of values that reflect the beliefs of most Americans about building a strong and caring society.

Summary

The roots of nonprofit activity in the US

- Nonprofit organisations were originally established under the British Statute of Charitable Uses Act of 1601
- Initially there was no clear distinction between profit-seeking and nonprofit organisations as both operated in similar spheres
- States in New England tended to be supportive of nonprofit activity – states in the South were more hostile
- Private nonprofit corporations were placed under federal law in 1844.

Key developments in the twentieth century

- Welfare capitalism was the dominant model of social welfare during the first quarter of the twentieth century, involving the construction of company towns and investment in people to make them more productive
- After the Second World War the government assumed greater responsibility for social welfare, and it often employed nonprofit organisations to deliver the services required
- By the late 1970s nonprofit organisations were delivering a larger share of government-financed human services than all levels of government combined
- Following a boom in the late 1990s, the sector faced a tougher period at the start of the twenty-first century.

The size and shape of the sector today

- The sector is the largest in the world with greater revenues than the nonprofit sectors of Japan, Germany, the UK, the Netherlands, France, Australia, Argentina and Brazil combined.
- Sector income is dominated by health care (51%), education and research (19%), and religion (12%)
- Private donors give most of their funding to religion (44%), education (14%), health (10%) and human services (9%).

The current policy issues

- Policy issues affecting the context in which managers and board members operate include:
  - debate over the role of the sector
  - demands for greater accountability
  - questions over tax exemptions
  - pressure for further commercialisation
  - argument over the role of faith-based organisations
  - pressures for foundations to increase payout rates
  - growing competition from for-profit organisations.

References

1 Murray Weitzman *et al.*, *The New Nonprofit Almanac and Desk Reference*, San Francisco, Jossey-Bass, 2002

2 Lester Salamon, *America's Nonprofit Sector – A Primer*, New York, Foundation Center, 1999

3 Lester Salamon, *The State of Nonprofit America*, Washington, Brookings Institution, 2002

4 Centre on Philanthropy – Indiana University, *Giving USA 2002*, Indianapolis, AAFRC Trust for Philanthropy, 2002

5 Peter Hall, *A Historical Overview* in *The Nonprofit Sector - A Research Handbook*, New Haven, Yale University Press, 1987

6 Peter Hall, *The Organization of American Culture 1700–1900*, New York, New York University Press, 1982

7 Lester Salamon, *The United States* in *Defining the Nonprofit Sector: A Cross National Analysis*, New York, Manchester University Press, 1997

8 Herbert Hoover, *American Individualism*, Garden City NY, Doubleday, Duran & Co, 1922

9 Foundation Center, *Foundations and the Tax Reform Act of 1969*, New York, Foundation Center, 1970

10 Waldemar Nielson, *The Endangered Sector*, New York, Columbia University Press, 1979

11 Lester Salamon, *The Nonprofit Sector and Government: The American Experience in Theory and Practice* in *The Third Sector: Comparative Studies of Nonprofit Organizations*, New York, Walter de Gruyter, 1990

12 Lester Salamon and Wojciech Sokolowski, *Global Civil Society — Dimensions of the Nonprofit Sector*, Baltimore, MD, Johns Hopkins Comparative Nonprofit Sector Project, 1999

13 Nonprofit Times, *The Nonprofit Times Top 100 Organizations*, Parsippany NJ, November 2002

14 Center on Philanthropy – Indiana University, *Giving USA 1999*, Indianapolis, AAFRC Trust for Philanthropy, 1999

15 Margaret Gibelman and Sheldon Gelman, *Should we have faith in faith-based social services?* in *Nonprofit Management and Leadership*, San Francisco, Jossey-Bass, Fall 2002

16 OMB Watch Analysis of Charitable Choice Provisions, www.ombwatch.org

17 Paul Jansen and David Katz, *For Nonprofits Time is Money* in *The McKinsey Quarterly*, Number 1, 2002

18 Pablo Eisenberg, *Congress Should Increase the Amount Foundations Must Give* in *Chronicle of Philanthropy*, Washington, June 27 2002

2 Building organisation capacity

Efficient and effective management has been a characteristic of nonprofit organisations in the US since they first emerged as distinct entities in the nineteenth century. Many formed themselves into the great national networks such as the YMCA and the Salvation Army that are now the cornerstones of much nonprofit activity. More recently nonprofit organisations have striven to raise the quality of their management through organisation development, strategic planning, management training and board development. The idea people are talking about most in the US now is capacity building.

Building organisation capacity is about systematically investing in developing an organisation's internal systems (for example its people, processes and infrastructure) and its external relationships (for example with funders, partners and volunteers) so that it can realise its mission and achieve greater impact.

Capacity building has to be viewed in the context of the organisation's objectives and its values. It is not about strengthening organisations for their own sake. It is about creating organisations with the ability to have significant impact in achieving their desired mission. Nor is it about being business-like because that is viewed by some as a characteristic to be valued. It is about being impactful within the context of values and beliefs that are cherished by people who champion nonprofit enterprise.

Cynics might say that capacity building is just a repackaging of established ideas. It is true that the ideas are not all new. But the energy and momentum behind capacity building are indicative of the enthusiasm with which it has been embraced. The most compelling reason for its ready acceptance is a recognition that the nonprofit sector is failing to have the impact it could have on the pressing social issues the nation faces. Across the US there is no shortage of organisations with effective programmes for assisting people in need, but their potential impact is often restricted by shortfalls in both funding and capacity. They want to deliver quality services, to reach more people, to mobilise better campaigns or just keep pace with rising expectations for competitive salaries, effective technological support and accountable boards. But they just don't have the capacity to do it, and this is particularly marked among the many under-resourced organisations in the social services part of the nonprofit sector.

Capacity building is a matter both for service delivering and for campaigning organisations. To have significant impact both need effective boards, strong management teams and good relationships with their funders. Service organisations need the capacity to manage quality, to measure performance and to manage risk. Campaigning organisations need the capacity to publicise their cause, to hold disparate groups together and to manage talented and creative people who often believe more in the cause than their organisation. They may need different types of organisation capacity, but neither can be effective without it.

What is most notable to a visiting outsider is the energy, enthusiasm, commitment and funding that is being directed at capacity building. Capacity building used to be seen as a cost. Now it is seen as an essential investment that lies at the heart of effective management. It is no longer just a continuation of past efforts to strengthen organisations. Organisations at the leading edge are undertaking thorough, systematic and rigorously evaluated capacity building initiatives. Their aim is to increase the overall impact of the nonprofit sector by creating organisations that are much more effectively and efficiently managed. They seek a step change in performance, not just gradual and half-hearted attempts at making improvements.

Clearly this depends on commitment and funding. As this book goes to print some of the foundations most committed to capacity building face reduced income and have cut their capacity building programmes. However, progress to date has convinced many people that capacity building is not an optional extra. It is an essential ingredient of effective management.

This chapter

Chapter 2 provides evidence from leading-edge organisations showing that they:

- recognise that lack of capacity is a critical constraint
- invest in capacity building
- identify the key elements of capacity required
- adopt new approaches to capacity building
- pursue explicit strategies for increasing impact
- measure the impact of capacity building.

2.1 Recognise lack of capacity as a critical constraint

History of capacity building

Since the early 1980s, there has been a growing realisation that nonprofit organisations need significant investment in organisation capacity if they are to have greater impact.

Forward-looking grant-giving foundations were amongst the first to raise the issue. They started asking questions about what nonprofit organisations were achieving and what could be done to increase their impact. Many people trace the start of capacity building efforts in the US to the launch of the David and Lucile Packard Foundation capacity building programme in 1983.

The theoretical context for capacity building gained much credibility from Robert Putnam's groundbreaking study of civic society organisations in Italy. He demonstrated that the potential for a community to grow and thrive depended on the richness of its associations and civic society organisations.[1] The book popularised the idea of 'social capital'. So today capacity building is viewed as an essential element of increasing social capital and hence of creating strong democratic societies that have the infrastructure to develop socially and economically.

'The quality of the connections between people and institutions provides the basis for civil society and healthy communities,' according to Urban Institute Researcher Carol de Vita.[2] 'From this perspective, capacity building's ultimate goal should be to achieve and sustain high performance in meeting the needs of a complex rapidly changing society.'[3]

Together, then, a well-grounded theoretical framework combined with the practical efforts of foundations, umbrella organisations, nonprofit boards, venture philanthropists and public pressure have pushed capacity building right up the management agenda. 'A national infrastructure for capacity building is now taking shape'.[2] It includes a wide range of management support organisations, a variety of for-profit and nonprofit consulting firms and, increasingly, resources that can be downloaded from the web.

Forces that hinder capacity growth

Until recently a common approach to management in the US was to spend as much money as possible on services and as little as possible on administration. This paradigm was supported by both foundations and government who believed that their funding would be most effective if it was spent on programmes, and that meant funding specific services. Whilst government contracts often provided a fixed percentage for overheads, foundations generally assumed that 'other' sources of funding would pay for the central overhead that was required. Neither saw the funding of capacity as a strategic investment aimed at strengthening organisations' ability to have significant long-term impact.

Donors also wanted their money to be spent directly on services and campaigns. Private donors have always been acutely sensitive about nonprofit overhead costs and expected administration to be kept to a bare minimum. They did not want their funds spent on office overheads. Their desires were often fuelled by organisations themselves. When desperate for funds, they promised that every cent would be spent on beneficiaries.

Charity watchdog groups and the press provided a further disincentive to investment in organisation infrastructure because they publicise ratios of administrative expenditure to programme expenditure. Such figures imply that programme expenditure is good and administrative expenditure is bad.

The interests of board members and employees also discouraged investment in the organisation itself. People sit on boards or work for nonprofits primarily because they are interested in the causes, not because they have an innate interest in building organisation capacity. There has therefore always been a very real and acute tension between spending money on programmes and investing in organisation capacity. Short-term pressures to deliver services to people in desperate need or to campaign on pressing social and environmental issues can be intense. 'The service and the organisation are considered to be competitors in a zero sum struggle for limited resources.'[4]

So the pressure on organisations to spend as much of their funding as possible on services was, and continues to be, intense and complicated by the difficulty of separating out essential organisation infrastructure from unnecessary administrative expenditure. 'The difference between building an organisation's capacity for success (muscle) and assembling a self-serving empire (fat) remains hard to distinguish'.[4]

Lack of capacity – a stumbling block to effectiveness

The intensive thinking about this in some quarters of the nonprofit sector has contributed to a widely held view in the US that capacity is the crucial issue for organisations wanting to make any significant impact on the major social issues they exist to resolve. Lack of management capacity is seen by many as the bottleneck that thwarts the growth and development of nonprofit organisations and consequently their potential to have a greater impact. 'The missing ingredient in the prevalent program-centred conception of social impact is organisational capacity. It is the capacity for strong performance in organisations – the ability to develop, sustain and improve the delivery of a mission – that provides the foundation for lasting social benefits'.[4]

Failure to attend to organisation and internal management issues is particularly acute in campaigning organisations. Focused as they often are on rapidly changing external agendas, and staffed by people who are passionately committed to the cause, they often overlook many of the basic requirements of effective organisation. Many of these organisations pay a high price in terms of poor staff retention, inefficient use of staff time as people retreat into their own agendas, and under-investment in technology that could give organisations greater efficiency and impact.

Foundations in particular see lack of capacity as a bottleneck. As they began to pay more attention to evaluating the impact of their grants it became clear that lack of organisation capacity was a critical obstacle to achieving the desired results. Evaluation after evaluation concluded that internal capacity was a key constraint. For example, the Boston Foundation's capacity building investments grew from a realisation that many of the homeless and battered women's shelters that they were funding were failing in their first five years of operation through not building sustainable organisation capacity.

Associations representing various groups of organisations providing social care also see lack of capacity as a stumbling block to effectiveness. In many fields organisations have to register with a recognised umbrella association for their field to be eligible for government funding. The Commission on Accreditation of Rehabilitation Services is an example. Organisations have to demonstrate that they meet the association's requirements, and these increasingly include management standards.

2.2 Invest in capacity building

Spurs to developing capacity

Despite the many disincentives, the case for significantly increased investment in organisation and management has grown exponentially in recent years. Commitment to creating stronger organisations sprang from many sources. Public pressure has led board members and managers to begin asking questions about how they could increase the impact of their organisations. In the past a common response might have been to raise more funds. Whilst greater funding is clearly essential to increasing impact, organisations have learned that it is insufficient on its own. Leading organisations recognise that the organisation itself can be a major barrier to achievement, and that significant amounts of both attention and financial investment are justified to develop its effectiveness.

A further development was the creation of the Alliance for Nonprofit Management, a professional association devoted to building the capacity of nonprofit organisations. Its members include management support organisations, management consultants and consulting firms, academic centres, policy makers, management assistance programmes and grant makers, all concerned with, 'raising the bar on quality', the strap-line of the Alliance.

The capacity building movement gained further momentum with the arrival of venture philanthropists in the mid 1990s (see Chapter 5). More often than not, these were highly successful business people who had made their fortunes establishing and then selling businesses. They wanted to invest some of their money in social causes and they knew from their business experience that building organisation capacity was an essential ingredient of success. The venture philanthropy movement gave capacity building a major boost, and it also brought new funds to pay for it.

So, from small beginnings, the capacity building movement has now become a hot topic in the nonprofit sector. The best evidence of the rate at which it has grown comes from the Foundation Center which reports that grants for 'management development', 'technical assistance' and 'programme evaluation' totalled $440 million in 2000. This is up one third on the previous year and up from $132 million in 1994, representing a constant dollar increase of $269 million. Although funding may fall from its peak following the decline of the stock market, it is likely to remain above the levels of the mid 1990s.

A fresh paradigm for effectiveness

As a result a new paradigm of organisation effectiveness has emerged. The key characteristics of this new paradigm are:

- continuous strategic investment in the development of the organisation itself, its people and its relationships to give it the power to have greater impact
- charging the full cost of programmes to funders and being comfortable about making 'surpluses'
- using unrestricted income and foundation grants to invest in the capacity of the organisation itself
- using unrestricted income to subsidise services only when there is a compelling case and a demonstrable connection with the organisation's strategic priorities.

2.3 Identify the critical elements of organisation capacity

The term capacity building emerged from the international development field where it was, and still is, used extensively to describe the empowerment of communities, the recognition of human rights and the development of the civil society sector. The terms management, governance and organisation were, however, not part of the lexicon of capacity building.

The term was subsequently adopted by managers and theorists and applied to organisations operating within the US. The widest use of the term refers to strengthening organisations' internal systems and their external strategies. External strategy determines what organisations set out to achieve, how they fund their activities and who they work with, and internal capacity is concerned with how they organise their affairs to deliver the strategy.

Experience from the US leads to the conclusion that the key elements of internal capacity include, amongst other things:

- the mission
- the board
- people
- management skills
- physical infrastructure
- technology
- evaluation.

The elements of external capacity include:

- relationships with funders, partners and stakeholders
- definition of relevant high value services
- orchestration of creative campaigns for social change
- creativity in identifying and exploiting new sources of funds and income generation opportunities.

Where to begin capacity building

Some researchers have attempted to identify which elements of capacity are most critical to organisations' success. In theory, every aspect of an organisation would benefit from investment. Better plans, more staff training, improved financial management systems and more powerful IT systems could all make an organisation stronger. So where should capacity building start, and how much time and money should be invested in each aspect of capacity?

A Brookings Institution survey of 250 researchers and providers of management assistance in the US highlighted **leadership** as the single most important ingredient of effective organisations: 'It is impossible to overstate the importance of the leader to the high performing organisation. Leadership was seen as the number one, and almost only, place to begin the journey from poor performance to high'.[5]

This survey also identified the elements of **internal structures** that were critical to high performing organisations. The most frequently mentioned characteristics were that these organisations:

- exploit information technology (74%)
- give staff the authority to do their jobs (66%)
- have few barriers between organisation units (54%)
- stay flat with few layers between the top and bottom of the organisation (51%).

They also identified the critical **internal management systems** of high performing organisations. These organisations:

- use the board (90%)
- clarify responsibilities (77%)
- plan for the future and have strategic plans in place (73%)
- use data to make decisions, despite all the difficulty of measuring performance (63%)
- invest in training (52%)
- have an accurate, fast accounting system (47%).

Respondents' answers to questions about **external capacity** suggested that high performance organisations:

- collaborate through strategic alliances, sharing services and sharing information
- make money by generating unrestricted income
- diversify their funding base
- measure the outcomes of what they achieve and compare themselves with the outside world.[5]

Christine Letts and her colleagues at Harvard compared high performing nonprofit organisations with high performing businesses. They concluded in their book *High Performance Nonprofit Organizations*[4] that there are four areas that are critical to capacity building:

- **Quality processes** – activities that translate commitment to quality into results by helping organisations determine whether and how a programme is satisfying clients. Strengthening these processes requires management and staff to identify practical and measurable ways to improve services.
- **Product development** – activities that help organisations search for good ideas and turn them into services.
- **Benchmarking** – processes for comparing key aspects of performance with other organisations.
- **Human resource development** – processes for motivating people specifically to advance the objectives and mission of the organisation and managing the human resource function in a strategic way.

William Ryan, one of the authors of the book, said they chose these four because "they fit in the middle of the spectrum between high level strategic planning and specific programme management". He argues that "nonprofit managers are good at managing at either end of the spectrum, but they neglect critically important capacity development work in the middle of the spectrum".

McKinsey, the management consultancy, conducted case studies on 13 nonprofit organisations that engaged in capacity building over a 10-year period. This research was conducted for Venture Philanthropy Partners, a nonprofit philanthropic investment organisation.[6] The research led to the creation of the 'Capacity Framework' which defines seven essential elements of nonprofit capacity.[6] The elements are:

- **Aspirations** – an organisation's mission, vision, and overarching goals, which collectively articulate its common sense of purpose and direction.
- **Strategy** – the coherent set of actions and programmes aimed at fulfilling the organisation's overarching goals.

- **Organisational skills** – the sum of the organisation's capabilities, including such things as performance measurement, planning, resource management, and external relationship building.
- **Human resources** – the collective capabilities, experiences, potential and commitment of the organisation's board, management team, staff and volunteers.
- **Systems and infrastructure** – the organisation's planning, decision making, knowledge management and administrative systems, as well as the physical and technological assets that support the organisation.
- **Organisational structure** – the combination of governance, organisational design, inter-functional coordination and individual job descriptions that shape the organisation's legal and management structure.
- **Culture** – the connective tissue that binds together the organisation, including shared values and practices, behaviour norms, and most important, the organisation's orientation towards performance.

McKinsey saw these elements as being related in a hierarchy.

They used this research to develop a Capacity Assessment Grid which provides a model of excellence against which organisations can assess their capacity. It can be used to identify areas of capacity requiring most attention. It is set out in more detail in Appendix 1.

The McKinsey Capacity Framework

Source: McKinsey & Company, *Effective Capacity Building in Nonprofit Organizations*[6]

More recently umbrella organisations operating at the state level have established a series of standards for nonprofit performance. These are published on the Internet and in some states funders are using them as criteria to determine whether organisations are fit to receive government money. The most well-known examples are the standards published by the Maryland Association of Nonprofit Organisations and the Minnesota Council of Nonprofits (see website references at the end of this chapter for details).

So the essential elements of capacity have been identified, tools for assessing organisation capacity have been developed and there is some evidence about which are generally perceived to be the most critical. The challenge for managers and board members is therefore one of assessing the capacity and making wise judgements about which elements to prioritise.

2.4 Adopt new approaches to capacity building

Whilst there is much anecdotal evidence and commonly accepted wisdom that top quality management and governance lead to better organisation performance, there is less understanding of the types and duration of capacity building initiatives that really work. 'There appear to be multiple starting points for improvement, several general strategies for growth, and a menu of characteristics that nonprofits can draw upon as target destinations for building capacity.'[5]

Evidence about the ingredients of successful capacity building is growing rapidly. New research by Paul Light and Elizabeth Hubbard[3] gathered data from eight funders who together spent $28 million on approximately 380 capacity building grants that financed over 500 projects. The types of projects in their sample are as shown on page 48.

They propose that four key elements shape the ultimate success of a capacity building project:

- the desired outcome or goal of the capacity building activity
- the change strategy selected to realise that goal
- the champions guiding the effort
- the time, energy and money invested in the process.

Type of capacity building project	Number of projects	%
Internal management systems		
Planning, strategic planning	104	21
Fundraising, financial management	71	14
Governance, board development	62	12
Organisational assessment	42	8
Technology planning, training, acquisition	35	7
Evaluation and other	17	3
Total	**331**	**65**
External relations		
Communications, marketing	33	7
Mergers, alliances and joint ventures	17	3
Mission	13	3
Strategy	8	2
Constituent relationships	7	1
Business venture and programme development	3	0.6
Total	**81**	**16**
Leadership		
Executive director transitions	34	7
Executive leadership, management skills	14	3
Total	**48**	**10**
Internal structure		
Human resources, staff development	40	8
Structure, management issues	3	1
Total	**43**	**9**
Totals	**503**	**100**

Source: Paul Light and Elizabeth Hubbard, *The Capacity Building Challenge*[3]

The first step when approaching capacity building is to recognise that these four elements are all inter-related. Although the desired outcome should determine the change strategy, which informs who should champion the effort and how much time and money it requires, in practice all four are in a dynamic relationship. The resources available will affect the choice of outcome and the champion may influence the chosen change strategy.

Elements of a capacity building project

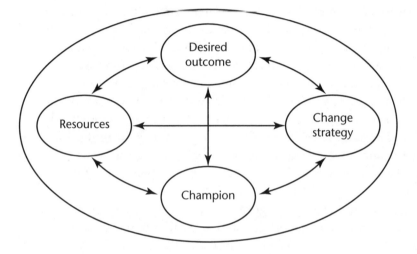

Source: Paul Light and Elizabeth Hubbard, *The Capacity Building Challenge*[3]

The desired outcomes

The desired outcomes of capacity building projects in this research fell into four categories:

- **Internal management systems** such as the strategic planning process, financial management systems, information systems and performance management processes.
- **External relationships** such as collaborations with other organisations, fundraising, volunteer recruitment, changes in demand for a service, clarification of the mission and improved marketing.
- **Leadership** such as top management and board skills, the clarity of responsibilities and the ability of the chief executive.
- **Internal structures** including management and governance structures, delegation, access to technology and diversity amongst staff.

BUILDING THE FOUNDATIONS FOR GROWTH: USA CHILD CARE

USA Child Care was established in 1995 by nationally known childcare professionals to be 'a national voice for direct service providers who serve low and moderate income children and families'. Initially they developed a national campaign to increase childcare reimbursement rates and a training programme for provider associations and an information network. These were delivered through two separate organisations.

A review by TCC Group (formerly The Conservation Group), a leading consultancy to nonprofit organisations, identified that people were confused by there being two organisations, resources were not being used efficiently and the missions of both organisations were suffering. They planned a rigorous and systematic approach to strengthening the organisation. The first step in capacity building was to resolve the structural issue. At the same time a new strategic plan was developed. The plans were crystallised at a weekend retreat. Each element of the strategy was then worked up in detail. For example, the strategy related to the merger identified what needed to be done, who would do it, when it would happen and what it would cost.

The organisation's capacity was greatly enhanced when the merger of the two organisations was completed and new board committees were established. Rick Hulefeld, a board member said, "We are much more focussed now and have a real feeling for where we are going".

Source: Gold Book Committee, *Gold Book – Success Stories in Nonprofit Management*[7]

Change strategies

The second of the four key elements of capacity building was the change strategy.

The approach organisations take to capacity building was seen as critical to its overall success. 'Discerning what kind of change strategy is likely to be most effective at any given time is a crucial skill for both nonprofit leaders and capacity building funders alike.'[3]

However, there is no straightforward methodology for moving from the analysis of the problem to the creation of an appropriate change strategy. Heterogeneity is a defining characteristic of the nonprofit sector, so it is hardly surprising to discover that it is difficult to generalise about effective intervention points and capacity building strategies. One model, prioritising human resource management, is given in the next case study.

CITIZEN SCHOOLS INVESTS IN HUMAN RESOURCES

'Citizen Schools is a Boston-based organization that seeks to educate children and strengthen community ties through improved after-school programs. Its program quality depends critically on the quality of the teaching staff and volunteers, which means human resources is at the top of this organization's capacity building priorities.

Citizen Schools was launched in 1995 by Ned Rimer and Eric Schwarz, two social entrepreneurs fresh from a successful personal experience teaching public school children first-aid and journalism. They had seen what difference they could make in the lives of children in a few short hours of their innovative after-school program but at the time Boston offered parents few high-quality or affordable after-school options.

Schwarz and Rimer's model for tackling this problem was based around a cadre of "Citizen Teachers". These volunteers would help children between the ages of 9 and 14 develop skills in such areas as leadership, writing, public speaking, and using the scientific method. By framing these activities as "apprenticeships" and making them fun and educational, Schwarz and Rimer felt that Citizen Schools could meet an un-served need and at the same time improve Boston's poor educational testing results.

Citizen Schools quickly learned that a major challenge in the after-school sector was attracting and recruiting enough talented part-time teaching staff to populate the program. Schwarz and Rimer overcame this hurdle by creating an innovative employment model that relied on staff-sharing agreements with several leading Boston area nonprofits. Citizen Schools designed 1- to 2-year full-time positions, complete with benefits and professional development opportunities, and branded them as a prestigious "Fellows Program".

Citizen Schools then sought and secured corporate funding to under-write the program. Under this program, each Fellow splits his or her time equally between Citizen Schools and another nonprofit organization. The Fellows now comprise one-third of the Citizen Schools staff, which has risen sharply from 13 to its current level of 57.

Citizen Schools' overall investments in capacity building – including its focus on human resources – have been rewarded handsomely. On the financial front, it has leveraged its new strategic clarity and corporate part-nerships into $3.5 million in additional funding. The program is reaching many more children, as well – from 560 in 1998 to more than 1,200 in 2000.

In terms of social impact, Citizen Schools can point to some very promising trends. In early tests, for example, children who have gone through Citizen Schools demonstrate significant improvements in writing skills. Furthermore, the product is in demand. There has been a 50 percent increase in the number of licensed after-school slots in Boston schools since 1995; one-third of the increase is attributable to Citizen Schools.'

Source: McKinsey & Company, *Effective Capacity Building in Nonprofit Organizations*[6]

The temptation is to conclude from any analysis of capacity that many components require attention and to attempt to address them all. However, organisations have limited capacity to build capacity. The constraints are usually a combination of senior management time and money. So the leadership has to make tough choices about the amount of capacity building that the organisation can sustain and how to allocate these critical capacity building resources.

Managers acknowledge that sustainable development usually requires continuous effort over a period of time to change people's habits and behaviour and to create new ways of working. There is an ever-present danger of putting insufficient effort into building each component of capacity. Effort spread too thinly over too many fronts may result in none being advanced in a significant and sustainable way.

There is a strong tendency for nonprofits to underestimate the time and funds required. The advice from Mary Ann Holohean, formerly of the capacity building Meyer Foundation is to "make fewer, larger changes and take more time over them and make greater use of external support".

Another strategic decision concerns the type of the intervention that is required and whether external assistance is needed to achieve the desired result. Whilst much management assistance is delivered by external consultants and trainers, there is growing evidence that peer-to-peer exchanges such as networking, mentoring and information sharing also play an important role in capacity building.

Champions

The third key element of a capacity building programme is the need for a champion. One or more people have to have the capacity building initiative at the top of their agenda, be planning the overall approach, driving the implementation timetable and promoting it to everyone affected. One of the reasons capacity building fails is the lack of a champion who has the skills, time and resources to make a success of the initiative. All capacity building initiatives ultimately have to become embedded into the organisation's culture – its way of doing things – and this requires the sustained effort and dedication that is best provided by a champion.

Resources

The fourth key element is resources. Capacity building is resourced very largely from varying combinations of grants by foundations and internal resources such as unrestricted income and surpluses from previous years. According to the Brooking's Institution Nonprofit Effectiveness Project around one-third is supported by external funding, one-third from the organisation's own resources and one-third uses a combination of both.

Research into a sample of funders that have capacity building programmes showed that 'high' resource funders spent an average of just under $200,000 per organisation and 'low' resource funders spent an average of $27,500 per organisation.[3]

One of the consequences of larger and longer-term capacity building funding is that funders tend to be in regular contact with recipients – often talking on a weekly basis. This provides external pressure to maintain the momentum of the initiative and an ongoing source of advice and support.

To summarise, capacity builders need to clarify the desired outcomes of the initiative, develop an appropriate change strategy, appoint a leader who will be its champion and ensure that it is supported by significant resources.

Further insights come from research undertaken by McKinsey. They draw three conclusions about the overall approach to capacity building from their work:[6]

1 Resetting aspirations and strategy is often a first step in dramatically improving an organisation's performance. The organisations that achieved the greatest increase in their capacity were those that created a new vision and a new strategy for the future. It is important to emphasise that a new aspiration or strategy can only be transformative if it is then used to align the other aspects of organisational capacity. If done thoroughly, this alignment process provides a tight institutional focus and road map for the organisation to use with both internal and external audiences, which help to keep everyone on track during the long and difficult process of building capacity.

2 Commitment to capacity building and ownership amongst senior management are essential. Progress in effectively resetting aspirations and strategy, institutionalising sound management processes and improving systems to work at scale requires managerial ability as well as good leadership. In many cases, the appointment of someone to take

line management responsibility for a large proportion of the organisation's internal affairs (often known as a chief operating officer) was key to ensuring that the organisation worked efficiently and effectively.

3 Patience is essential. Almost everything about capacity building took longer and was more complicated than expected. Capacity building can feel like a never-ending process because improvements in one area place new demands on other areas. There are few quick fixes in capacity building.

Principles of successful capacity building assistance

Organisations in the US seek assistance from many sources including large for-profit consulting firms, for-profit and nonprofit consulting boutiques, solo practitioners, volunteer brokers, management support organisations, foundations, associations and academic centres.

An intensive study of the most committed and successful providers by the Environmental Support Centre and the nationally recognised nonprofit Innovation Network concluded their approaches could be boiled down to nine principles:

1 **Every organisation is capable of building its own capacity** – the most successful providers of capacity building carry a deep respect for their client's ability to build their own capacity and genuinely recognise that an organisation is in charge of its own capacity building.

2 **Trust between the organisation and the provider is essential** – both parties must feel free to communicate openly, to ask for help beyond the usual, to risk disapproval, to listen and to learn.

3 **Organisations must be ready for capacity building** – exhibiting the following qualities:
   ■ the organisation is open to change and willing to question itself
   ■ the organisation can clearly describe its mission
   ■ key members believe that capacity building will help to further the mission
   ■ the organisation is prepared to commit the necessary time and resources to capacity building.

4 **Ongoing questioning means better answers** – the provider facilitates a climate in which questioning and feedback are encouraged.

5 **Team and peer learning are effective capacity building tools** – working in pairs and learning experiences for people who work in teams are good for capacity building.

6 **Capacity building should accommodate different learning styles**
– some people learn by doing, some by experimenting, some need to
talk, some need to think, some are more visual and some more verbal –
all need to be taken into account.

7 **Every organisation has its own history and culture** – the better a
provider's understanding of an organisation's situation, the more
powerful the capacity building.

8 **All people and all parts of an organisation are inter-related** – no
matter how specific the issue, it connects with the rest of the organisation
and must be dealt with in that way. Change has a far better chance of
success if it involves people from many levels, staff, constituents and
board members.

9 **Capacity building takes time** – intensive long-term training and
apprenticeships prepare people to build organisations and can take place
in stages.

Source: Allison Fine, Nancy Kopf and Colette Thayer, *Echoes from the Field*[8]

2.5 Pursue explicit strategies for increasing impact

Across America there is a widely held view that the country has many
well-tested ideas for tackling most of the social problems the nation
faces. However, most operate on a local, small and under-funded basis
and whilst valuable on their own, together they are not having a significant impact on the fundamental problems that they seek to address.

Considerable thought is being given to the different generic strategies
organisations can pursue to increase their impact. Although the
thinking is at an early stage of development, particularly when
compared to the business thinking on generic strategic options, some
strands are emerging. They are pulled together here because each
generic strategy has implications for the approaches organisations take
to capacity building.

The evidence suggests that there are four fundamentally different
strategies organisations can pursue to increase their impact. They can:

- diversify
- specialise
- scale up
- scale deep.

These strategic options can be related as illustrated below:

Generic strategies for increasing impact

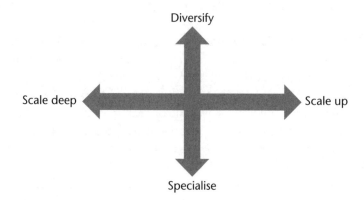

Diversification strategy

Most nonprofits diversify and they do so because they seek or are presented with new opportunities. They expand the range of services provided and they offer services to related groups of people. For example, organisations that assist people with health problems, diversify into research about the causes of the problem and organisations that assist children diversify into similar services for young adults.

Diversification is perhaps the most common strategy for increasing impact because it does not threaten existing services. It is often pursued incrementally and may not be a conscious strategy. Diversification enables organisations to exploit economies of scope – the ability to reach one group of people with a range of different services. It also enables organisations to attract additional resources, either through selling new services to purchasers or by appealing to different groups of donors.

Diversification is an attractive strategy because it is generally funded by new resources and therefore avoids the need to make hard choices about the re-allocation of existing resources. As a strategy is does not threaten the coalition of stakeholders that has been established to support current activities.

Many organisations begin by providing services and then diversify into campaigning because they recognise that their own efforts will always be small compared to those of government. They believe that they can get greater leverage in achieving their mission by campaigning for new legislation or changes to government spending priorities.

Diversification does have significant drawbacks as a strategy. There is a danger that the organisation attempts to undertake an ever-wider range of activities, and does not have the capacity or the skills to provide effective management and support for everything it does. The lack of capacity often exhibits itself as ever-increasing meeting agendas, incomplete projects, stressed staff, increased sickness and problems with staff retention.

Specialisation strategy

An alternative strategy is to specialise and become more focused on the organisation's existing field of operation. This might involve enhancing existing services to meet the needs of service users better or it could involve improving service quality.

Christine Letts quotes the example of the Vera Institute of Justice, an organisation that designs and operates demonstration programmes as a means of improving justice in the US. It conducted in-depth field research into the causes and dynamics of violence amongst youth. Instead of testing a specific programme, the organisation is tracking, over several years, the lives of a select number of inner-city teenagers. It is working in a focused way in its own area of specialisation and delving deeper into the underlying issues that the organisation exists to address.

Sometimes a specialisation strategy is a response to a diversification strategy that has become too broad. Organisations may add additional services, reach out to new groups and then conclude that they do not have the capacity and the competence to manage a wide range of services. Alternatively they may conclude that some services would be more successful if they were located in other organisations or if they were established as independent organisations. This would enable the organisation to concentrate its resources on a more limited number of people or services.

However, specialisation also has its drawbacks. It can lead to loss of funding streams, as money is often linked directly to a service. It can also narrow the organisation's potential donor base as the remaining activities may appeal to fewer funders.

Scaling up strategy

Scaling up is the generic strategy receiving most attention in the US at present. It is a strategy for replicating successful approaches so they can benefit more people. The proponents of scaling up argue that the nonprofit sector could have greater impact if organisations spread successful methods of addressing social issues more widely around the country. They see potential economies of scale resulting from more widespread application of the most effective models.

'Few nonprofit organisations today have the scale and organisational ability to tackle the most challenging social problems effectively. Only 18% of non-profits have a budget of $1 million or more. Most use their limited resources to market themselves to the same donor groups, to compete for the same foundation grants, to recruit the same people and ultimately to reach the same populations.'[9] So the potential for the sector as a whole to increase its impact is significant.

There are many examples of organisations that have successfully scaled up in the past such as the Red Cross, Volunteers for America and Big Brothers Big Sisters. Going to scale is therefore not an entirely new challenge. It was achieved by organisations that are now the backbone of the nonprofit sector because they had great ideas that resonated with people all over the country and who grasped the opportunity to establish a service in their area.

Harvard Business School researcher, Jane Wei-Skillern, asked a sample of managers why some nonprofits are reticent about going to scale. She concluded:

- social entrepreneurs tend to focus on perfecting their ideas and tend not to think about the strategic alternatives for rolling out a programme
- nonprofit people find it less exciting to take other people's ideas – they want to create their own
- setting up a new programme and 'going to scale' require entirely different skills and these are seldom found in one person.

Scaling up has its critics. Some see it as a business perspective that is concerned only with efficiency and impact. They argue that good ideas can be promulgated across the sector by publicising successful programmes and encouraging networking between organisations. Dennis Derryck of New School University in New York argues that "neighbourhoods are very specific, culturally, ethnically and spiritually, so approaches to social problems have to be tailored to individual circumstances".

He also argues that great social changes such as the granting of civil rights, the promotion of women's rights and actions to protect the environment have been brought about by disparate groups of organisations that have remained institutionally independent. He is supported by Michael Edwards of the Ford Foundation who says "creating federations and encouraging networking can be a more effective growth strategy," and Rosni Posner of the Alliance for Nonprofit Management who says, "big is not always better in the nonprofit world".

One problem for organisations attempting to go to scale according to Mary Ann Holohean, formerly of the Meyer Foundation, is that they find that they are not embedded in the local community. Some of the best projects 'grow out of the community'. She sees a big difference between a 'community based' organisation and a 'community occupying' organisation.

Jane Wei-Skillern's research[10] looked at different ways to scale up and identified three different approaches:

- scaling up principles (by promoting an idea for others to follow)
- scaling up specific programmes (by working through affiliated organisations)
- scaling up an entire organisation (by creating an integrated national branch structure).

She argues that each has advantages and disadvantages. Promoting ideas can involve speaking at conferences, writing up experience, publishing best practice guidance and a raft of other approaches to interest organisations in the idea or the service. Learning can be shared through networking. It is inexpensive, but it does not allow organisations to exploit economies of scale and the scaling up process cannot be managed in an integrated way.

Working with affiliated organisations allows for more varied approaches and more creativity in the way the service is scaled up. It can be adapted more easily to suit local circumstances. Some organisations have different levels of affiliates ranging from using a common name and having a close relationship, to giving an idea away and offering periodic support.

Most organisations in her research wanted to scale up through branches. She believes social entrepreneurs want to 'own' their creation and are reluctant to let go. They are concerned about other people taking their model and not delivering it to the same standards. Branch structures also allow best practice to be spread in a controlled way, supported by technical assistance and training.

The appeal of branch structures is that they offer the greatest opportunity to create a brand and potentially a virtuous circle in which a growing brand attracts more funds that in turn further strengthens the brand. However branches also require standards and a means of monitoring performance so they are much more complex to establish.

A number of conclusions emerge from her research into scaling up. First, replication is about taking good ideas and modifying them for different circumstances. It is not about rote application of a good idea.

Second, when organisations scaled up they learned more in a shorter time than organisations undertaking an activity at one site. This is an important but under-recognised benefit of scaling up.

Third, scaling up must be 'demand pulled' by the local community not 'supply pushed' by a national organisation. Sustainable organisations need local energy, supported by a peer-to-peer approach, because nonprofit leaders learn best from each other.

Fourth, leaders need to come across as doing solid work in their community not as working primarily to scale up their ideas. This is supported by Mary Anne Holohean, "humility is required, and a non-hierarchical approach works best".

Finally, performance measurement is a critical aspect of scaling up effectively. Managers need to be completely clear about how they will measure their success and create transparency across the whole organisation. This should involve a few simple, useful and pragmatic measures.

WOMEN'S WORLD BANKING – SCALING UP THROUGH AFFILIATES

Women's World Banking's (WWB's) mission is to expand the economic participation and power of low income women by opening access to finance, information and markets. WWB works towards achieving its goal in three ways:

- by providing and organising support to affiliates who in turn offer direct services to low income women
- by building learning and change networks comprised of leading microfinance institutions and banks
- by working with policy makers to build financial systems that work for the poor majority.

When Michaela Walsh founded the organisation she wanted to create a global organisation with decisions made from the bottom up. Instead of creating a global institution she established a network of affiliates – independent country-based organisations with local boards.

At the end of 2002 the organisation had 40 affiliates in 34 countries, over 400,000 active clients, the average loan was $415, the average repayment rate was 98.5% and costs were 21 cents for every $1 lent.

This is how the organisation built capacity through an affiliate model:

1979 – Founder established the organisation using her own savings.

1981 – First affiliates established in Colombia and Kenya.

1986 – Requirements to becoming an affiliate (small local capital fund, business plans consistent with WWB principles, board and management dominated by women) established.

1989 – Training programme established for affiliates (10,000 clients).

1990 – Affiliate management programmes launched in which affiliate presidents and executive directors critique each other's business plans with the aim of enhancing financial skills.

1994 – Affiliate/Network Partnership Agreement approved. At the same global meeting key performance indicators and standards were adopted. The Partnership Agreement process involved affiliate members, the global team and neighbouring affiliates in an annual review and strategic planning process (100,000 clients).

1996 – Global meeting agreed one-third of the organisation's funds be spent serving existing affiliates, one-third expanding the network and building broader networks and one-third on policy work, knowledge building and dissemination.

1997 – Strategy to 2000 agreed to spend more on tailored services for affiliates, disaffiliate non-performing affiliates and to give associate organisations access to WWB workshops and policy forums.

1998 – Revised Partnership Agreement created by consensus with affiliates establishing performance standards to be achieved by 2000.

1999 – Established programme to pilot innovations with leading affiliates, part funded by WWB.

2001 – Launched the Global Network for Banking Innovation in Microfinance – engaging leaders of mainstream financial institutions that are committed to microfinance as a profitable business opportunity.

2002 – The Capital Fund used to back loan guarantees for Affiliates exceeded $44 million.

According to Nancy Barry, President of WWB, "We have spent a lot of time and effort building this common culture. Through annual global or regional meetings, affiliate leaders from around the world have built our shared mission, vision, and value statements. These values include a belief that poor women are entrepreneurs, clients, and change agents – and should not be treated as passive beneficiaries of social services. They include a shared belief in business approaches to economic and social changes, with all affiliates expected to build sustainable, responsive services and institutions serving large numbers of poor women, not short-lived projects".

"Our values include a belief in the power of self-determined organisations, bound by mutual accountability for results, rather than donor-driven approaches or top down controls."

Source: based on Harvard Business School case study: Catalytic Change Through Networks

Scaling deep

Organisations that pursue a strategy of scaling deep focus their activities in a limited geographic area and with a well-defined user group. They might aim to reach a higher percentage of their user group, to offer them a wider range of services or to enhance the effectiveness of their service. They can focus their attention on strengthening their local relationships and their local brand. 'Scaling deep is about the "best of breed" in your field.'[11]

Scaling deep has the advantages of maintaining staff and board attention on more limited and well-defined objectives and of concentrating resources. It is less demanding of organisation capacity. Management may be more straightforward and administrative overheads lower. However, scaling deep may not allow an organisation to exploit economies of scale and might limit the pool of donors interested in supporting the organisation.

2.6 Measure the impact of capacity building

Clearly, with all this interest in capacity building, people are asking whether the results are worth the effort. Does better governance or better planning enhance organisation performance? Indeed, as Light and Hubbard ask 'what are the measurable outcomes of a measurement outcome system?'

They argue that there are at least three levels of outcomes:

- **Outputs** – which demonstrate whether the immediate objectives of the initiative have been met (such as a new system implemented or technology installed).
- **Organisational outcomes** – which show whether the initiative improved the functioning or performance of the organisation (such as greater productivity or increased efficiency).
- **Mission impact** – which establish whether the initiative resulted in the organisation achieving greater impact (such as more people housed or better-informed users).

In an ideal world managers, board members and funders would prefer to see results in terms of mission impact – and there is growing demand for such evidence. However, many capacity building initiatives are small compared to the overall size of the organisation, so the impact may be hard to discern amongst all the other internal and external changes taking place simultaneously. As one funder said 'it would be the height of hubris to say that our $30,000 planning effort resulted in better client services in a $2.5 million direct service organisation'.[3]

Whilst there is a need to 'take stock' of the effectiveness of capacity building before and after each initiative and review whether it achieved the desired results, this is not always easy because of the temptation to inflate the outcomes of initiatives to justify the time and effort invested.

Light and Hubbard suggest a 360-degree survey of key stakeholders before and after the capacity building initiative to assess perceptions of outcomes against expectations. They go further to propose that if a number of organisations carried out such reviews evidence of the impact of different initiatives in organisations of varied sizes, ages and types could be examined to determine which types of initiative are perceived to have the greatest impact.

Demonstrating the success of capacity building is not easy. Even when organisations attempt to measure its effectiveness, it is hard to assess its impact. A number of studies of re-engineering in the private sector suggest that an average success rate might be in the region of 25–50%. So a seemingly low success rate might be expected in the nonprofit sector as well. Furthermore, it is difficult at this stage to produce a body of evidence that organisations impact has increased due to capacity building. Experience to date does not answer the key questions posed by Connolly and Light in their article, *Building to Last: The Grantmaker's Guide to Strengthening Nonprofit Organizations*, 'what kinds of capacity building interventions get the best results?'[12]

Overall, there is a growing commitment to invest more effort into measuring the results of capacity building and an expectation that as organisations gather data, the evidence base about different approaches to capacity building will increase. Those organisations that contribute to that effort will be best placed to exploit the benefits and apply the learning that will inevitably emerge over the coming years.

Summary

Recognise that lack of capacity is a critical constraint
- Government funders, private donors and charity watchdogs unintentionally pressurise organisations to under-invest in organisation capacity
- Lack of capacity is seen as the bottleneck that is constraining nonprofit organisations from having greater impact on the pressing social issues that the nation faces.

Invest in capacity building
- The case for significant investment in organisation and management has grown with exponential interest
- A new paradigm of organisation effectiveness has emerged involving:
  - continuous strategic investment in the organisation
  - charging funders the full cost of programmes
  - using unrestricted income to invest in the organisation capacity
  - subsidising services only when there is demonstrable connection with the organisation's strategic priorities.

Identify the critical elements of organisation capacity
- Internal capacity building focuses on developing the mission, the board, people, management skills, physical infrastructure, technology and evaluation
- External capacity building is concerned with taking new initiatives, developing new strategies and attracting new and more diversified income sources.

Adopt new approaches to capacity building

- The four key elements that shape the ultimate success of a capacity building project are:
  - the desired outcome
  - the change strategy selected
  - the champions guiding the effort
  - the time, energy and money invested in the process
- Most capacity building projects are concerned with strategic planning, fundraising and financial management, board development, communications and marketing
- Key ingredients of successful initiatives include new aspirations, commitment from senior management and plenty of patience.

Pursue explicit strategies for increasing impact

- There are four generic strategies for increasing impact: diversification, specialisation, scaling up and scaling deep
- Diversification is the most common and least threatening to current activities but risks over-stretching the organisation's management capacity
- Specialisation involves greater effort with an existing group of users but can reduce access to funders and donors
- Scaling up has the potential to increase organisation impact but there are dangers of not being properly connected to the local community
- Scaling deep involves focusing in a geographic area but may not allow the organisation to exploit economies of scale.

Measure the impact of capacity building

- There are three levels of outcomes:
  - the output of the initiative
  - the impact on the organisation
  - the impact on the organisation's mission
- Organisations need to take stock of the effectiveness of capacity building before and after each capacity building initiative.

References

1 Robert Putnam, *Making Democracy Work – Civic Traditions in Modern Italy*, Princeton, NJ, Princeton University Press, 1993

2 Carol De Vita and Cory Flemming, *Capacity Building in Nonprofit Organizations*, Washington, The Urban Institute, 2001

3 Paul Light and Elizabeth Hubbard, *The Capacity Building Challenge*, Washington, Brookings Institution, 2002

4 Christine Letts, William Ryan and Allen Grossman, *High Performance Nonprofit Organizations*, New York, Wiley, 1999

5 Paul Light, *Pathways to Nonprofit Excellence*, Washington, The Brookings Institution, 2002

6 McKinsey & Company, *Effective Capacity Building in Nonprofit Organizations*, Reston VA, Venture Philanthropy Partners, 2001 (download from www.vppartners.org)

7 Gold Book Committee, *Gold Book – Success Stories in Nonprofit Management*, Washington, Alliance for Nonprofit Management, 2000

8 Allison Fine, Nancy Kopf and Colette Thayer, *Echoes from the Field*, Washington, Innovation Network, 2002 (download from www.innonet.org)

9 Bill Meehan and Les Silverman, *For Charities, Performance is the New Ethic* in *Leader to Leader*, New York, The Drucker Foundation, Fall 2001

10 Gregory Dees, Jane Wei-Skillern *et al.*, *Pathways to Social Impact – Strategies for Scaling Out Successful Social Innovations*, Durham, Centre for the Advancement of Social Entrepreneurship, 2002

11 J. Gregory Dees *et al.*, *Strategic Tools for Social Entrepreneurs*, New York, John Wiley & Sons, 2002

12 Paul Connolly, *Building to Last: The Grantmakers Guide to Strengthening Nonprofit Organizations*, New York, TCC Group, 2000 (download from www.consco.com)

Websites

Maryland Ethics and Accountability Code for the Nonprofit Sector (download from www.mdnonprofit.org)

Minnesota Council of Nonprofits (download from www.mncn.org)

3 Managing performance

More than ever before, Americans want to know what nonprofit organisations are accomplishing. Foundations, government and major donors want to know that their resources have achieved the desired results. They are less interested in what the organisation did and more interested in the outcome and impact of the funding. The movement to transparency and accountability in all walks of life means that nonprofit organisations reporting on the outcomes of their work will be regarded more highly and therefore receive more financial support.

Whilst performance measurement has proved to be easy in theory, and it has been much more difficult in practice. As one chief executive in a survey commented "Measuring mission success is like the Holy Grail for nonprofits – much sought after but never found". The authors of the resulting report comment 'Nonprofits simply have not been able to duplicate the crisp, straightforward way that businesses measure their performance'.[1] Professor Michael Cortes of the Institute for Nonprofit Management at the University of San Francisco concurs, "Performance management is in its early stages of development and is not a settled area yet". McKinsey's Paul Jansen agrees, "No one has cracked the code for performance metrics. We are in the evolutionary stage and the challenge is to get people to begin a journey that will take 10 or more years".

Leaders in the field acknowledge that performance management will become increasingly important as organisations strive to ensure all efforts are focused on achieving their objectives as efficiently as possible. However, they are conscious that the catalytic effect of an organisation's work on a whole field can be more important than its outputs or outcomes. Inevitably it is much harder to ascribe causality for these wider impacts. "We know when we have played a role," says Kim Smith of New Schools Venture Fund, "but we don't know the extent of our contribution".

Furthermore, there are concerns about the wider impact of performance management on the sector: 'There are few actionable assessment tools that measure impact at a community-wide level or can describe the impact of policy, research, advocacy and other efforts in tackling the more complex and intractable problems of society'.[2] Some fear that relentless focus on outcomes will further dry up funds for organisations seeking to make constructive change on a community-wide, issue-based or systemic level.[2]

Despite these acknowledged limitations, the focus of attention has moved from measuring outcomes to managing impact. According to Alan Abramson, Director on the Nonprofit Sector and Philanthropy Program at the Aspen Institute, "the next step is to move from measuring outcomes to managing impact". The key to managing impact is assembling information on the organisation's outcomes and using it systematically in management and board decision making. Knowledge about performance can then be used in an active way to inform decisions that enhance organisations' effectiveness.

This chapter

Chapter 3 provides evidence from leading-edge organisations showing that they:

- grasp the opportunity to manage performance
- recognise legitimate concerns
- select measures that fit the organisation's mission
- use results to drive decisions at every level
- embed performance management into organisation culture.

3.1 Grasp the opportunity to manage performance

Performance management – its origins

Measuring performance in nonprofits has a long history, beginning with reporting on financial performance. People wanted to know how organisations spent their money. That was followed by measurement of outputs, because people wanted to know what the organisation did with its funds. Interest in outputs can be traced to the late 1950s and the advent of the Great Society social programmes of the 1960s, principally the Model Cities and the Community Action Programs.

In 1976 United Way's programme specification system defined 587 categories of human services and suggested measures for each. More recently there has been much interest in setting standards and measuring quality to provide information about how well organisations deliver their services. In the early 1980s the idea of key performance indicators became popular, particularly in public service organisations. Later in the 1980s accrediting bodies began requiring service providers to measure participant satisfaction.

Outcome measurement is seen to follow naturally from these previous developments and addresses the question 'what was achieved?' It is viewed by many as the next brick in the wall of performance measurement. There is a widespread view in the US that outcome measurement is here to stay. The distinction between inputs (money, staff and volunteer time), outputs (the number of people served and campaigns run), outcomes (the results of the service for individuals) and impacts (the results of services and campaigns community-wide) is widely accepted. 'Any scan of nonprofit publications, academic and trade journals and even mainstream media, reveals a popular fixation on results and accountability. Whatever the term – the message is the same: a demand for clear measurement of impact.'[2]

The growth of interest in outcomes and impact took off in the early 1990s when United Way of America made significant investments in developing outcome measurement tools and promoted them across the sector. In 1992 Harold Williams and Arthur Webb of the Rensselaerville Institute published a significant book *Outcome Funding – A New Approach to Public Sector Grantmaking*[3] that added to the momentum. Many national organisations picked up these initiatives and encouraged and supported their regional and local chapters (branches) to take steps to measure outcomes.

By 1998 the American Cancer Society was providing training on outcome measurement for its local units, the American Foundation for the Blind Annual Leadership Conference focused on outcomes and the American Red Cross reported that 100 of its chapters were currently working on outcome measurement. According to Elizabeth Boris of The Urban Institute "Foundations, government and United Ways have all come to the same views around the need to measure impact".

Most recently the debate has moved from measuring outcomes to the use of data to manage performance. Implementation of performance management has been pushed particularly hard by venture philanthropists. They wanted to see numbers that demonstrated growth and effectiveness. They expected the organisations that they funded to produce reports similar to investment reports with graphs and charts showing the numbers of people served and the outcomes of the services. They drove the organisations they funded to make significant improvements to their performance management systems.

However, according to Bill Ryan of Harvard's Hauser Centre, "There has been a backlash against the types of performance metrics foisted on organisations by the new philanthropists". The numbers were sometimes seen to be too simplistic and failed to represent the subtleties and complexities of providing services to people who often have multiple problems that are not amenable to simple measures.

Forces driving organisations to manage performance

There are many external forces driving nonprofit organisations to develop performance management systems. First, there are growing demands for greater transparency and accountability. People increasingly expect nonprofits to be clear and honest about what they are doing and accountable for their achievements and failures. Some call for 'radical transparency' that would enable anyone to see precisely what a nonprofit is doing. According to Charles Lyons, Chief Executive of Unicef USA, "Radical transparency may be the key to improving performance".

Second, funders want to know what has been achieved with their money and, critically, are more willing to pay for the costs of gathering and reporting on performance. There is some scepticism about the value of 'in-depth' evaluations, but a great deal of interest in low-cost systems that provide information that is 'good enough' to demonstrate outcomes and inform future decision taking.

Third, the widespread move to funding individuals who require state health and social services, rather than funding the suppliers, has emphasised results-oriented service delivery. Outcomes for individual participants are usually recorded and can be a requirement in care contracts. The availability of this data is encouraging organisations to assemble information on the overall performance of a service and use it to gain insights into which actions achieve the desired results.

Finally, nonprofits are subject to continuous attention from the press who are always ready to highlight wrong-doing. This feeds public cynicism about nonprofits which is hard to counter without evidence of solid achievements. The vacuum of information about accomplishments leaves nonprofits wide open to criticism. Performance management offers an opportunity to create widespread understanding of long-term successes that buttress organisations against such media challenges.

Although the demands for improving performance are primarily external, boards and managers recognise that performance management is a powerful tool for keeping organisations focused on results. 'Nonprofit board members have a well known tendency to stray, to promote pet projects and initiatives, and nothing combats such hobbyism better than a clear, commonly agreed upon set of institutional measures.'[1]

Similarly managers find that the presence of performance metrics helps to focus the efforts of their staff. They are also finding that good performance measures help in seeking grant funding. 'The majority of philanthropic institutions are not yet demanding this level of sophistication…but the trend definitely favours those who can show tangible results.'[1]

Beyond the pragmatics, there is a compelling theoretical case for performance management. Resources are always limited so organisations need to evaluate their work to understand which services deliver the best results. This information should inform resource allocation decisions which in the past have often been based more on well-crafted funding applications than on rigorously tested evidence of achievements. Funders can then invest more heavily in those programmes that are proven to be effective and withdraw from those that are shown to be less effective.

A further strand in the theoretical case stems from the flow of funds to nonprofits. Unlike for-profit organisations, nonprofits do not have an in-built organisation reward system. When a for-profit is successful its sales and profits increase, so successful organisations prosper while unsuccessful ones eventually fail. In the nonprofit world it is possible for an organisation to be highly successful at fundraising and deliver poor services. Performance management is therefore the missing link that connects results to future rewards, in the form of new and extended funding.

Measuring outcomes at Toolworks

Toolworks, a San Francisco-based agency providing services to increase economic and social opportunities for disabled people, makes extensive use of outcome measures.

"We promote the measures when we are approaching funders," says Executive Director Donna Feingold. "We also use them to identify gaps in our services. For example, our community support services developed because our outcome follow-ups identified that although we had got people into work they were lonely and had poor quality home life."

The twelve outcome measures for Toolworks' 2000–01 employment programme come from seven separate sources:

Measure	Data source	Goal	Outcome
Effectiveness			
No. of clients placed in new jobs	Placement reports	72	73
% earning $8 or more per hour	Placement reports	75%	67%
% maintaining job for 90 days or more	Placement reports	85%	84%
% securing subsidised housing	Case records	25%	30%
No. of new contracts secured	Contract files	10	12
Efficiency			
No of clients with reduced reliance on public benefits	Case records	175	219
% of clients placed within 90 days of intake	Placement reports	80%	74%
% of clients receiving support from generic resources	Case records	50%	64%
% of employees maintaining an accident-free workplace	Claim reports	95%	91%
Satisfaction			
% of clients who are satisfied with the service	Satisfaction surveys	75%	76%
% of satisfied staff	Staff survey	75%	86%
% of satisfied referring agencies	Survey	75%	89%

A summary of all outcome measures is presented at the annual meeting and the measures are reported regularly to staff.

So, are organisations grasping the opportunity to manage performance more systematically? In 1997 a survey of outcome measurement suggested that 'there has been an explosion of outcome measurement activity in recent years'.[4] In 1998 a survey by Independent Sector of 1,700 organisations found that 43% were collecting information on changes in client conditions or behaviour and 67% reported that they were routinely collecting information on clients' satisfaction with services.[5]

More recently, Paul Light's 2002 survey of Executive Directors[6] found that 92% reported an increased emphasis on outcome measurement and of 79% reported that the increase was 'a great deal' or 'a fair amount'.

It is clear that outcome measures are here to stay. Leading organisations are now focusing on implementing performance management systems that enable managers and boards to determine what they have accomplished and to keep staff attention on achieving their missions.

3.2 Recognise legitimate concerns

Although the case for performance management is strong, and it is widely accepted that the move to measure has been valuable, there are significant challenges in implementing such systems. Research into performance management for foundations has demonstrated that as measurement moves away from outcomes at the level of the individual organisation and towards policy change, there are fewer models or systems for measuring impact.

Different levels of outcome measurement for foundations

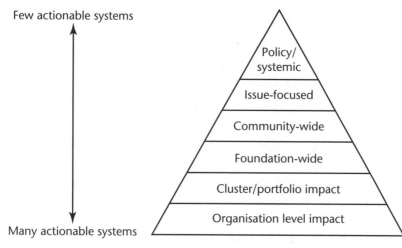

Source: Global Leaders for Tomorrow, *Philanthropy Measures Up*[2]

Recent research into outcome measurement in nonprofits came to a similar conclusion: 'leaders of nonprofit organisations face a particular bind in responding to the demands for results-based accountability. If they focus only on the project-level outcomes over which they have the most control or for which indicators are readily available, they risk default on the larger question of accountability to publicly valued goals. On the other hand, if they try to demonstrate the impact of their particular projects on community-wide outcomes, they risk taking credit inappropriately or shouldering the blame for indicators beyond their control'.[7]

Practitioners recognise that whilst measurement is comparatively easy in some parts of the nonprofit world it is much more difficult in others. Preventative work is frequently raised as a problem. For example, measuring how many teenagers did not get pregnant as a result of a teen sexual health programme is only possible over a long time scale, and even then it is virtually impossible to link the programme with the results. In this circumstance intermediate indicators are seen as more valuable in preventative work. For example, measuring changes in people's attitudes before and after the service is delivered can provide valuable information to service providers.

Some activities are more amenable to measurement and some are more qualitative in nature. The outcome of an employment programme can be measured relatively easily in terms of the number of people obtaining employment of the type desired and staying in post for a stated period. The outcomes of a counselling service are inherently less easy to measure since they are very dependent on the quality of the interaction between people holding confidential discussions.

"People are aware of the dangers of relying on numbers alone," according to Audrey Alvarado of the National Council of Non Profit Associations, a network of state and regional associations representing 17,000 nonprofits throughout the country. "The challenge is to articulate achievements in ways people can understand – and this requires a combination of numbers and case studies."

The challenge of balancing quantitative and qualitative measures is reflected in evidence on the types of organisations that are most likely to measure outcomes. A joint Independent Sector and Urban Institute study found that employment training, vocational rehabilitation, home health care and nursing home care were more likely to track outcomes related to clients' condition.[8] In these cases reporting is required by external agencies including funders and accreditation organisations such as the Joint Commission on Accreditation of Healthcare Organizations.

Other challenges are recognised and taken into account in the development of performance management systems. They include:

- the risk that performance management could disadvantage areas of work that are less easily measured
- the danger that staff might be encouraged to target services where successful outcomes are more likely rather than at areas of greatest need
- excessive interest in short-term results that could be at the expense of the longer term sustainability of initiatives – a particular concern in the nonprofit sector where change can take many years or even decades.

There is also the challenge of establishing the primary purpose of a performance management system. As Peter Shiras of the Independent Sector says, "There is a difference between what organisations need from measurement (honest, critical appraisal that feeds into organisations' learning) and what they need to give funders (evidence of success to get more money)".

PREVENTING PERFORMANCE FROM DISTORTING PRIORITIES: CHILDREN'S INSTITUTE INTERNATIONAL

Children's Institute International provides a home visiting service. They recognised that the 'best outcome' for individuals varies. In most cases, keeping young people out of foster care is a desired outcome, but in a few cases, foster care might be the best option.

To overcome this problem they take a two-level approach. They conduct individual assessments on all children using standard child psychology development measures. In addition, they establish goals for each child and family and assess individual achievement of the agreed goals. They use a goal attainment scale to measure the percentage of children achieving the stated goals and assimilate this data to produce programme level results. They benchmark their results against similar programmes delivered by other organisations.

According to Chief Executive Mary Emmons, "A strong organisation culture is required to avoid creaming the easy cases. Our aim is to help the most difficult cases that we are capable of assisting. We do turn down some families because their problems are too complex for our skills and resources. Even with this boundary, we recognise that very difficult cases do make heavy use of resources so we top up state funding for these cases with donor income".

There are concerns about the resource implications of improving performance management. Some approaches are expensive, and managers are acutely aware of the danger of spending time and money on performance systems that ultimately never quite measure achievement of the organisation's mission and may not deliver value concomitant with the cost of implementation. "Start up costs are high and it is difficult to access resources to develop performance management systems," according to Alan Abramson of the Aspen Institute. There are many reports of expensive evaluations that do not turn out to be useful. The key according to Abramson is to "find low cost ways of collecting and using data".

When the data is collected in usable forms, ways have to be found to make effective use of it. "The big challenge is to incorporate measuring into everyday activities and then to adjust what the organisation is doing when the measurements suggest change is necessary," says Abramson.

Performance management in action – some practical advice

United Way offers valuable advice about having realistic objectives when establishing performance management systems:

'1 Requiring program managers to set outcome targets before they have at least a year of baseline outcome data is counterproductive. Programs with no experience in outcome measurement generally have no basis for setting an appropriate target, and their targets will likely be little more than guesses.

2 Fund allocators do not yet have enough experience with outcome measurement to judge whether a particular level of achieved performance is good, bad or in between.

3 Comparing seemingly similar programs to reward those with the "best" outcomes is tempting but misguided. Even "similar" programs have meaningful differences in mission, target audience, geographic location, staffing, service methodology and funding level.

4 In judging outcome findings, the best comparison for a program is itself: Is the program improving? Is it learning from earlier outcome findings, making adjustments, and having better results?

5 Despite the hope of many fund allocators, outcome findings will not make the allocation decision easier. Decisions about where to direct resources will remain complex and value based, and funding decisions always will need to consider more than outcome performance.'

Source: Margaret Plantz *et al., Outcome Measurement: Showing Results in the Nonprofit Sector*[9]

Despite the many challenges, there is no doubt that performance management will become an essential part of management activity for most organisations. "There are no ultimate answers in performance metrics," according to Stephanie Lowell, Nonprofit Practice Manager at McKinsey. "But having metrics does focus an organisation on what it should be achieving. Understanding how a nonprofit service affects people in its client group is a valuable discipline." So whilst they will be most valuable when they are used as aids to decision making, performance metrics are not substitutes for good judgement.

LAUNCHING A PERFORMANCE MANAGEMENT INITIATIVE: BOYS AND GIRLS CLUBS OF BOSTON

Boys and Girls Clubs of Boston is an $11 million organisation that exists to help boys and girls, generally from disadvantaged circumstances, develop the qualities needed to become responsible citizens and leaders. They provide activities and support services designed to assist in the educational, emotional, physical and social development of 6 to 18 year olds and they serve 8,000 children in the Boston area.

They decided to take a significant initiative to develop a performance management system and culture. As they had little information on service users, the initiative began by modernising their membership database. This involved changing enrolment forms and developing a balanced scorecard of outcome indicators. These were piloted with a sample of clubs that were enthusiastic about the initiative. The challenge then was to take the initiative 'to scale' and involve all their clubs.

Linda Whitlock, the Chief Executive, assembled a team of line managers to lead the project and involved a board member with particular expertise in outcome measures. She decided that she would personally lead the initiative to ensure it was seen as a priority for everyone.

The organisation raised $300,000 from foundations to finance implementation of the initiative. They formed a partnership with a university and established a long-term longitudinal study to attempt to measure the overall impact of club experience on people's lives. It will measure the impact of clubs on children's educational, emotional, social and moral development.

"We have an obligation to know what impact we are having," said Linda Whitlock. "I have systematically built this initiative to ensure that it is sustainable – for ever! It will enable us to differentiate ourselves significantly from other organisations seeking funds to do similar work."

3.3 Select measures that fit the organisation's mission

According to the survey carried out jointly by Independent Sector and The Urban Institute, organisations are collecting two types of outcome indicators. First they are gathering **information on service outcomes**. This measures the quality of a service or the perceptions of users. The key question they address is whether users were satisfied with the service. They ask participants how they rated the each aspect of a service such as its quality, timeliness, responsiveness and staff attitudes.

Second, they are gathering **information on end outcomes**. This measures the actions or changed conditions of users that result from the delivery of the service. They capture the numbers and percentages of people who exhibit the changes that the programme was designed to achieve. The majority of organisations in their survey collected both types of indicator.[8]

Research by McKinsey concluded that organisations have three options for measuring their success in achieving their mission. They can be used in combination. First, they can **narrowly define the mission so progress can be measured directly**. The example of Goodwill Industries is frequently cited. Its mission is to help disabled people by providing job training and employment services, and with an income of over $1,600 million per annum is the country's seventh largest nonprofit. It measures the number of people served, the number gaining employment and the salaries that they earn.

Second, organisations can **demonstrate through research a direct connection between their service and the desired results**. Jump $tart Coalition, a nonprofit dedicated to improving the educational outcomes of poor children is an example. It takes the lowest achievers from the Head Start programme and provides a basic literacy skills programme. Academically robust studies have demonstrated that children who attend their programme at the age of four have better educational outcomes throughout primary school. The number of children attending their programme is therefore a good measure of the achievement of their mission.

Third, organisations can **develop micro-level goals that imply success on a grander scale**. The Nature Conservancy has a grand mission to increase global biodiversity – which it cannot measure. But its main activity is to purchase and protect important sites and it is currently responsible for over 11.5 million acres of land. It measures the biodiversity health at its own sites by evaluating the condition of plants and animals it is trying to save and tracks efforts to counter the most critical threats to environmental health.

Examples of outcome measures

'■ Number and percent of vocational rehabilitation participants placed in employment who retained their job for 90 and 150 days
■ Number and percent of youth service participants who went on to attend 2 or 4 year college courses
■ Number and percent of Alzheimer's clients with improvements or no change in walking steadily, self feeding, interacting with others
■ Number and percent of mental health clients placed in less restrictive settings
■ Number and percent of people screened for drugs who show a decreased amount of substances 3, 6 and 12 months after a drug treatment programme
■ Number and percent of clients who retained housing in which they were placed 3, 6 and 12 months after leaving the programme
■ Pounds of material recovered and recycled by environmental programmes.'

Source: Elaine Morley *et al.*, *Outcome Measurement in Nonprofit Organizations*[8]

For many nonprofits, following up service users 3, 6, 12 and more months after the service has been provided is seen as important because the outcome of the service may not show immediately. Though difficult in cases where it is hard to keep track of recipients (such as homeless services), follow-ups can provide high quality information about outcomes. Clearly, data gathering becomes increasingly difficult and expensive as the time gap between the delivery of the service and the follow up grows.

Another aspect of choosing performance indicators is the need to capture the unique features of nonprofit activity. These include:

■ reaching under-served populations
■ opportunities for volunteering and 'citizen participation'
■ the results of advocacy work
■ opportunities for spiritual activity.

ASIAN NEIGHBORHOOD DESIGN'S INDIVIDUAL AND FAMILY TRACKING AND EVALUATION TOOL

'Asian Neighborhood Design (AND) has worked for over 20 years in the San Francisco Bay Area, sponsoring a variety of programs to help individuals and families get out of poverty. They use a Tracking and Evaluation Tool with many of their clients.

Each project participant, with an AND support person, crafts a personal self-sufficiency plan. Staff track the new participant's status in each of seven categories – from "income/assets" to "personal attributes" – with a score of -2, –1, +1, or +2. A score of –2 represents a high risk or crisis situation, while a +2 represents a strong, stable situation. At regular intervals they meet with their AND support person and assess their progress in each of the seven categories.

The tool is not only used for tracking and evaluation. It also guides the discussion between the AND support person and the participant, and it helps the participant to develop and carry through the self-sufficiency plan.

The tool helps AND evaluate how a participant is progressing and how long AND can continue to support the participant. The idea assumes that a person needs several strong supports to be considered self-sufficient and can handle no more than one or two risk areas at the same time.

This evaluation tool focuses on outcomes – on changes in people's lives that may be partly due to AND and other programs. It involves no expectation of precise measurement, and there is (intentionally) a large element of judgment in the numbers it yields. Nevertheless, (and this is critically important to the value of the tool) large score differences, such as between a total score of –8 for one participant and +5 for another, should reflect easily recognizable differences in levels of self-sufficiency.'

	Income/ assets	Education/ skills	Housing/ food	Safety/ environment	Human service	Relationships	Personal attributes
Major life issue:							
Assets: +2							
+1							
Barriers: −1							
−2							
TOTAL							

Source: Global Leaders for Tomorrow, *Philanthropy Measures Up*[2]

A comprehensive performance management system will capture data on these special dimensions of nonprofit activity as well as the more obvious benefits to service users. 'Agencies should tap many perspectives when identifying program outcomes. Program volunteers, current and past participants (and perhaps family members), persons such as teachers and employers, and other agencies can point out important outcomes.'[9]

This should be balanced with the need to keep performance measures simple. "The key issue is not ever greater focus on the technicality of output measures or of ascribing causality," according to James Austin, Chair of Harvard Business School's Initiative on Social Enterprise. "It is more important to identify meaningful measures and discover how to integrate them into management systems."

The importance of agreeing measures with funders before work begins is also stressed. Leading organisations ensure that they have explicit agreements with their funders about both the measures and the targets. This allows assessment of performance to focus on learning for the future rather than retrospective debates about what the most appropriate measures should have been.

Finally, the desire to learn from experience and continuously improve should be balanced against the need to keep some consistency from year to year so that trends can be measured and achievements celebrated.

SOCIAL RETURN ON INVESTMENT: ROBERTS ENTERPRISE DEVELOPMENT FUND

Roberts Enterprise Development Fund (REDF) is a venture philanthropy fund that invests in social enterprises. Investors want the enterprises that they support to be financially viable, but more importantly to create significant social benefit. Investors therefore want to calculate which investments produce the greatest financial returns and which have the greatest social impact.

In the business world, methods for calculating financial returns are well understood and are based on discounted cash flow analysis. This takes the cash flow that the enterprise is expected to generate over coming years and 'discounts' the value of future cash flows to allow for the fact that cash next year is worth less than cash now.

The significant breakthrough that REDF made was to calculate social returns in a similar way. To value social returns they calculate the reduction in social security payments and the reduction in the use of community clinics, mental health treatment, hospital emergency rooms, legal services, prison services, substance abuse treatment and other public services that will result from an organisation's services. They then discount these values in the same way that businesses discount future cash flows.

As their focus is employing people in social enterprises, they also add the value of the taxes that previously non-tax-paying employees will pay. Together these two amounts are a proxy for social value.

To create a total picture of the value of a social enterprise, they add the financial value of the enterprise with the social value to create a 'blended value'. They have calculated the financial and social returns of the 11 investments that the fund has made. They are well worth reading.

Industrial Maintenance Engineers – an example of social return on investment

Industrial Maintenance Engineers (IME) is a social enterprise that exists to provide professional cleaning services delivered by people with psychiatric disabilities, ex-offenders and people with a history of substance abuse.

It provides janitorial services for 38 buildings and is expected to have sales of $1.4 million by 2004. It employed 77 people at the start of 2000.

Social purpose results (per target employee)	1999 $
Public savings	23,531
New taxes paid by employees	890
Wage improvement of each employee	5,931
Financial improvement (wage improvement less reduced social security)	3,594

At the time of the report (winter 2000) just over $300,000 had been invested in the enterprise. The financial value of the enterprise was $477,000 and the social purpose value (over the life-time of the enterprise) was a mighty $58 million, primarily because the overwhelming majority of employees were people who, before employment, were heavily dependent on social security and a range of public services.

Source: *SROI Reports*[10]

3.4 Use results to drive decisions at every level

Two broad approaches to measuring performance are emerging from initiatives taken to date. The first and most common is a results-based approach that quantifies outcomes in relation to inputs, activities and outputs. These can be reported on a balanced scorecard or a corporate dashboard. The second is comparative and uses benchmarks to review performance against similar organisations or services. They can both be applied simultaneously.

Approach	Reported in
Result oriented	Balanced scorecards
	Corporate dashboards
Comparison oriented	Benchmarking reports

The results-based approach is rooted in the well-established idea that **inputs** of resources support **activities** that lead to service or policy **outputs,** which in turn produce the desired **outcomes**. In this model, outputs are about the programmes that organisations deliver and outcomes are about the benefits to participants.

There is a widespread view in the US that the choice of what to measure needs to be rooted in a theory of social change. The first step according to Alan Abramson of the Aspen Institute is "to be clear about the underlying model of change that the organisation is attempting to achieve. It can then use performance measurement to test whether the resources applied are having the desired effect".

The chain of relationships between activities, outputs and outcomes is referred to as the 'logic' or 'theory' of how a programme brings about benefits to its participants. United Way talks of a series of 'if-then' relationships and gives the example of pregnancy programmes:

- 'If a program provides prenatal counselling to pregnant teens, then the teens have increased knowledge of good prenatal care
- If the teens have increased knowledge of good prenatal care, then this leads to changed behaviour: the teens eat the proper foods, take a prenatal vitamin each day and avoid cigarettes, alcohol and other drugs
- If the teens follow these practices, then the result is that the teens deliver healthy newborns.'[9]

The balanced scorecard

Some organisations have adopted the idea of the balanced scorecard, originally developed by Robert Kaplan and David Norton for use in the private sector. It is based on the notion that traditional corporate sector financial measures only capture past performance and that it is more important to measure the drivers of future performance.

The aim is to measure performance on a range of dimensions, each chosen because they will assist the organisation to achieve its overall mission. So the balanced scorecard focuses managers on both outcomes and the health of the organisation that is producing the outcomes.

Their ideas have been widely implemented in the for-profit world. In the nonprofit sector the scorecard puts the organisation's mission at the heart of four types of measures:

Balanced scorecard

Dimension of performance	Measuring
1 Service users/policy changes	Achievements of the organisation's mission
2 Internal processes	Planning and service delivery processes
3 Learning and growth	Organisation capacity, evaluation and learning
4 Financial	Fundraising, cost control, productivity improvements

According to Kaplan 'the balanced scorecard has enabled nonprofit organisations to bridge the gap between vague mission and strategy statements and day-to-day operational actions. It has facilitated a process by which an organisation can achieve strategic focus, avoiding the pathology of attempting to be everything to everyone. The measurement system has shifted the focus from programs and initiatives to the outcomes the initiatives and programs are supposed to accomplish'.[11]

The balanced scorecard acknowledges aggregating performance data is often not appropriate in the nonprofit world. "The key benefit of the balanced scorecard," according to Jeff Bradach, Managing Director of Bridgespan Group, the successful nonprofit consultancy, "is that it helps to organise data. Operating data is very important and having it well organised enables effective accountability".

Three of the performance perspectives are concerned with measuring internal performance. According to Harvard Business Professor Allen Grossman, "There is evidence that if nonprofit organisations have good plans, quality assurance systems, measurement systems and mechanisms for improving performance then they will have better delivery of their service".

New Profit Inc requires the organisations it funds to use balanced scorecards. They report the following traits amongst the organisations they fund:

- the management team will talk more about strategy and less about tactics
- staff of the organisation know and understand the strategy and how their job fits into it
- organisations develop the capability to refresh and create their own scorecards
- evaluation becomes more integrated with and embedded in the organisation's operations.

Source: Global Leaders for Tomorrow, *Philanthropy Measures Up*[2]

Just as people counsel against attempts to make performance indicators unrealistically scientific, so there is a view that it is more important to have a workable scorecard than to strive after the perfect scorecard. "The precise categories of what to measure on the scorecard are not the critical issue," according to Allen Grossman. "The point is to understand the drivers of performance and get the board and staff to discuss these drivers. They need to go beyond fundraising and good governance to get insights into the ecology of how nonprofits function."

Some organisations are taking the approach one step further. Kaplan and Norton extended the notion of the balanced scorecard and proposed that organisations should use their key performance indicators to create a 'strategy map' that helps managers to see the connections between each of the drivers of performance and the intended results.

The idea of a strategy map builds on the work many organisations have done on strategic planning. Strategic plans establish organisations' missions, objectives and the overall strategies for achieving the mission. Strategy maps take this one step further. They attempt to reduce the strategy to its essential elements and to show how the organisation will deliver the desired mission.

STRATEGY MAP FOR A VENTURE PHILANTHROPY-FUNDED
ORGANISATION: NEW LEADERS FOR NEW SCHOOLS

New Leaders for New Schools aims to improve the performance of state
schools by recruiting, training, placing and supporting a new generation of
outstanding school principals.

The organisation trains and places school principals in urban schools. It
plans to place 500 school principals by 2010. In 2002 it expects that
30,000 children will have enhanced educational prospects following the
appointment of its highly trained school leaders. Its $2 million start-up
funding was generated by seed funding from three venture philanthropy
organisations: Boston-based New Profit Inc., San Francisco-based New
Schools Venture Fund, and the Los Angeles-based Broad Foundation.

Their strategy map and the associated performance indicators are evolving.
At the time of writing it was as follows. It is somewhat overwhelming at first
glance as it reduces the organisation's strategy and performance to one
diagram. It is easiest to read it from the bottom upwards.

New Leaders for New Schools – strategy map 2001–02 ⅢⅢ➤

The corporate dashboard

One of the dangers with performance information is that managers are
quickly overwhelmed with data. To overcome this, a number of organisations have implemented the idea of a 'corporate dashboard' – a
limited number of key indicators that can be read, like a car dashboard,
at a glance, and give an overview of the organisation's performance.

The dashboard contains data on the key outcomes the organisation is
achieving. It is typically produced quarterly and distributed to board
and staff – and sometimes to external funders as well.

The dashboard reflects the notion that no one indicator can quantify an
organisation's achievements and that a range of measures is needed to
get an accurate overview. 'A single outcome indicator seldom provides
a sufficiently comprehensive perspective on an organisation's
outcomes.'[8]

Dimension of performance	Strategy			
Social impact	Foster high academic achievement for all students led by NLNS Fellows and alumni		Catalyse changes in public schools through demonstrated success of the NLNS model	
	■ Identify measures to evaluate school performance		■ Identify measures & communications to demonstrate success of NLNS model	
Organisation outputs	Cohort of new leaders	New training and support	Placement in new schools	
	■ Quality of fellows ■ Mix of cohort (background, school type)	■ Quality of foundations ■ Quality of residency ■ Fellow satisfaction with ongoing support	■ Retention of partners ■ Number of placed fellows with authority over budget and hiring ■ Fellow satisfaction with placement	
Internal process	Recruit, select and sign fellows	Deliver training, mentorship and support to fellows	Site selection, placement and community partnerships	Affect school leadership & policy programmes
	■ No. of applicants for fellow position ■ No. of fellows signed	■ Faculty signed, courses revised ■ No. of mentor principals selected ■ Support plan developed and approved	■ No. of partners ■ No. of residency agreements signed ■ No. of fellows placed as administrators	■ Articles on NLNS ■ Participation in conferences ■ Meetings with thought leaders
Growth and learning	Build organisation capacity	Ensure effective governance (National & local boards)	Evaluation and organisational learning	
	■ Staffing and organisational structure ■ Technology and communication plan ■ Process codification	■ Board structure and responsibilities defined ■ Local advisory board formation	■ School evaluation metrics developed ■ Balanced scorecard completed and in use ■ Rubrics developed	
Financial perspective	Fundrasing and revenue generation		Cost control	
	■ Meet fundraising goals ■ Balance national & local fundraising		■ Maintain expenses on or below budget	

Key ■ Potential performance measure

Jewish Vocational Services (San Francisco) – Dashboard Indicators

Founded in 1973, Jewish Vocational Services (JVS) San Francisco is a non-sectarian organisation that links employers and individuals together to achieve their employment goals by providing the skills needed in today's workplace.

Ten years ago JVS established a sophisticated client database and seven years ago it began building a performance culture. The organisation has over 100 performance indicators covering all aspects of its work. These are boiled down to 12 that are most closely aligned with the corporate strategy. These 12 form the corporate dashboard. Their dashboard is derived from a balanced scorecard approach to measuring performance, and the four headings of performance come from their strategy map.

The dashboard is produced quarterly and sent to all staff twice a year with a commentary from the chief executive. The dashboard results provide a key input into the annual operating planning process. The results are published no more than 30 working days after the end of the quarter. They are reported half-yearly to the board along with bullet points summarising progress in achieving annual goals. Board meetings are scheduled to coincide with publication of the dashboard.

Data from the performance system is also used in personal performance reviews and in the salary setting process.

A performance measurement committee of volunteers meets three to four times a year to help refine measurement tools and analyse performance. This committee consists of experts from the foundation sector and 'veterans' of McKinsey and Bain consulting practices, who bring corporate expertise and fresh eyes to their tools and performance outcomes.

In future JVS San Francisco is planning to link client service usage data with their contract invoicing system and to introduce a bar code swipe system so that attendance data is input by their clients.

"Creating an integrated performance system enabled us to respond efficiently to the differing requirements of our funders," said Executive Director Abby Snay. "It also enabled us to provide key information for managing the organisation more effectively."

JVS San Francisco quarterly dashboard – year-end results

	2000/01 performance	Target	2001/02 performance
Adults and youth with challenges to employment			
Number of job placements secured	740	814	705
% of students completing skill building programmes	76%	85%	81%
% of students demonstrating gains in pre/post tests	86%	92%	90%
% of clients placed in full-time/ benefited positions	36%	40%	34%
Average wage at placement	$11.47	$12.45	$11.95
% of available programme capacity filled	93%	95%	91%
% stakeholder satisfaction with services	90%	95%	94%
Build organisation capacity			
Capital funds generated	$0.84m	$3.78	$1.01m
Number of courses certified	1	2	0
Learning and growth			
Average staff turnover	24%	23%	27%
Finance			
Total fee-based revenue	$ 46k		$84k
Contribution of unrestricted revenue	$530k		$480k

Abby Snay admits it is not yet perfect, and is planning further improvements based on their experience and feedback from their stakeholders.

Benchmarking

In addition to gaining a tighter understanding of their own performance, some organisations are using benchmarking to compare their performance with that of other organisations. Benchmarking has particular appeal to nonprofit organisations because it builds on a tradition of cooperation. People value such collaboration because it reflects underlying missions that transcend the roles of individual organisations.

There are a number of different approaches to benchmarking. Some organisations allow others to visit and discover differences in their processes and their results. Some organisations do 'study tours' with each other or in small groups. Some engage in more formal benchmarking based on systematic data collection across a range of organisations to compare performance and some form 'clubs' to learn collaboratively about driving improvements.

According to Christine Letts and her colleagues 'benchmarking is an organisational learning process that bridges the gap between great ideas and great performance'. They argue that organisations should invest time and resources in benchmarking because 'nonprofits must maximise the value of what they do with the resources they use. A learning process like benchmarking enables them to measure and improve value. For most nonprofit professionals a process like benchmarking enables them to increase the organisation's problem solving capacity'.[12]

"We are due for a wave of interest in benchmarking," according to McKinsey Director of Nonprofit Practice Paul Jansen. "It usually starts with industrial tourism. This develops into a desire to collect meaningful measures, and often a fight over which numbers are the most pertinent. Only after it has gone through these two stages do opportunities for real insight emerge – when organisations understand the various practices that lie behind differences in performance."

Creating and maintaining the momentum for benchmarking is not easy. As Letts and her colleagues note 'in most organisations there is a tendency for doing to eclipse planning and for planning to eclipse learning'.[12] They argue that the 'burden of developing a compelling case for benchmarking falls to the leaders of a nonprofit. They must be willing to risk exposing their organisations' strengths and weaknesses...to define their organisational learning needs...and present their case to funders and staff'.[12]

Some lessons for funders

Some funders have encouraged the organisations that they fund to develop outcome measures. United Way offers experienced advice to funders:

'■ Funders will play a key role in the nonprofit sector's move to a focus on outcomes. To be most constructive, funders should view their role as helping each program develop the outcome measurement approach that provides the most useful information for that program. To the extent that funders impose outcomes, measures, or timetables that do not align with agencies' efforts, they impede successful implementation.

■ Funders serve their own best interests by helping agencies develop capacity for outcome measurement.

■ Local funders can collaborate with each other very effectively to support agency efforts. They can, for example, pool resources to underwrite training and technical assistance. They also can agree on outcome measurement terminology, methodology and implementation timetables. Common application and reporting forms go even further in clarifying expectations and reducing the burden of paperwork on local agencies.

■ Funders can help agencies by providing an outside perspective on the reasonableness of agencies' outcome measurement plans and working collaboratively to help improve the proposed approach. Funders should accept outcomes, indicators and measurement methods established by relevant national organizations and accrediting bodies unless they fail to meet essential criteria.

■ As funders add outcome data as a reporting requirement, they should drop existing reporting requirements that do not match the focus on outcomes. If benefits for people are the critical emphasis, then some reports designed to monitor internal processes (for example, quarterly cash flow statements, detailed line-item budgets, salary information for specific staff, staffing structures, minutes of board meetings, internal policy and procedure manuals) should be eliminated. This action also helps offset the added burden for agencies of collecting and reporting outcome data.'

Source: Margaret Plantz et al., *Outcome Measurement: Sharing Results in the Nonprofit Sector*[9]

3.5 Embed performance management into organisation culture

Action to take

By themselves, measures do not deliver performance improvements. Results are achieved by putting performance at the heart of management. This requires actions by the board, senior management and service managers.

At the board level, some organisations give their programme committees responsibility for performance management. The Urban League, the influential organisation that enables African Americans to secure economic self-reliance, power and civil rights, has a board committee on programmes and affiliates whose main purpose is to monitor performance. It reviews each programme every year and is chaired by the senior vice chair. The League also has an annual board retreat that monitors the organisation's performance. Similarly, Big Brothers Big Sisters of Long Island has a programme committee of the board that monitors outcome evaluations of the individuals it serves and of the organisation as a whole.

Jewish Vocational Service adopts a slightly different approach. It has a board committee specifically on performance measurement. It meets quarterly to review the results and to refine the performance management system. Some boards take another approach and combine the strategy and performance functions, so one board committee oversees the development of both the strategic plan and the performance management system.

Continuous support from the chief executive and senior management is seen as essential to maintain the momentum of a process that takes years rather than months to implement. Children's Institute International, for example, discovered that it needed to create two promotion routes for its staff to achieve the performance focus it required. "Two different types of people are needed to enhance performance," said Chief Executive Mary Emmons. "One has the professional skill set and the other the managerial perspective. So we created the two routes and then invested heavily in training on topics such as finance and contract compliance to give programme managers the tools they needed to manage performance. We also invested heavily in IT so they had the information they needed to manage performance."

Many organisations stress the importance of stories to bring the performance system to life. The REDF social return on investment reports all contain an employee highlight that tells the story of how one person's life was transformed by the social enterprise.

The key point to learn is that creating a performance management system and culture requires sustained effort over many years. It also needs significant resources, both financial and staff time. To overcome the challenges and implement successful performance management systems, organisations have found that they need to explain the rationale for putting resources into it and to address people's legitimate concerns. This is a topic which benefits from extensive discussion before new initiatives are launched. In practical terms it is usually necessary create a project, appoint a project leader and establish clear and realistic objectives. The team should report to senior management and it should involve line management at every opportunity. Its final objective should be to embed the arrangements into the organisation's culture so it can disband having completed its work.

The lessons of performance management

So what has been learned by organisations that have set out to embed performance management in their organisation culture? The most common point made by interviewees was that it will lead organisations to be more modest in their aspirations and to simplify their activities. Virginia Hodgkinson, Professor at the Center for the Study of Voluntary Organizations and Service at Georgetown University, said that, "Performance management does lead to re-assessment of goals and to clearer separation of long and short-term goals".

"Efforts to improve performance will lead organisations to simplify," according to Harvard's Allen Grossman. "Having impact requires focus and unfortunately nonprofits use the veil of the nobility of their cause to justify a wide range of activities. This is unlikely to lead to optimum performance."

Alan Abramson of the Aspen Institute gave a similar message, "Performance management will lead organisations and foundations to simplify what they are attempting to achieve and be more modest in their aspirations. This is a necessary change because there is often a significant mismatch between organisations' aspirations and their resources".

The McKinsey research found that the existence of a system of measures helps to establish a culture of accountability. 'For years, the independent sector has gotten a free ride in this regard; very few donors or boards ever held management accountable for results and on the rare occasions when they did, it took a long time to gather the necessary evidence to act. Performance measures…vastly simplify that process for boards, senior managers and program managers alike.'[1]

Finally, experienced commentators stress simplicity. "Focus on practical, pragmatic measures, avoid perfection and don't be academic," according to Mary Ann Holohean, formerly of the Meyer Foundation. "Keep it simple, accessible, computerisable and efficient," advises Elizabeth Boris of the influential Urban Institute in Washington.

Summary

Grasp the opportunity to manage performance
- Demands for greater transparency, clearer accountability and sharper focus on achieving objectives are all leading organisations to put greater effort into performance management
- Performance information helps funders to invest in programmes that are proven to be effective and withdraw from those that are less effective. It is the link that should connect current results with future funding
- Organisations are integrating outcome information into corporate performance management systems and using it in decision taking.

Recognise legitimate concerns
- Measuring performance is easier:
  - at the level of individual organisations
  - for some types of services
  - in some sectors
- Organisations need to be aware of the dangers of only focusing on measurable outcomes, only accepting easy cases and taking a short-term view
- Performance management needs to be adapted to suit the circumstances and to balance quantitative and qualitative outcomes
- Organisations need to use existing data, focus on low cost ways of generating new data and ensure that the results are incorporated into everyday decision taking.

Select measures that fit the organisation's mission

- Organisations are collecting information on service outcomes and end outcomes
- Mission success can be measured by narrowly defining the mission, using research to demonstrate the connection between services and the desired results and developing micro-level goals that imply success on a wider scale
- Following up users 6, 9 and 12 months after the service has been delivered is important because the outcome of many nonprofit activities may not show for many months
- The unique features of nonprofit activity such as reaching under-served populations, opportunities for citizen participation and advocacy work also need to be captured
- The desire to learn from experience and continuously improve has to be balanced by the need to maintain consistency from year to year.

Use performance results to drive decisions at every level

- The two approaches to performance management are results based and comparison based
- Leading organisations clarify the logic or 'theory of change' that underpins high performance
- The balanced scorecard and the corporate dashboard are two common methods for summarising an overview of corporate performance
- The different approaches to benchmarking build on the sector's tradition of collaboration. Benchmarking is a systematic learning process. It requires consistent top-management support to ensure that it delivers long-term impact.

Embed performance management into organisation culture

- Leading organisations make a board committee responsible for monitoring performance and overseeing improvements to the performance management system
- Chief executives and senior managers act on the results of the performance system
- Performance management leads organisations to simplify their objectives, focus their activities and be more accountable
- Introducing performance management requires a project team with a leader, sufficient resources to ensure the initiative is sustainable over the long term and a brief to embed the process into line management.

References

1 John Sawhill and David Williamson, *Mission Impossible? Measuring Success in Nonprofit Organizations* in *Nonprofit Management and Leadership*, San Francisco, Jossey-Bass, Spring 2001

2 Global leaders for Tomorrow, *Philanthropy Measures Up*, Davos, World Economic Forum, 2003

3 Harold Williams and Arthur Webb, *Outcome Funding – A New Approach to Public Sector Grantmaking*, New York, The Rensselaerville Institute, 1992

4 K.E. Newcomer, *Using Performance Measurement to Improve Public and Nonprofit Programs*, San Francisco, Jossey-Bass, 1997

5 Susan Wiener *et al.*, *Balancing the Scales: Measuring the Contributions of Nonprofit Organizations and Religious Congregations*, Washington DC, Independent Sector, 2001

6 Paul Light, *Pathways to Nonprofit Excellence*, Washington, Brookings Institution, 2002

7 David Campbell, *Outcome Assessment and the Paradox of Nonprofit Accountability* in *Nonprofit Management and Leadership*, San Francisco, Jossey-Bass, Spring 2002

8 Elaine Morley *et al.*, *Outcome Measurement in Nonprofit Organizations*, Independent Sector, 2001 (download summary from www.IndependentSector.org

9 Margaret Plantz *et al.*, *Outcome Measurement: Showing Results in the Nonprofit Sector,* in *New Directions for Evaluation,* Jossey-Bass, reproduced by United Way, 1999 (download from www.unitedway.org)

10 *SROI Reports*, San Francisco, The Roberts Enterprise Development Fund, 2000 (download from www.redf.org)

11 Robert Kaplan, *Strategic Performance Measurement and Management in Nonprofit Organizations* in *Nonprofit Management and Leadership*, San Francisco, Jossey-Bass, Spring 2001

12 Christine Letts, William Ryan and Allen Grossman, *High Performance Nonprofit Organizations*, New York, Wiley, 1999

Websites

www.redf.org A wide range of material on Social Return on Investment is available from this site including:

Analysing the Value of Social Purpose Enterprise Within a Social Return on Investment Framework, which describes the underlying methodology

An information OASIS which describes how to implement a social return on investment system

Sample Social Return on Investment Reports

www.unitedway.org United Way's Outcome Measurement Resource Network and a wealth of reports and material on measuring outcomes.

4 Creating strategic alliances

Nonprofit organisations in America are forming strategic alliances because they believe that they can achieve their missions more effectively through collaborations with other organisations.

There has always been a high level of inter-dependence between organisations, as they formed umbrella bodies, professional associations, purchasing clubs, insurance cooperatives and advocacy organisations to further their interests. Indeed, the first Amherst Wilder Foundation publication to promote collaboration appeared in 1915.

From the mid to late 1970s pressure from funders stimulated mounting interest in collaboration. Many states encouraged the development of collaborative networks to address welfare, poverty and employment issues. According to the Wilder publication, *Collaboration – What Makes it Work*, 'autonomy and "going it alone" are frowned upon in complex systems such as mental health, services for the handicapped and youth employment'.[1]

Towards the end of the 1980s interest in mergers began to grow as funders became concerned about duplication of services and the effectiveness of organisations that lacked critical mass. However, with some notable exceptions, many 'mergers' turned out to be 'takeovers' of struggling organisations by stronger ones. Whilst there was a strong case for mergers, there were seldom sufficiently strong external pressures to drive organisations to overcome the fear of loss of their autonomy and independence.

Since the 1990s there has been growing interest in partnerships as organisations realised that they frequently lacked the skills and resources to address increasingly complex social problems. Combining resources can create programmes with greater impact, integrating back office functions can increase efficiency, and introducing ideas and knowledge from other sectors can transform an organisation's perspectives on social issues.

Strategic alliances are increasingly common. A survey of a random sample of 400 nonprofits discovered that 24% had experience of strategic re-structuring. They reported that it had enabled them to cut costs (through volume buying and sharing employees), hire more experienced staff and provide them with improved compensation and greater career opportunities.[2] Further evidence of interest in alliances comes from Mandel Center for Nonprofit Organisations that published a book of 'lessons from the trenches' setting out case studies of different types of alliances.[3]

These strategic partnerships are now seen as having great potential to enhance the effectiveness of the nonprofit sector. 'The twenty-first century will be the age of alliances' declares James Austin, Chair of the Initiative on Social Enterprise at Harvard Business School, in the first sentence of his groundbreaking book *The Collaboration Challenge*.[4]

Managers have come to realise that there are many different types of alliances between total independence and full merger. These relationships are seen to exist on a continuum with a low level of commitment and small loss of autonomy at one end and a high engagement and greater integration at the other. Exploring these intermediary relationships is more common than entering into the complications of mergers, with all their associated structural, legal and personnel challenges.

It is widely acknowledged that managing partnerships is even more challenging than managing single organisations. The preparatory stage demands thorough research to establish the capacity and stability of each organisation to the satisfaction of the others. They take time to establish and require dedication if they are to be successful. As Mary Pearl, Executive Director of the Wildlife Trust explained, "the return in terms of impact has to be much greater than the time the organisation has to invest in establishing the partnership".

This chapter

Chapter 4 provides evidence from leading-edge organisations showing that they:

- establish strategic alliances to increase impact
- choose alliance types to suit the circumstances
- create alliances with the corporate sector
- build alliances on trustworthy relationships
- merge to build strategic capacity.

Defining terms

Many different terms are used to describe organisations working together and there is no universal agreement on their definitions. The following is a guide to the application of different terms and is used in this book.

The terms **strategic alliance** and **collaboration** refer to significant long-term relationships between two or more organisations that share resources to achieve their mission more effectively.

Other words used interchangeably with those above include **partnerships** and **coalitions**.

Strategic re-structuring occurs when two or more independent organisations reorganise themselves to establish an ongoing relationship to increase the administrative efficiency and/or further the mission of one or more of the participating organisations.

The results of the above activities include:

Administrative consolidations – alliances that involve sharing, exchanging or contracting administrative functions
Joint programmes or projects – alliances that involve launching and managing one or more programmes or projects to further participating organisations' missions
Management service organisations – new organisations to further the administrative efficiency of two or more organisations
Joint ventures – new organisations to further the administrative or service aims of two or more organisations where the partners share the governance of the new organisation
Group structures – new organisations, or designation of existing organisations, as a 'parent' that governs the functions of a number of other organisations – the 'subsidiaries'
Merged organisations – combining the assets of two or more organisations under one corporate structure.

These definitions draw closely on those given in the evaluation report on the Strategic Solutions initiative.

Source: Paul Connolly and Peter York, *Pulling Together: Strengthening the Nonprofit Centre through Strategic Restructuring*[5]

4.1 Establish strategic alliances to increase impact

The dramatic growth in strategic alliances is being driven by organisations' desire to:

- increase mission impact
- exploit economies of scale
- achieve cost savings
- attain critical mass
- respond to mounting competition.

Increase mission impact

Greater impact can often now be achieved only by organisations combining their skills and resources. The case for collaboration is that the most complex problems society faces cannot be tackled by any one organisation acting alone. Issues of poor educational achievements, drug misuse, crime and poverty are inherently complex and inter-related, and are often best addressed by agencies working in an integrated way.

'In her highly regarded 1989 book, *Collaborating*, Barbara Gray notes that the quality of results often increases when a problem is addressed through inter-agency collaboration. This happens because the organisations working jointly are likely to do a broader, more comprehensive analysis of the issues and opportunities. They also have complementary resources that diversify their capability to accomplish tasks.'[1]

Strategic alliances are often created to improve the quality and range of services offered. This can involve:

- joint bids for contracts for the provision of a human service
- joint ventures in fundraising where two or more organisations working together can raise more funds than those organisations working separately
- creation of a 'one-stop-shop' bringing services together in one building.

The University of Chicago carried out a survey of 192 organisations with recent experience of strategic re-structuring. They found that organisations re-structured more often to improve the quality and range of what they do and the efficiency with which they do it, rather than because of any immediate threats of closure or pressure from funders.[6]

The most common benefits that respondents to this survey reported were increased programmatic collaborations with partner organisations, increased services, increased administrative capacity and quality and increased market share.[6]

Exploit economies of scale

Strategic alliances are also created to exploit economies of scale, for example where a local service wishes to 'scale up' to provide the service at a regional or national level. This allows the overhead costs to be spread over a larger number of service users and thus reduce the overhead unit costs. For example, Citizen Schools, an organisation that offers after-school support for under-privileged children, knows that it needs to increase the number of schools it runs to cover the organisation's central overhead costs. It has a detailed analysis of the cost structure of different growth strategies and knows that it will need new partners to achieve the required economies of scale.

Achieve cost savings

Another reason for forming an alliance is to achieve cost savings. There are opportunities to reduce costs in both programmes and core administration costs. Paul Jansen of McKinsey reminds organisations that "they have to consider the size of the prize. Administration costs are around 10% of total costs but programme costs can be around 70–80% of total costs. So if economies can be found in delivering programmes the potential prize is much larger".

To address administration costs, nonprofits are coming together to share administrative systems and forming management service organisations. This gives opportunities for saving 'back office' costs by combining the provision of finance systems, information technology and human resource services. According to Harvard's James Austin 'many nonprofits will be propelled into austerity alliances…to economise on scarce resources'.[4] However, strategic re-structuring expert David La Piana cautions that "although cost reduction is a major motivator, cost savings are seldom a short-term outcome of mergers and consolidations".

Attain critical mass

Organisations are also creating strategic alliances to give themselves critical mass. The nonprofit sector includes many small organisations that survive on minimal resources and huge individual commitment. There are many opportunities to combine management and governance and create fewer units with greater capacity to compete for funds and deliver greater impact. McKinsey's Paul Jansen believes that "Organisations with income of less than $500k per year are too small to have any economies of scale or economies of skill. They need to re-structure to create critical mass".

National organisations with branch and chapter structures have led the way in persuading smaller branches to merge and create critical mass. United Way of Los Angeles, for example, merged 39 branches into one, leading to a significant increase in effectiveness.

"Alliances are the way forward for lobbying work," says Anita Aaron of Lighthouse. "Most organisations can not afford a separate lobbying function, but we can all contribute towards the creation of larger and more effective organisations that specialise in lobbying."

Respond to mounting competition

Many nonprofits are considering a fundamental change in organisational structure because of the economic pressures of increased competition from other nonprofits and from business. "Competition from for-profits is driving nonprofits to form partnerships," according to Peter Manzo, Executive Director of the Centre for Nonprofit Management in Los Angeles. He cites the example of 13 child care organisations in Los Angeles that came together because of competition from for-profit organisations.

The point is confirmed by the University of Chicago survey which reports that 'Competition is a key factor in strategic re-structuring. Organisations are attempting to temper competition by co-operating or merging'.[6]

The rationale for the growth of strategic alliances can be seen as a natural development of the sector. "Strategic re-structuring is natural as the nonprofit sector matures" according to David La Piana. "When a business's re-structuring is successful its stock value rises dramatically. When a nonprofit's re-structuring is successful, its ability to fulfil its social mission rises dramatically."

The role of funders

Funders have a particularly delicate role in re-structuring. On the one hand they are uniquely positioned to require organisations that should form strategic alliances to re-structure and increase their impact. No other external stakeholder holds the power needed to force this change. Organisations are being driven to form alliances by funders who are 'frustrated with overlapping programs, service gaps, turf battles and lack of co-ordination'.[7]

On the other hand funders can push organisations into inappropriate and unwanted relationships. 'The past decade has included "collaboration mania" among some people who set policy and offer funding. Unfortunately, it has also become a nostrum among some nonprofit organisations desperate to attempt anything to survive in a challenging environment.'[1]

Views are divided according to the evaluation of the Strategic Solutions initiative. 'Many experts maintain that funders should not drive the move to re-structure because their grantees will be less likely to "own" the process and the results. However, others thought that unless nonprofit organisations were pushed, they would resist even considering strategic re-structuring, let alone implementing it.' [5]

Some nonprofits point out somewhat wryly that many foundations find it easier to require the organisations to form alliances than they are able to form partnerships amongst themselves. Even foundations that make the funding of alliances a priority appear less enthusiastic about forming alliances themselves. The critics argue that the gains from funders forming strategic alliances may be as great as the advantages from alliances between the organisations they fund.

4.2 Choose alliance types to suit the circumstances

There is a range of types of strategic alliances, each of which fits different circumstances. The lowest level of joint working involves cooperation and coordination agreements. These allow organisations to share information and sometimes plans, refer service users to each other and to avoid unnecessary competition. Such arrangements can be short term and often depend on personal relationships between people in the cooperating organisations. They are not strategic alliances and do not involve strategic re-structuring.

All the other types of collaboration are longer term, involve significant resources and usually require legal agreement to formalise the relationship or the establishment of new legal entities.

The continuum of types of strategic alliances

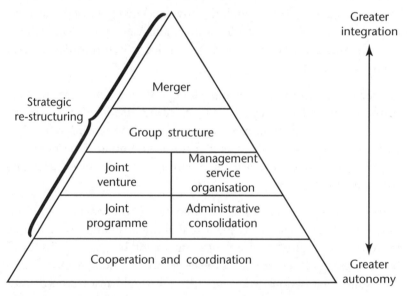

Source: Ideas combined from Jane Arsenault, *Forging Nonprofit Alliances*[8] and David La Piana, *Beyond Collaboration – Strategic Re-structuring of Nonprofit Organizations*[7]

Joint programming

The lowest risk and most prevalent type of relationship is called the joint programme. These relationships are often time limited and can take the form of a contractual agreement. They allow two or more organisations to work together without affecting their ultimate autonomy. They can involve service delivery and fundraising activity.

Joint programme delivered by management

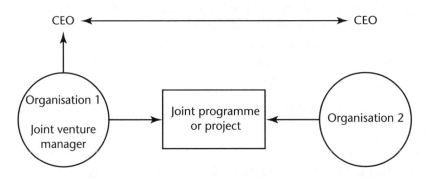

In joint programming, both parties contribute staff and resources, the joint venture is the responsibility of a manager in one organisation and oversight is provided by the chief executives of both organisations.

JOINT PROGRAMMING

Century Health, an Ohio-based community health centre, decided to work with Open Arms, a domestic violence and rape crisis service, to provide a domestic violence offenders programme.

Community leaders had decided that the town of Findlay should have a visitation centre where offenders could have supervised visits with their children.

The chief executives of both organisations recognised that Century needed Open Arms' expertise with domestic violence and that Open Arms needed Century's experience with drugs misuse because 80% of offenders have substance abuse problems.

Century House is responsible for Harmony House, the visitation centre, and Open Arms is responsible for the offenders programme. The two chief executives jointly supervise the manager, who is technically on the staff of Century. No funds are exchanged between the two agencies.

Source: Amelia Kohm *et al.*, *Strategic Re-structuring*[6]

Administrative consolidation

A similarly low-risk option is to consolidate back office activity. This can involve one organisation selling spare capacity such as computer space, excess financial management or human resource management capacity to another. It might be an intermediary step before creating a management service organisation.

These arrangements are established by creating joint operating agreements.

SHARING BACK OFFICE SERVICES IN RHODE ISLAND: SELF HELP AND NEW VISIONS

Self Help and New Visions are two social service agencies providing substance-abuse programmes, food banks, homeless shelters, health clinics and child care in Rhode Island. In 1997, when the executive director of New Visions retired, the executive director of Self Help was appointed to lead both organisations.

Together, the two organisations employ 275 people and have a combined budget of $15 million. However the two organisations remained separate because it was important to maintain their identities which were linked to the communities they served.

The two groups signed an agreement to create a joint human resources department. In addition they saved money by purchasing health insurance, telephone services and medical supplies together.

After five years they considered continuing their agreement indefinitely. The opportunity to seek new funding from a source that favoured larger organisations persuaded them to consider a merger – despite the misgivings amongst clients and staff.

Source: David Whelan, *Chronicle of Philanthropy*[9]

Joint venture

Jane Arsenault says in her excellent book *Forging Nonprofit Alliances* that the most common reasons for creating joint ventures are for:

- **knowledge sharing** – where organisations recognise that each has a distinctive competency, innovative approach or specialised knowledge that, if shared, will contribute to higher quality service outcomes for both

- **market access** – where organisations can reach a new user group or extend their geographic reach
- **new product or programme development** – where development costs can be shared between organisations.

There are two types of joint ventures, one controlled by a legal agreement and the other by the establishment of a separate organisation. In both cases the partners separate the joint venture from ongoing operations. Both types are appropriate where neither organisation has the required skills, where the joint venture requires a different culture or where the joint venture is physically separated from the partners.

In the arrangement controlled by a legal agreement, there is a **joint oversight group** consisting of members of the partner organisations. The joint venture manager reports to this group. The model gives the manager a greater degree of autonomy and therefore requires all parties to have a high level of confidence in the manager's skills. A system of rotating the role of the chair is common in this arrangement.

Joint venture governed by a joint oversight group

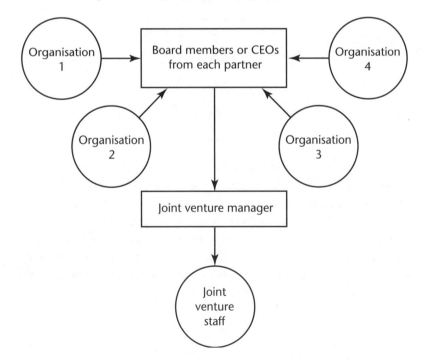

An example of this type of arrangement can be seen in four organisations in San Francisco that created a fifth to carry out client assessments for all of them.

The other arrangement is a **separately incorporated joint venture** with its own board. Each partner has an agreed number of seats on the joint venture board and the constitution of the joint venture can only be changed with the agreement of the partners. This model is appropriate where there are significant financial or liability risks.

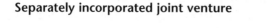

Separately incorporated joint venture

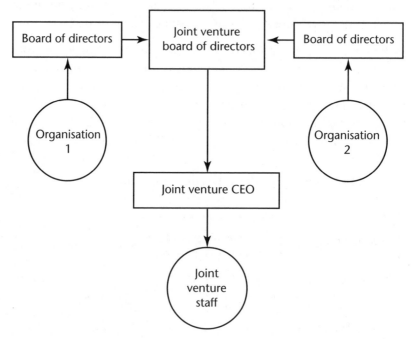

The desire of some government authorities to reduce the number of providers with whom they contract has given joint ventures a significant boost, because nonprofits can combine together to bid as one organisation. That organisation can then manage the contract, allowing members to focus on the provision of the service. This arrangement enables greater management capacity to be incorporated into the service without distorting the sensitive administrative cost ratios of the nonprofits delivering the services.

TREASURE ISLAND – HOMELESS DEVELOPMENT INITIATIVE

A group of agencies worked together with the City of San Francisco to use a Defence Department site to provide services for homeless people. They established a joint venture to provide housing, employment and economic development services.

According to Donna Feingold, Chief Executive of Toolworks, one of the partners, the success of the joint venture depended on:

- having an overarching goal that was greater than the objectives of the individual agencies
- keeping focused on the mission
- developing good working relationships between the partners
- paying attention to what was communicated and how it was communicated
- accepting give and take between agencies.

The greatest challenge was working with the City authority, as it was a key funder and its culture was different from that of the other partners.

Management service organisations

Management service organisations, known as MSOs, are another form of strategic alliance. MSOs are being established because there are opportunities to provide some management and administrative services more efficiently in groups of organisations rather than separately.

There are two types of MSO. The first is a partnership between a number of organisations that come together to create a separate body to provide all the partners with one or more services. The MSO may be a for-profit or a tax-exempt organisation (as the tax authorities have relaxed the rules on the status of MSOs that service nonprofit organisations).

The second type is created within an existing nonprofit to sell excess capacity in some of its administrative services to other nonprofits. It is known as a wholly-owned MSO.

MSOs typically provide a range of services that can include:

- **personnel management** – recruitment, staff training, purchasing of benefits, payroll and legal compliance
- **facilities management** – lease management, building maintenance, provision and service of equipment

- **financial services** – fully integrated financial systems, invoicing, management and financial accounts, group purchasing
- **fundraising** – raising funds jointly for all partners or for each organisation individually
- **planning** – data analysis, supporting planning committees
- **contracts management** – for leases and equipment
- **marketing** – market analysis, developing communication strategies, design and production of print
- **quality assurance** – establishment of quality standards, monitoring, management information system support, improvement efforts and outcome studies.

Source: Jane Arsenault, *Forging Nonprofit Alliances* [8]

Whilst MSOs offer opportunities to provide back office services more efficiently, they nevertheless have their own challenges. 'The greatest challenge in the wholly-owned MSO is to engender a sense of customer service in the staff on the front line.'[8] Jo Haggerty of United Way of Los Angeles concurs: "the problem with MSOs is that they lack a charitable mission".

There is also a danger in wholly-owned MSOs that servicing the parent organisation will take priority over the often smaller purchasers of the MSO's services.

ESTABLISHING PARTNERS FOR COMMUNITY

Partners for Community (PfC) is an MSO in Massachusetts with two founding partners and three affiliate organisations. It was established by two social service-providing organisations that were struggling to cover their overhead costs as cost of living expenses rose faster than income from government grants and contracts.

PfC provides financial, human resource, information, technology, space, procurement and organisation development services. It emerged after discussions clarified that a merger would jeopardise contracts and that neither organisation wanted to lose the reputation associated with their names.

The first savings came when the two organisations moved into one building. Later a language centre, a small community development corporation and an employment training centre contracted to have their administration provided by PfC.

A key decision was the appointment of a chief operating officer. He oversaw the transfer of all financial information to one accounting programme and re-organised the flow of work so that financial staff worked according to function rather than agency.

"Improving our information technology was reason enough for us to come together" claimed one of the original partners. "Economies of scale really make sense in this area."

Source: Amelia Kohm *et al., Srategic Re-structuring*[6]

Group structures

Group structures or parent corporations allow a number of separate organisations to operate under the umbrella of the parent. They are appropriate when the activities of the subsidiaries are different, but they all want to be part of the one organisation. The subsidiaries can be offered different degrees of autonomy, depending on whether the parent wishes to exercise tight control or give them freedom to pursue their own activities within agreed boundaries.

Group structure

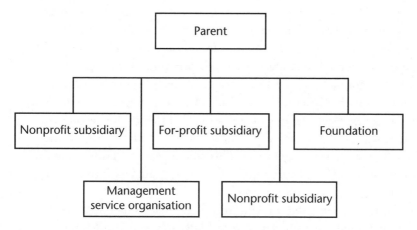

Some organisations registered as charitable and religious organisations (known as '501 c (3)s') are creating social welfare subsidiaries that have a separate tax status (known as '501 c (4)s') to enable them to carry out lobbying activities without risking regulatory interventions when expenditure on lobbying exceeds the legal limits for charitable and religious organisations. Some are creating subsidiaries to offset risks or potential liabilities, for example those arising from trading activities. Yet others are establishing social welfare subsidiaries when regulations require that a majority of the board membership consists of service users and the organisation believes that this requirement is not appropriate for their circumstances.

Parent corporations are becoming more popular as organisations become larger and more complex, and they want to divide their activities into more discrete units, each with its own governing board. They are undoubtedly more complex to manage and govern, but they do provide significant opportunities for exploiting economies of scale. Those services that are most effectively provided by the parent, such as finance, IT and property can be delivered by the centre, and those that are best provided by the subsidiaries can be located there.

The arrangement also separates the strategic role of the centre – such as deciding what services the group as a whole should provide – from the operational roles of the subsidiaries, which concern themselves primarily with the provision of each service. It also provides for greater accountability, as the parent can nurture its subsidiaries and hold them to account for achieving agreed objectives.

PHMC AND THE BRIDGE

The Bridge is a substance abuse treatment centre whose budget grew to $2 million by the early 1990s. Following retirement of key staff and loss of a key contract it ran into financial difficulties. It recognised that survival depended on finding a partner so it investigated several options for its future.

PHMC, a nonprofit public health organisation that provides health and human services in the Delaware Valley, had grown to a budget of $15 million.

Negotiations between the two organisations led to the conclusion that, whilst there was a good fit between their services, the relationship would have to be a parent/subsidiary model. This would protect PHMC from the financial liabilities of The Bridge and the risks associated with running a residential drug treatment programme.

PHMC is the sole member of The Bridge and selects its board. The first board included representatives from PHMC as well as previous members of The Bridge board. PHMC is contracted to provide finance, marketing, human resources, information system and programme development functions.

The integration was not easy because there were cultural differences between the two organisations, some redundancies were unavoidable and staff benefits were reduced. However, The Bridge now gives PHMC a wider range of services and a stronger reputation for supporting underserved populations and The Bridge has benefited from PHMC's many services, including a fundraising campaign that raised over $200,000.

Source: based on case study on Strategic Solutions website

4.3 Create alliances with the corporate sector

Nonprofit organisations in America are forming a wide range of successful partnerships with for-profit organisations. These relationships came to particular prominence in the early 1980s with the often - quoted example of American Express's promise to donate one cent for every transaction and $2 for every new card issued to finance the renovation of the Statue of Liberty.

Harvard Business Review reported in 1996 that 'since American Express's pioneering ventures, the number or alliances between nonprofit and for-profit organisations has skyrocketed. Avon, American Airlines, Ocean Spray, Polaroid, Ramada International Hotels, Arm & Hammer, Wal-Mart Stores and many other corporations have joined forces with national nonprofit institutions such as the American Red Cross, the YMCA, the American Heart Association, and the Nature Conservancy as well as local agencies tackling problems in their communities. Today, it is unusual to go into a supermarket, fast-food restaurant or drug store without encountering posters and other promotional materials for a social program co-sponsored by one or more private sector organisations'.[10]

By 2002, nonprofit/for-profit relationships were big business. Although the total value of these relationships is impossible to calculate, *Giving USA 2002* reports that corporate philanthropy totalled over $9 billion, representing 1.3% of pre-tax profits. Corporate sponsorships generated a further $700 million in 2001.

Business undoubtedly now recognises the value of creating strong relationships with the nonprofit sector. Business for Social Responsibility makes the following observations. 'Corporate community involvement can:

- **Increase employee morale, retention, attendance, and performance** Boston College's Center for Corporate Citizenship found that 84% of employees felt that a company's image in the community is important; 54% felt that it was very important. The study found that "the more an employee knows about the company's programs, the more likely he or she will be loyal and positive about the company."
- **Develop employee skills** The business benefits of employee community involvement help to develop a variety of competencies, including teamwork, planning and implementation, communication, project management, listening skills and customer focus.

- **Enhance company reputation** Americans think most favorably of companies that focus their philanthropic efforts on donating products and encouraging employee volunteering in the community.
- **Attract investors** More than 12.5% of investment in U.S. companies is screened for social factors such as community investment. U.S. assets in socially screened portfolios rose to $2.6 trillion in 1999 from $639 billion in 1995.
- **Increase customer goodwill and loyalty** A 1997 Cone/Roper study found that 76% of consumers would switch their purchases to a retail store associated with a good cause.
- **Improve relationships with the community** Many companies find that community involvement can open new markets, reduce local regulatory obstacles, provide access to the local political process, generate positive media coverage and increase company or brand awareness within the community.'

Source: www.bsr.org © 2001–2004 Copyright: Business for Social Responsibility – All rights reserved

Many businesses are therefore seeking to establish longer-term and more strategic relationships with nonprofit organisations. In his book The Collaboration Challenge James Austin established the notion of a continuum of types of relationships between nonprofits and for-profits. They begin with a philanthropic stage, in which the company is a charitable donor. The resources may be significant to the nonprofit, but are not strategically significant to the company.

When the philanthropic stage is successful, the relationship moves to the transactional stage. This is a more active relationship in which both parties expect more significant benefits. Activities can include cause-related marketing, event sponsorship, product certification, licensing agreements and employee volunteering. Many such relationships begin at this stage.

Nonprofit organisations that have leading-edge relationships have reached the integrative stage. In these cases missions, people and activities are increasingly integrated. The relationship becomes more deeply embedded in both organisations' corporate strategies and the resources involved are progressively more significant. See table opposite.

Austin reports that a particular benefit of these relationships is the opportunities that they create for partners to learn from each other. 'Cross-sector partnering was distinctive because the participants in such alliances were likely to have noticeably different performance measures, competitive dynamics, organisation cultures, decision-making styles,

The collaboration continuum

Relationship stage		Philanthropic	Transactional	Integrative	
Level of engagement	Low	⇢	⇢	⇢	High
Importance to mission	Peripheral	⇢	⇢	⇢	Strategic
Magnitude of resources	Small	⇢	⇢	⇢	Big
Scope of activities	Narrow	⇢	⇢	⇢	Broad
Interaction level	Infrequent	⇢	⇢	⇢	Intensive
Managerial complexity	Simple	⇢	⇢	⇢	Complex
Strategic value	Modest	⇢	⇢	⇢	Major

Source: James Austin, *The Collaboration Challenge*[4]

personnel competencies, professional languages, incentive and motivational structures, and emotional content'.[4]

These relationships frequently develop organically over a period of years. Children's Institute International (CII) has a strategic alliance with management consultants Accenture. The Institute benefits from a mentor for the chief executive, assistance with strategic planning and assistance with marketing; all of which has made a significant contribution to building the organisation's management capacity. Accenture benefited from being able to show that it contributed to the Los Angeles community and from opportunities for its staff to work on projects that they felt were important. The success of the relationship has been recognised with a prize at the National Philanthropy Awards.

More recently, CII has successfully bid with a for-profit partner for a contract to deliver mental health services. The for-profit organisation will deliver the high-end psychiatric work in hospitals and CII will deliver a range of associated community services. It is currently a small commitment, but shows further evidence of the opportunities for private and nonprofit organisations to work together in strategic alliances.

So the connections between businesses and nonprofits are moving on from the traditional philanthropic model to a more sophisticated set of relationships that deliver quantifiable benefits to both parties. People at the frontiers of these relationships report that the greatest challenge is meshing the cultures of the corporate and nonprofit sectors. For-profit organisations move faster and have clearer lines of accountability. Nonprofit organisations have more consultative approaches and have multiple stakeholders to consider.

KaBOOM!

KaBOOM! exists to create healthy play opportunities for children by bringing together individuals, organisations and businesses to lead community-building playground projects, to educate the public on the value of community-centred play, and to advocate for more safe and accessible playgrounds.

Established in 1995, KaBOOM! has created 400 playgrounds and enhanced a further 1,100. Much of the $20 million investment it has spearheaded has come from corporate partners including Ben and Jerry's Homemade, Snapple Beverages, Computer Associates and Motorola.

Chief Executive and Co-founder Darell Hammond says, "one of the lessons we've learned is to pick the right partners. We jokingly say that we start our best partnerships by dating our sponsors. We invite potential partners to see us in action at a playground or skate park construction day or presenting at one of our training conferences. Then we ask if we can meet to learn of their intentions. We hear what motivates them and as with any honest courting couple, we tell them everything about us that we can".

He advises for-profits and nonprofits to be curious about each other; "I think that in our rush to raise funds and meet business goals, organisations fail to learn enough about each other to ensure that their missions and goals match. Our most powerful sustainable project results come when we are able to build a relationship between a company and a community that is driven by a shared vision, shared power, shared resources, shared responsibility and shared accountability".

Source: case study on Independent Sector website

4.4 Build alliances on trustworthy relationships

Managing strategic alliances presents special challenges because there are always two or more sets of staff, managers and board members involved. The University of Chicago research into 192 strategic restructurings found that the higher level integrations required in joint ventures and management service organisations presented more challenges than the less demanding alliances of joint programming and administrative consolidations.[6]

The most common challenges they identified were:

- managing conflicting organisational cultures
- adjusting staff to new roles/positions
- allaying concerns about loss of autonomy
- building trust among organisations.

Most actions needed to deliver a successful strategic alliance are ultimately concerned with building and maintaining trustworthy relationships between the partners. "Increasing trust is the key and should be an explicit objective," according to Professor Michael Cortes of the Institute for Nonprofit Organisation Management at the University of San Francisco.

Organisations need to reflect on some essential pre-requisites before establishing or joining a strategic alliance:

- none of the partners should be in a crisis of any form, because the pressures will inevitably 'spill over' into the alliance
- partners should have 'spare' organisation capacity to meet the demands of the alliance or the resources to create new capacity
- there should be good relations between the boards and managers in all the organisations that will be part of a strategic alliance
- organisations that are committed to working in partnerships should have a strategic plan that emphasises partnerships.

In addition, according to Donna Feingold, Chief Executive of Toolworks, "managers need to understand that sometimes they are collaborating and sometimes they are competing with the very same organisations".

Practical experience with strategic alliances

United Ways are often catalysts in creating and supporting strategic alliances. United Way of Greater Los Angeles has considerable experience negotiating its own alliances as well as catalysing others. Chief Executive Jo Haggerty recommends the following:

- involve the chief executive from the start
- make a member of the permanent staff responsible for negotiating the agreement and appoint a board member to provide oversight
- ensure that there will be continuity of staff in partner agencies
- expect all parties to deliver on their commitments
- encourage board members to visit the partnership in action
- limit the number of strategic alliances that the organisation develops
- recognise that alliances will increase administrative overheads
- be tough on turning down offers for alliances if they are not appropriate or consistent with the organisation's values
- base all alliances on written agreements.

Seven features of successful alliances

For organisations that meet the pre-requisites and are considering an alliance there are seven essential attributes of successful alliances.

1 The first is **values**. To be successful in an alliance the organisations need to hold a shared set of values about the cause they are championing and about ways of working together. These values will influence the way the parties approach the alliance and how they work together.

2 The second requirement is **leadership**. Partnerships require champions in each of the participating organisations, and these individuals need to take direct responsibility for achieving the partnership goals. Partnerships also require the unequivocal support of the leaders of the participating organisations. Boys and Girls Clubs of Boston appointed a vice president (a post on the senior management team) with responsibility for partnerships to ensure that they are given senior management attention.

3 The third important feature is clarity of **mission and strategy**. Strategic alliances need a compelling mission, realistic objectives and a clear strategy for achieving them. "Each partnership needs to have great clarity over its goals, achievable objectives with win-win opportunities for both organisations" according to Linda Whitlock, Chief Executive of Boys and Girls Clubs of Boston.

4 The fourth essential attribute is **board** commitment. The boards of all participating organisations need to be strongly committed to the partnership and willing to support it through the good times and the difficult times. For some alliances, Bill Tyman, Chief Executive of Big Brothers Big Sisters of Long Island, establishes a sub-committee consisting of members of both boards and staffs. For others he goes even further – each partner has a seat on the other's board. To ensure that each organisation has an overview of the partner's organisation, board minutes are circulated to partners. He also requires that counterparts (board members, CEOs, managers and staff) meet each other frequently to encourage good personal relationships.

5 The next requirement is **resources**. To be successful strategic alliances need to be properly resourced, and there needs to be great honesty and realism about the time and financial commitments each organisation will have to make to the partnership. When it comes to reporting on how the resources have been applied, the financial reports need to be tailored to the needs of the partnership and not to follow the standard reporting formats of the participating organisations.

6 Then there are the challenges of creating open and honest **communications** between partners. Managers need to recognise that many different stakeholders, such as funders, board and committee members, staff, chapters and volunteers, may be affected by a strategic alliance. Each requires regular and thorough communication. Formal communications should be supported by plenty of informal communication, ideally at board, senior management and staff levels. Sharing information across two or more organisations to keep staff, managers and board members of all organisations in touch with progress and problems requires even more effort and attention than communication within organisations, itself no small challenge.

7 Finally, there should be an explicit commitment to good faith **negotiations** when the alliance is being established. David La Piana has learned much from the many discussions he has facilitated. He now uses three ground rules when discussing the establishment of an alliance. Without the prior agreement of all partners:

- there should be no material changes in the partnership proposition
- negotiators must be named and there should be no changes during negotiations
- there must be no negotiations with other external parties.

He recommends establishing an open list of issues being worked on and communicating update regularly to negotiators and other stakeholders, so people can see the progress and the status of each issue at a glance.

These seven attributes all create the foundation for trustworthy relationships between the partners. They enable all parties to admit failures when things go wrong and to celebrate success frequently when milestones and objectives are achieved.

Dealing with autonomy and self-interest

Autonomy is a precious attribute for many nonprofit organisations and self-interest cannot be ignored.

'Successful collaboration involves some degree of letting go of personal ego and the needs of individual organisations to meet the larger agenda of collaboration. It is essential that all of the players know what they or their organisations are willing to invest, what they are willing to give up and what they simply cannot compromise on.'[11]

The following advice comes from the highly successful BoardSource publication *Beyond Collaboration:*[7]

Self-interest is neither inappropriate nor unethical in a nonprofit context. It is a legitimate and major issue in strategic re-structuring negotiations. The challenge is to identify and address participants' legitimate self-interest concerns so that they do not move underground to re-emerge as sabotage.

Autonomy and independence are much cherished rewards in a sector where compensation is not a primary motivator. Most impasses encountered in the course of strategic re-structuring efforts can be traced to inadequate attention having been accorded to this emotional and potentially explosive issue. One way to defuse this potent issue is to ask the proponents of autonomy to detail their concerns and fears. Without interruption, argument or rebuttal – indeed with great and sympathetic care – they should be encouraged to articulate their worst fears for their organisation, for their constituency and for themselves. Subsequent thorough discussion of each concern can result in compromises, cleared-up misunderstandings, and well-informed agreements to disagree. Equally important, these discussions will reveal the motivations of the parties and thereby begin to build mutual trust, an essential foundation for a successful outcome in any strategic re-structuring process.

Thomas Backer, President of the Human Interaction Research Institute has a particular eye for the people issues in creating strategic alliances. 'Few partnerships are created with appropriate attention to the behavioural and management science that has accumulated over the last few years – both about how to create partnerships or collaborations and about how to sustain them over time.'[12]

He sees the biggest problem as unrealistic expectations. He recommends that organisations start by thinking about how the partnership will assist the other partners, and not their own organisation. "Seeing the situation from other people's perspectives is invariably helpful."

Factors influencing the success of strategic alliances

The Wilder Foundation recently updated its authoritative review of the research into what it calls 'collaborations'. The 10 most frequently mentioned factors that contribute to the success of strategic alliances in the research findings were:

1 **Mutual respect, understanding and trust** – for the culture and the limitations of members
2 **Sufficient funds, staff, materials and time**
3 **Appropriate cross-section of members** – representing each segment of the community affected by the collaboration
4 **Multiple layers of participation** – board, management and staff
5 **Members see collaboration as in their self-interest** – advantages exceed loss of autonomy
6 **Development of clear roles and policy guidelines** and an understanding of how members discharge their responsibilities
7 **Open and frequent communication**
8 **Shared vision**
9 **Skilled leadership** – an individual with organisational and interpersonal leadership skills, who carries out the role with fairness and is granted legitimacy by the collaborative partners
10 **History of collaboration in the community** – with members understanding expectations of each other in the collaboration.

The authors of the study emphasised that the frequency with which factors are mentioned did not necessarily equate with impact on the success of the collaboration, but it did give an indication of their importance.

Source: Paul Mattessich *et al.*, *Collaboration: What Makes it Work*[1]

4.5 Merge to build strategic capacity

Although there are no official statistics, mergers are much less prevalent than other forms of strategic alliance. Nevertheless there is significant merger activity and growing interest in mergers as a strategy to strengthen organisations' strategic capacity. 'Nonprofit leaders generally agree that the sector is witnessing a dramatic increase in the frequency with which mergers are being considered and executed'.[13] Newspapers mention mergers more frequently and surveys of chief executives demonstrate much enthusiasm for mergers, though most say other organisations should merge and not their own.

'The consensus among people studying mergers seems to be that economic conditions are driving the sector toward a shake-out and consolidation. Factors include the growth of the nonprofit sector, competition with businesses and other nonprofits, devolution, welfare reform, upward pressure on salaries, and the realisation by a growing number of nonprofit managers that mergers are viable options.'[13]

The number of mergers is growing despite the evidence that many business mergers do not deliver the anticipated benefits. 'The real benefits of a merger are not short term and tactical but medium to long term and strategic:

- better market positioning
- a larger market share
- a higher public profile
- greater political influence
- more strategic fundraising
- a larger staff allowing greater specialisation of functions and the provision of more service
- the creation of a continuum of services under unified control
- better economies of scale.'

Source: David La Piana, *The Nonprofit Mergers Workbook*[13]

Paul Jansen of McKinsey sees additional advantages: "the strategic benefit is that scale allows organisations to hire better quality managers and that is the key. In my experience mergers also allow organisations to transfer best practice both in programmes and in management".

Whilst strategic mergers are espoused, they are comparatively rare. Mergers of last resort are much more common. 'Merger or consolidation is seldom the first thought of leaders of a troubled organisation; instead they deplete reserves, even restricted endowments, live in expectation of the next grant; defer facilities upkeep, and reduce services and salaries; in short, they hang on and hope for a miracle.'[7]

Types of organisations merging

Mergers are most prevalent in the mental health, substance abuse, child welfare and homeless fields, and the typical type is 'strong joins weak' in what amounts to more of a takeover than a merger. As organisations take a more strategic approach, some are merging with their competitors. Others are responding to donor pressures.

An increasingly significant area of activity is the acquisition of nonprofits by for-profits. Private hospitals in particular have been buying nonprofits. Nursing homes, home health agencies, child welfare, substance abuse and mental health organisations are also being acquired, with the income from these sales being used to create endowments and so transform the original nonprofit into a grant-giving foundation.

Typology of mergers

Type	Merger of	Aims	Example	Comment
Horizontal	Organisations in the same field	Economies of scale Increased service reach	Homeless organisations Hospices	Common for larger bodies to 'take over' ailing agencies
Vertical	Organisations offering sequential services	Continuity of relationships with users	Hospital and home care agency Infant and toddler centre and a pre-school	Frequently implemented with parent corporation model
Conglomerate	Organisations in unrelated fields	Diversify income sources Economies of management	Group homes for adult developmentally disabled and a school for behaviourally disordered children	Not common and not thought to yield significant benefits
Concentric	Organisations in related field, but not competitive	Satisfy users with multiple needs Create new service opportunities	Drug misuse and mental health agency	Used to integrate services into a one-stop-shop

Source: Jane Arsenault, *Forging Nonprofit Alliances* [8]

Four key steps in a successful merger

The key to a successful merger is to build trust and confidence. Most mergers involve partners who know each other and there is often a history of poor relationships. Tom Backer, President of the Human Interaction Research Institute recommends making "an assumption that people are not really friends at the start of the process".

There are four essential steps that contribute to a successful merger.

1 First, **define 'the prize'**, the vision of a merged organisation assisting more people, mounting stronger campaigns and providing better quality and more integrated services. The prize should become the touchstone which everyone can hold on to when negotiations become difficult.

2 Second, **establish a process and timescale** for negotiations. David La Piana says "Timescale is important. It should be neither too long nor too short. The ideal is 4–6 months". He recommends that organisations should "identify all the issues that might arise at the first meeting and then agree which ones need to be solved before the merger can proceed". The proposed process should anticipate that there will be difficulties and should therefore include a mechanism for resolving insuperable obstacles. He sets out detailed advice for each stage of a merger process in *The Nonprofit Mergers Workbook.*[13]

3 Third, **address the biggest obstacles early on** in the process. Two areas that commonly present difficulties are the name of the merged organisation and who should fill the key roles of chair and chief executive. Inability to agree on any major points can bring the whole process to a grinding halt. These issues need to be raised early in the process, but not before good personal relationships have been established.

4 Fourth, recognise that **cultural integration is the greatest challenge.** 'There is ample evidence that a significant reason why mergers fail is the inability of the two organisations to integrate at a cultural level.'[8] People bring their own organisation cultures to the negotiating table and expect others to share their point of view, not realising that their organisation has different beliefs and norms.

Failing to deal with difficult and sensitive issues, particularly those concerned with redundancies, relocation and re-defined jobs can often re-emerge as problems years after the formal completion of the merger. Experts refer to 'un-consummated' mergers, where the organisations have been merged but the people have not integrated. They also caution that organisations have a remarkable ability to re-create within themselves the very problems that they were established to solve.

Even when these steps are followed, experience shows that it is easy to underestimate the time and effort required to bring a merger to a successful conclusion. 'Charity leaders and consultants say they now realise just how much time, care and attention the people involved with both organisations are required to make the efforts successful' according to a feature article in the *Chronicle of Philanthropy*.[9]

VOLUNTEERS OF AMERICA

Volunteers of America is a national, spiritually based human services organisation with over 11,000 staff and income exceeding $500 million per year. It assists over 1 million people and benefits from the efforts of over 40,000 volunteers.

Over recent years it has been approached by a number of local agencies that wished to come together with Volunteers of America. Twelve have successfully merged and according to National President Charles Gould "there will be more in the future. Although economics drives some organisations to seek mergers, we are actively pursuing them. They get the advantage of joining the Volunteers of America brand, and we achieve economies of scale and greater promotion of the brand".

Summary

Establish strategic alliances to increase impact
- Leading organisations are seeing opportunities for increasing impact that can be exploited only by combining their skills and resources
- Strategic alliances enable organisations to improve the quality and range of their services, exploit economies of scale and create critical mass
- Funders are uniquely positioned to encourage, and sometimes require, organisations to collaborate, but they need to ensure that the process is fully owned by the participants.

Choose alliance types to suit the circumstances
- Organisations are establishing different types of strategic alliances which sit on a continuum with cooperation and coordination at one end, strategic alliances in the middle and mergers at the other end
- Joint ventures, management service organisations and group structures can all contribute to increasing impact.

Create alliances with the corporate sector
- Nonprofit organisations are forming a wide range of successful partnerships with for-profit organisations
- Relationships exist at three levels – the philanthropic stage, the transactional stage and the integrative stage
- Connections between businesses and nonprofits are moving from traditional philanthropic towards transactional and integrative relationships
- Alliances present learning opportunities because organisation cultures, decision-making styles and performance measures are different.

Build alliances on trustworthy relationships
- Managing strategic alliances presents challenges of conflicting cultures, adjusting staff to new roles and allaying concerns about loss of autonomy
- The seven essential attributes are shared values, strong leadership, clarity of mission and strategy, board commitment, sufficient resources, open communications and good faith negotiations.

Merge to build strategic capacity
- Most mergers are driven by economic conditions, but some organisations are merging to strengthen their market position and increase public profile, extend their political influence and increase strategic fundraising
- The four steps in a successful merger are to define the prize, establish a process and timescale, address the biggest obstacles early on and recognise that cultural integration is the greatest challenge.

References

1 Paul W. Mattessich *et al.*, *Collaboration: What Makes it Work*, Saint Paul, Amherst H. Wilder Foundation, 2001

2 David La Piana and Amelia Kohm, *In Search of Strategic Solutions*, Washington, Grantmakers for Effective Organizations, 2003

3 John Yankey *et al.*, *Nonprofit Strategic Alliances Case Studies*, Cleveland, Mandel Center for Nonprofit Organizations, 2001

4 James Austin, *The Collaboration Challenge*, San Francisco, Jossey-Bass, 2000

5 Paul Connolly and Peter York, *Pulling Together: Strengthening the Nonprofit Sector through Strategic Restructuring*, New York, TCC Group, 2002

6 Amelia Kohm *et al.*, *Strategic Re-structuring*, Chicago, Chapin Hall Center for Children, University of Chicago, 2000

7 David La Piana, *Beyond Collaboration – Strategic Re-structuring of Nonprofit Organizations*, Washington, National Centre for Nonprofit Boards (now BoardSource), 1998

8 Jane Arsenault, *Forging Nonprofit Alliances*, San Francisco, Jossey-Bass, 1998

9 David Whelan, *Re-thinking Nonprofit Partnerships* in *Chronicle of Philanthropy*, Washington, June 27 2002

10 Alan Andreasen, *Profits for Nonprofits: Find a Corporate Partner*, in *Harvard Business Review*, Boston, Nov–Dec 1996

11 Florence Green, *When Collaborations Go Bad*, Boston, *The Nonprofit Quarterly*, Third Sector, New England, Fall 2001

12 Thomas Backer and Alex Norman, *Partnerships and Community Change*, Los Angeles, California Politics and Policy, 2000

13 David La Piana, *The Nonprofit Mergers Workbook*, Saint Paul, Amherst Wilder Foundation, 2000

Websites

www.independentsector.org for information about the Resource Centre for Effective Corporate Nonprofit Partnerships

www.lapiana.org for information about the Strategic Solutions project that is dedicated to achieving a major and lasting positive impact on the nonprofit sector's perception, underatnding and use of strategic re-structuring

www.bsr.org for information about all aspects of corporate social responsibility including community involvement, corporate philanthropy and corporate volunteering

5 Exploiting changing patterns of funding

The financing of nonprofit activity has changed significantly over recent years and it will change further over the coming years. Leading-edge organisations have spotted these changes and are grasping new opportunities to finance their growth and development.

Nonprofits in America receive 38% of their income from private payments for services. Models for managing these income streams broadly follow the theory and practices that are well established in the business community. Organisations compete for customers, charge prices that cover full costs and sometimes allow for a modest surplus. The laws of supply and demand prevail. Nonprofits receive a further 31% from government grants and contracts and 20% from private funders, including individual contributors, foundations and corporate donors. These are the unique feature of the sector since the provider of the funding is not the beneficiary of the service. Traditional business theory therefore does not help.

This chapter is about the fundamental shifts in the sources of finance which are unique to the nonprofit sector and which together account for just over half its income. Sources of nonprofit finance have diversified dramatically over the last 10 or so years. In the past the main sources of private funding were grants, direct mail, bequests and annual fundraising campaigns. Today, sources include programme related investments, venture philanthropy, community development finance institutions, loans, bonds, equity investments and a range of other financial instruments. Although they represent a small proportion of total funding, each is a significant development.

In addition to new sources of finance, striking changes have taken place in the organised funding community over recent years. Foundations have shown a growing interest in the effectiveness and impact of the organisations that they fund. The establishment of Grantmakers for Effective Organisations in 1997 as an affinity group of the Council on Foundations, funded mainly by the Packard Foundation, has captured funders' growing interest in capacity building and organisation impact. However, like other organisations funded by Packard, their future role is less clear following the dramatic decline of Packard Foundation grants.

Some foundations and high-net-worth donors have started to provide funded organisations with a much higher level of support and to expect in return greater accountability for achieving results. This is known as high engagement philanthropy. Venture philanthropists have taken this even further, translating venture capital approaches to the nonprofit world and demonstrating how an even higher level of engagement can work. Although small scale and controversial, the effects of these approaches are challenging conventional thinking across much of the sector.

This chapter

Chapter 5 provides evidence from leading-edge organisations showing that they:

- take advantage of fundamental trends in finance sources
- expect more demanding funders
- capitalise on new funding sources.

5.1 Take advantage of fundamental trends in finance sources

A brief overview of the financing of nonprofits shows that private funding has grown dramatically in real terms in the last 30 years from $21 billion in 1970 to $211 billion in 2001. Growth has been particularly rapid in the last 10 years with income from private funding more than doubling in this period (see figure at top of next page).

Individuals provided three-quarters of these funds in donations and a further 7.5% in bequests. Their generosity has grown during this period, rising from $327 per capita in 1970 to $511 in 1998 in constant dollars, 'fuelled by a booming technology industry that was fast producing new multimillionaires'.[1] This growth reflects increasing personal income. Giving by the nation as a whole has only varied between 1.6% and 1.9% of personal income during this 30-year period, and in 1998 stood at a high of 1.9%. So while people are giving more, they are not giving a significantly higher percentage of their income.

How much is given to US nonprofits?

Total private contributions $ billion

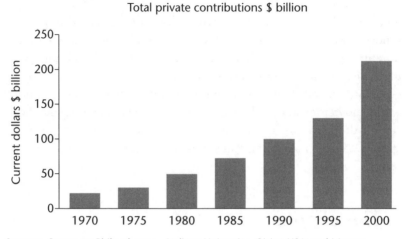

Sources: Center on Philanthropy – Indiana University, *Giving USA*[2] and Murray Weitzman *et al., The New Nonprofit Almanac and Desk Reference*[1]

Who gives to nonprofits?

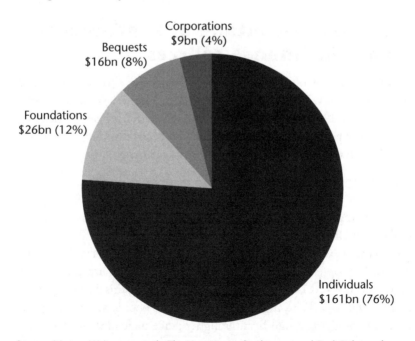

Source: Murray Weitzman *et al., The New Nonprofit Almanac and Desk Reference*[1]

The nonprofit funding 'market'

Within this overall pattern of considerable expansion, both the range and the number of organisations offering funds to nonprofit organisations are growing rapidly. The number of organisations seeking finance is growing just as fast. As a result academics are beginning to talk about the concept of a nonprofit funding 'market'. The concept mirrors the business world, with its business finance market, stock markets and other financial institutions. The market for nonprofit finance – known as the nonprofit capital market – has many providers and many recipients, and includes both primary providers and intermediaries such as United Way and Community Foundations.

This powerful idea is beginning to shape thinking about funding of the sector, though the name is slightly misleading because the notions of 'capital' and 'revenue' are not yet as clearly delineated in the nonprofit sector as they are in the business world.

The nonprofit funding market

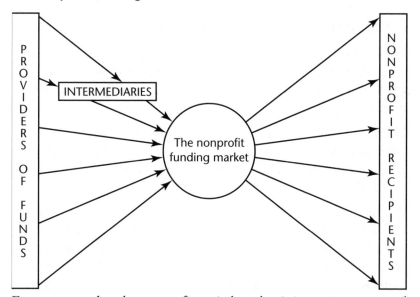

Experts argue that the nonprofit capital market is immature compared to the market for business finance. Feedback from recipients to providers is poor, so funders do not know which types of investments have greater social impact and which are less effective. There are few common performance metrics, so it is difficult to compare the impact of different 'investments' made by funders. Funding bodies are highly fragmented, so knowledge about what works best is not easy to obtain. Some analysts, therefore, envision a more rational, segmented and therefore more efficient and responsive nonprofit capital market.[3]

Experts further believe that changes are taking place which could have a significant impact on the recipients of funds. 'The nonprofit capital market is not a static organism, but is dynamic, with new players entering, old players exiting and new approaches to philanthropic strategies coming into play.' Jed Emerson, Stanford University lecturer, makes the case for organised re-structuring of the nonprofit capital market. 'The major challenge confronting the nonprofit capital market is that of how to organise itself more effectively so that one investment may build upon the next to maximise both the efficient use of charitable resources and the added value of various charitable investments.'[4]

In the more immediate future, the most significant changes for nonprofit organisations include:

- greater concentration of wealth amongst a small number of high-net-worth donors
- significant potential growth from bequests
- further increases in non-cash donations.

Greater concentration of donors

People who are earning money and therefore paying taxes give larger sums than non-earners. The average charitable contribution of tax filers was $3,163 in 1998. This has grown from $2,138 per person in 1986 – a constant dollar increase of 45%.[1]

The more people earn, the more they are likely to give. The American Association of Fund Raising Counsel estimates that a massive one-third of all income from individual donations comes from the wealthiest 1% of households.[2]

The potential rewards from identifying high-level donors, capturing and maintaining their interest and retaining their contributions are considerable. Fundraising will therefore become more targeted, and based on building more individualised relationships with donors. Furthermore, these are the very donors who will make greatest demands on the recipients. They are already asking questions about the effect that their donations are having and they will want more evidence of impact in the future.

Significant potential growth from bequests

Although bequests account for a small proportion of giving at present, researchers have calculated that over the next 55 years an extraordinary $73 trillion will be transferred between generations.[5] This wealth has been accumulated because of peoples' propensity to save, strong long-term stock market performance and increasing house prices. Its ownership is concentrated amongst a very small proportion of the population with 1% of households controlling 40% of the nation's wealth.[6]

The evidence of the 1980s is that people with substantial wealth are more likely to establish foundations (a third of all foundations were established in the 1980s). Assuming that donors continue to bequeath the same proportion of their income to charity as they do today, inter-generational wealth transfer will produce an extra $11.5 trillion for the nonprofit sector over the next 55 years.[5]

As a result some Americans are talking of a possible 'golden age of philanthropy', producing significant additional unrestricted funding for nonprofit organisations. Even the lowest scenario for inter-generational wealth transfer suggests that $41 trillion will pass down over the next 55 years. This figure has been the subject of much debate, particularly following falls in the stock market, but the original researchers have published a robust rebuttal of the challenges.[7] Whether or not such a 'golden age' materialises, the opportunity for organisations to capture the interest of this group and significantly increase their income from bequests is potentially enormous.

Further increases in non-cash donations

The nature of personal giving has also changed over the last 10 years. In addition to financial gifts, there has been a significant increase in non-cash donations. From 1987 to 1997 (the last year for which figures are available) non-cash donations increased from 12% to 28% of gifts. These gifts include property, jewellery, stocks, works of art, cars, food (from the food industry) and other items.

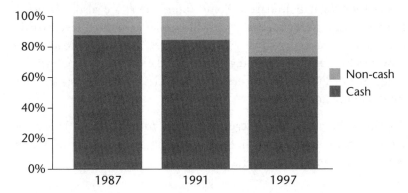

Source: Murray Weitzman *et al., The New Nonprofit Almanac and Desk Reference*[1]

Those nonprofits that organise to collect unwanted cars, obtain goods for recycling, accept jewellery and take stocks and shares as donations will be better placed to exploit these opportunities.

5.2 Expect more demanding funders

There is undoubtedly a trend for funders to become more engaged with the organisations that they support. They are recognising the power that they have, and the responsibility associated with that power. Despite criticism of 'top down' approaches to accountability, the strong trend is towards funders demanding evidence of the impact of the programmes and organisations that they finance. They are also offering greater support to those organisations.

Leading organisations are therefore expecting to:

- receive fewer, larger, more strategic grants
- engage in more partnerships
- provide greater accountability
- share more learning across the sector.

Expect fewer, larger, more strategic grants

Funders are realising that the scope of their previous goals far exceeded the available resources. They are therefore attempting to establish more realistic objectives for their programmes. Under pressure to demonstrate results, foundations in particular are likely to continue focusing their funding so they can more easily measure their impact.

Some foundations are replacing the traditional funding sectors such as arts, youth, environment and human services with cross-sector programmes – such as the reduction of poverty – that traverse the traditional functional boundaries. Some foundations are also taking the initiative, asking for proposals that will enable them to achieve a particular strategic objective. The volume of these focused approaches has now reached such a level that the Foundation Center publishes a 'Requests for Proposals' newsletter to publicise these requests amongst fund-seeking nonprofits.

Together, these trends are leading funders to offer fewer, larger and more strategic grants. This in turn is driving grant seekers to present larger, more strategic responses.

However, this more proactive approach has been the subject of some criticism particularly from people working at the front line. They believe that they know what is best for their communities and resent the arrogance of funders who define how social problems should be solved and focus their funding on explicit social objectives. "Locality differences are very important in the US" according to Rikki Abzug, Assistant Professor at the Milano Graduate School of Management and Urban Policy in New York. "Neighbourhoods are very specific culturally, ethnically and spiritually". She cites the example of the Casey Foundation programme on strengthening families where they ask organisations what they think is most needed in their communities.

So despite the general trend towards having fewer, longer-term and more encompassing relationships with grantees, some foundations have made an explicit decision to be responsive to grant seekers requests and to continue distributing a large number of small community grants.

Engage in more partnerships

Funders are encouraging grant seekers to work in partnership both with each other and with funders themselves. They are also encouraging applications from partnerships and from consortia of organisations. As a result some applicants are creating alliances to seek funds jointly that are then distributed to member organisations. Some funders are also forming partnerships and consortia with other funders to increase the resources available for a particular issue.

Some see themselves in long-term partnerships with grant recipients. Mary Ann Holohean, until recently of the Meyer Foundation, says "we offer organisations a menu of support including advice, loans and advances to cover cash flow difficulties as well as grants. Our relationship does not mean we will give them funds every year, but we will stay in partnership with them".

Provide greater accountability

In the past public accountability of nonprofits in the US has been light touch, and centred on the receipt of permission to operate from the tax authorities (the Internal Revenue Service) and submission of an annual tax return (known as the IRS 990). This began to change, following a small number of high profile charity scandals in the 1990s such as United Way of America and New Era Philanthropy.

'Nonprofits have (until recently) lived a relatively charmed existence in an unregulated environment' according to Kevin Kearns of the Graduate School of Public and International Affairs at the University of Pittsburgh. However, this has changed over the last 10 years. Periods of general lack of interest in public policy on nonprofits have tended to be interrupted by sudden explosions of scrutiny, usually following major scandals. As a result, 'The debate on accountability in the nonprofit sector has emerged from the chambers of legislatures and the courts and entered the living rooms of citizens across the country'.[8]

The issue of effectiveness has also become a matter of public policy. 'The question increasingly being raised by communities, scholars, the media, governments and politicians is whether the impact achieved by foundations…is sufficient to justify continuation of their privileged and protected status.'[9]

The most dramatic response to these challenges has been the rapid growth and influence of Grantmakers for Effective Organisations. Established in 1997, it now has 340 foundation members, including many of the largest and most influential foundations and Regional Associations of Grantmakers. It draws over 550 people to it biannual conferences and is dedicated to promoting learning and encouraging dialogue among funders working in the field of organisational effectiveness.

A further response has come from funders who are paying greater attention to the evaluation of the impact of individual grants and of programmes of grant making as a whole. Funding for evaluation is increasingly seen as an integral part of a grant.

'Related to the growing demand for greater accountability in philanthropy is the increased attention being given to program assessment and evaluation. Talk among foundation boards and staff these days is all about outcomes and how to measure them.'[9] The greatest attention is being paid to ongoing evaluations that are 'good enough' to demonstrate results rather than large-scale, post-project evaluations that are often seen as expensive and not offering good value for money.

This, however, creates some anxiety. 'There is the fear that the resulting preoccupation with measurable outcomes and objective evidence may prevent foundations from taking on the kinds of big issues they are so well positioned to address. Further, there is concern that foundations may be misleading themselves and others by attempting to apply scientific evaluation to areas that, by their very nature, are complex, ambiguous, and ever changing.'[9]

Nevertheless, the overall trend is clear. Organisations will be expected to build evaluation and impact assessment into their project proposals and funders will want to see and publish the results achieved with their funding. In addition, foundations, in particular, will be paying greater attention to assessing the overall impact of their funding programmes and the extent to which they are achieving the foundation's overall objectives.

YOUTH DEVELOPMENT AT THE EDNA MCCONNELL CLARK FOUNDATION

In 1999 the Edna McConnell Clark Foundation decided to focus its funding on helping to strengthen youth development organisations. It adopted a new approach to grant making called Institution and Field Building.

The heart of their process is a comprehensive, multi-stage process used to identify promising organisations, assess their overall capabilities and invest in those organisations that are best positioned to benefit from the McConnell Clark approach.

Typically the relationship involves:

- **Identifying** organisations by scanning various communities for successful organisations that meet predetermined criteria
- **Due diligence** work where the foundation studies the organisation's programme models, leadership and management, financial strength and internal performance measurement systems
- **Business planning** to specify the steps the organisation will take to achieve its growth
- **Investment** with substantial multi-year funding linked to agreements about the goals the organisation says it will reach and for which it will be held accountable
- **Performance tracking and evaluation** to monitor achievements and develop the organisation's capacity to evaluate its work and improve its operations.

Cash investment in each organisation ranges from $1–5 million for up to five years. Non-financial support includes professional and technical assistance, help with communications and introductions to other funders. When work has begun, a foundation portfolio manager – a senior level staff member responsible for managing relationships with grant recipients – maintains contact with the organisation, reviews its performance and provides ongoing support and assistance.

Characteristics of an effective foundation programme

Research into the views of foundation leaders and observers of philanthropy commissioned by Grantmakers in Health produced a seminal review of the trends and tensions inherent in grant making. Based on responses to the question, 'what are the characteristics of foundation programs that have really had an impact?' the author advanced the view that an effective foundation programme is one characterised by:

'**Coherent Sense of Purpose** – a clear understanding of intent and expectations articulated up front

Focus – targeting a specific societal issue, problem, or need that has been identified by the foundation as compelling as well as consistent with its mission, values, and priorities

Thorough Knowledge of the Field – basing action on an in-depth knowledge of the issue, problem or need being addressed

Clear Theory of Change – selecting an implementation strategy on the basis of a clearly articulated change theory and process judged to be the most effective one for achieving intended outcomes

Strategic Deployment of Resources – mobilizing and deploying all the resources available to the foundation so as to increase the likelihood of success and to attract and leverage the participation and resources of other partners

Timeliness and Duration – maximizing the potential for success by taking into account the realities of the environment in which the program will be operating and the readiness of actors to act; sticking with a program for sufficient time to make a real difference

Interaction with Key Constituencies – involving key constituencies from the initial conceptualisation through implementation and evaluation

Mobilisation of Communities – drawing, building on, and strengthening the capacity of communities to solve their own problems

Communications – including communication strategies and tools as integral elements of every program undertaken

Active Program Management – adopting a program management style that emphasises working with participants in foundation initiatives in such a way as to increase the effectiveness of each element of the initiative and the degree to which those elements add up to a productive whole

Staffing – building a staff of program officers who view their jobs as working in partnership with grant recipients and others to develop and implement programs directed toward the achievement of foundation goals and expectations; creating an organizational environment conducive to their creativity and productivity.'

Source: Dennis Prager, *Raising the Value of Philanthropy*[9]

Share more learning across the sector

Public pressure is also driving foundations to improve their communications. There is a growing feeling that in return for the tax breaks that foundations receive, they have a duty to report in an open, accessible and meaningful way on how they have spent their money and what it has achieved.

There is also an emerging view that evaluation should be less concerned with how well one grant has or has not been used and more concerned with the opportunity for organisations and funders to learn from each other. Consequently, some funders are requiring nonprofits working on similar issues to have more contact with each other. Others are taking the initiative by bringing organisations together to share experiences.

In this way everyone can learn more about what works and what does not work, and can use this knowledge to increase future effectiveness. Organisations that integrate shared learning opportunities into their funding applications are therefore more likely to be successful than those that ignore this significant trend.

5.3 Capitalise on new funding sources

The traditional reliance nonprofits have on income from donors, government and the sale of services is slowly changing. New sources of funds have become available over the last few years. Although small in proportion to the sector's total income, each presents new opportunities and challenges for nonprofit managers. How significant each will become in the future is hard to predict.

There is a parallel between funding of business and of nonprofits. Businesses select from a range of sources of finance, banks for low-risk and low-return funding, the equity market for medium risk and higher returns and venture capitalists for high-risk incubation of new ideas. Similarly, it is argued, nonprofits should look to a range of different financial instruments to fund organisations at their various stages of development or when different types of funding are needed.

The most interesting non-traditional sources of funds are:

- programme related investment
- high engagement funders
- venture philanthropy.

Programme related investment

Traditionally foundations have used the interest or gains on their investments to finance their grant-making programmes. More recently some foundations have begun investing a small proportion of their capital in nonprofit organisations in the form of loans. So instead of investing all their capital in mainstream financial institutions, some is invested in the organisations they wish to assist. These investments are an alternative to a grant and are known as programme related investments or PRIs.

The value of these loans grew dramatically in the late 1990s as a result of the stock market boom. In 1999, over $260 million was lent to nonprofit organisations. The largest category (40%) of these loans was for community development and housing, including housing development, neighbourhood revitalisation in urban centres and small business promotion in rural communities. A further 28% covered investment in health and education projects.[10]

Most PRI funding is used to support organisations through direct loans and loan guarantees and to capitalise development banks and venture funds. A small proportion is used to enable nonprofits to acquire or improve property used for charitable purposes.

Just under 200 foundations provide PRIs. Two-thirds of their loans were for more than $100,000 and 16% were for more than $1 million. Many of the recipients are financial intermediaries that in turn lend money to development and housing agencies, job training agencies, community organisations, arts groups and other borrowers. These intermediaries include loan funds, credit unions, development banks, microenterprise funds and venture capital funds. Half the funding made available financed capital projects.[10]

The case for greater programme related investment is based partly on the needs of organisations for different types of finance, and partly on a growing unease that the overwhelming majority of foundations' capital is invested to produce maximum financial benefit for the foundation as opposed to bringing wider social benefits. A small percentage of foundations do use ethical criteria to influence their investment strategies. However, most do not, and may inadvertently be investing in businesses that cause the very problems that grant recipients are trying to solve. So some foundations have decided that they can better achieve their social mission by investing in social projects, even if this means accepting a lower rate of return.

Indeed, some commentators argue that foundations should be paying much greater attention to the 95% of their assets that are not paid out each year, than to the 5% that are paid out. At present most staff and board effort is focused on grant making. This limits people's attention to around 5% of foundation resources. 'By not engaging in total foundation asset management we are consistently missing the point of philanthropy, which is not grantmaking itself, but the application of precious resources to support the creation of a more whole, just and peaceful world.'[11]

For any foundation the balance between maximising long-term return on funds and using them for immediate impact on major need is hard to get right. But PRIs do mean that some of the capital required by nonprofit organisations can be financed by loans, thus releasing hard-won donations and retained earnings to be used for other investments or programme activities.

High engagement funders

A small number of funders have begun to require a much higher level of accountability from grant recipients, and in return offer them a higher level of support. Some of these are new funders and some are existing foundations that have decided to take a high engagement approach.

The assumption behind high engagement funding is that enhancing organisation performance is critical to achieving social goals. 'Among all the options available to them as grant-makers – funding research, dissemination of best practice, training and education for professionals…, high engagement funders conclude that improving the work of a given number of particular nonprofit organisations will be the best means of achieving social goals.'[12]

High engagement philanthropy is 'a combination of three elements – strategy coaching, reliable grant money and alignment of funder and grantee interests – that produce a different balance of power in the grantor-grantee relationship'.[12] The aim is to create a more open and trusting relationship, with the funded organisation reporting both on achievements and on problems.

Strategy coaching aims to help organisations develop robust strategies and in particular to support them in developing 'business plans' that identify relatively short-term goals and establish how they will be achieved. The highly engaged funder acts as a sounding board, offering judgement and insight. The funder also expects to see the strategy converted into action and takes a keen interest in results.

In return, the funder offers long-term and flexible support for grant recipients which can include training and consultancy to support activities such as financial management, marketing and fundraising. Although high engagement funding is more expensive for the funder, these costs are treated not as grant administration costs, but as investments in organisations designed to achieve greater impact. They also place demands on the grant-making organisation itself because of the high level of skill and experience demanded from their own staff. This may require the grant maker to raise its own game and recruit or develop the required skills.

The result of this approach is that funders are making long-term investments in organisations, rather than providing one-off grants for individual programmes or projects. Nonprofits appreciate this approach, though with some caveats. An authoritative review of the impact of high engagement philanthropy concluded that grant recipients valued the high engagement approach but preferred the freedom to select the management support they required rather than accepting the funders' chosen suppliers.[12]

Venture philanthropy

Venture philanthropy is a particular type of high engagement philanthropy. It is modelled on the success of venture capitalists who invest in a portfolio of businesses, monitor their performance closely, provide frequent assistance, help to raise further funds and have a defined exit point, often five to seven years after making the initial investment. The resources for venture philanthropy tend to come from successful business people who wish to become involved in the organisations that they finance and to hold them accountable for their performance.

Venture philanthropy starts from the principle that this type of funding is an 'investment' and not a grant. The funders are committed to the organisation's objectives and usually want to back the organisation as a whole. They want to see rapid growth of the organisation and they want to ensure that the organisation develops its own capacity as well as its programmes.

Venture philanthropists believe that they can achieve greatest impact by offering a combination of multi-year funding, strategic coaching, assistance to build organisation capacity and access to local networks of business people and funders. Most importantly they expect tight accountability from the organisations in which they invest. They see themselves as entering a true partnership that depends on openness and trust. They share the risks of things going wrong and the satisfaction of seeing real achievements.

Two disparate trends created the conditions in which venture philanthropy could thrive. First, nonprofit organisations were increasingly aware of the need for entrepreneurial skills and for less restricted funding to invest in their own organisations. Second, the unprecedented wealth creation in the late 1990s produced a significant number of people with both a desire to put something back into the community and the time and the resources to realise their intentions.

Coming from the business world, venture philanthropists have the mindset of an investor. They want to see a 'social return' on their investment and they are often keen to get to the 'root cause' of an issue. According to Kelly Fitzsimmons, Co-founder of New Profit Inc, a Boston-based venture philanthropy organisation, "investors want to raise the bar of investment results. Our investors believe that these results are achieved by the compounding effect of good investment choices, high standards, good management and tight accountability".

A VENTURE PHILANTHROPY FUND: NEW PROFIT INC

New Profit Inc (NPI) is a venture philanthropy fund whose goal is to achieve large-scale social change by investing in and partnering with a select group of innovative, high-performing nonprofit organisations. It supports social entrepreneurs in bringing their organisations to larger scale by providing them with significant, performance-based growth capital as well as intellectual capital in the form of strategy consulting, growth planning assistance, management support and network access.

Established in 1998, NPI has raised capital of over $14 million and secured a further $10 million for the organisations in its portfolio. Its 43 investors put up a minimum of $100,000 each over four years and in return they participate in the investors' network, help to select recipients and offer expertise to recipients through mentoring and strategy advice.

NPI produces reports to update investors on the progress of each recipient against agreed performance measures for organisation growth and social impact. It has nine staff and an annual operating budget of $740,000, not including grants to its portfolio.

NPI funds eight organisations with four-year grants ranging from $500,000 to $2 million in intellectual and financial capital. Seven of the eight are in the education field and each organisation receives over 110 days of staff time per year. They are:

- **BELL (Building Educated Leaders for Life)** operates after-school programmes for minority students aged 8–11 years in disadvantaged communities to promote academic proficiency
- **Citizen Schools** that engage students aged 9–14 years through fun, challenging, hands-on, out-of-school apprenticeships with a focus on academic gains
- **Jump $tart** that delivers an early childhood literacy programme working one-to-one with at-risk urban pre-schoolers using a research-backed curriculum
- **New Leaders for New Schools** that recruits, trains, places and supports a new generation of outstanding school principals in urban state schools
- **Teach for America** that offers outstanding and diverse recent college graduates opportunities to teach for two years in under-resourced schools
- **Working Today** that is working towards the day when independent workers have access to a full safety net of affordable, portable benefits, workplace rights and legal protection
- **College Summit** that reaches low-income high school students with a programme that doubles their rate of enrolment in college
- **Computers for Youth** which provides computers and training to students aged 9–14 years (and their families) to teach computer literacy and engage them in learning.

NPI has a close working relationship with The Monitor Group, the international consultancy firm. Monitor does not charge for most of the strategic consultancy because the work gives their staff interesting and challenging personal development opportunities.

Their output and results are impressive. The annual average revenue growth of their portfolio of organisations in 2002 was 31% compared to 3% per annum for the average youth development organisation in the US. The number of people served by their organisations is growing by rates varying from 20% per annum to over 300% per annum for the smaller and newer organisations, with an overall average of 43% growth for 2002.

According to Kelly Fitzsimmons, one of the co-founders, "the greatest challenge has been attracting senior and talented people to work alongside the entrepreneur who is driving the enterprise."

Although venture philanthropy has gained a high public profile, it is new and the scale of the funding is still tiny. There are 42 venture philanthropy funds in the US and their total capital is estimated to be just over $400 million. Two-thirds of these organisations were incorporated after January 1999. They exist in 18 states, the majority being in California (11), New York (6) and Texas (4).[13]

In 2001 they made grants of $50 million, significant new money, but representing less than 0.2% of all grants made by foundations. However, non-monetary support is an important element of their offer, and 15 of the 42 estimate that their non-cash support is greater than their financial support. Social Venture Partners, a Seattle-based fund that has been modelled in 21 other locations, invests 500–600 hours of partner time in each recipient organisation.

Perhaps linked to their desire to 'get to the root' of social problems, venture philanthropists invest more in youth and education than any other field with 18 of the 42 focused on this area. Whilst some make grants in the $25,000–75,000 range, seven invest $1 million or more in each recipient organisation. Most grants are for between four and seven years.

The most common criterion for selecting recipients is strong leadership, reflecting venture philanthropists' belief in investing in individuals with the personal attributes and skills to achieve the desired social impact.

The 2001 Annual Review prepared by Community Wealth Ventures showed that the 42 venture philanthropy organisations identified:

- have an average of 3.4 staff
- measure outcomes using social return on investment and the balanced scorecard
- are interested in measures that track the performance of the organisation itself as well as the resulting impact on the community.

The role and potential of venture philanthropy is one of the more controversial topics in nonprofit America at present. Given its very small size, it has generated a remarkable quantity of heated debate. The case for both venture philanthropy and high engagement funding is that they:

- respond to flaws in the current funding arrangements
- provide a new approach to philanthropy that appeals to people who are not attracted by traditional grant making and who bring new resources to the sector
- offer 'core funding' that organisations say they desperately need

- provide a range of non-financial support such as coaching and technical assistance
- supply flexible funding
- provide the tough accountability that is often lacking in the nonprofit sector.

A RECIPIENT CASE: CITIZEN SCHOOLS

Citizen Schools was founded in 1994 to provide a network of after-school and summer educational programmes. These are based on an apprenticeship model of rigorous hands-on learning that unites volunteer adults with children aged 9–14 years. Citizen Schools believe that out of school time represents the greatest untapped opportunity for improving children's education and strengthening communities.

In 1999 they were serving 900 children and won a competitive bid to receive financial and strategic support from New Profit Inc, which:

- tightened their 'theory of change' (at the individual and field levels) and strengthened their evaluation system
- provided CEO coaching, facilitation for the leadership team and board meetings
- created a balanced scorecard as a simple quarterly action-planning tool
- developed detailed costings and financial models for 'scaling up' the service.

Since NPI became involved Citizen Schools has grown to serve 2,200 children in 2003. Its funding base has grown from $1.8 million to $6.6 million and a Citizen Schools University has been launched to replicate the model across the country.

According to founder Eric Schwartz "the clarity of our vision, tightness of our action plan and power of our evaluation metrics are demonstrably greater. More importantly we're building the capacity to continue to grow, improve and creatively impact the field. They provided $3.7 million towards our $25 million four-year growth plan – less than 20% of the total but vitally important to our momentum and ultimate success.

"It has worked for us – big time. We've more than doubled in size while improving quality and starting to replicate nationally. We're serving twice as many children and serving them better. Venture philanthropists have brought us tough-minded concentration on results."

Beyond that it is clear from the requests which these funders receive from nonprofits, that there is simply a big demand for this type of investment.[14] Furthermore venture philanthropy "should be an attractive alternative to both sides of the political spectrum" said Wendy Kopp, founder of Teach for America. "For conservatives we're bringing private sector and entrepreneurial approaches to public problems. For liberals we're all about social change and improving the welfare of the least privileged people."

The case against the venture philanthropy approach is most powerfully articulated by Bruce Sievers, former Chief Executive of the Haas Foundation. He argues that there are four assumptions underlying venture capitalism that become deeply problematic when applied to philanthropy. First, venture capitalism depends on a single 'bottom line' test of success. 'Nonprofit activity has a complex and intangible range of aims that often elude simple classification and measurement'.[15]

Second venture philanthropy is based on the assumption of 'going to scale' – replicating services at regional, national or even international levels. This should lead to economies of scale, but nonprofits exist to meet highly differentiated social needs, to fill niches that are not satisfied by the public sector.

Third, venture capitalists are actively engaged in the management of the enterprises they finance and so have high level of 'control'. But nonprofit organisations are independent and have to maintain a balance of power between a range of stakeholders. An overly intrusive investor can threaten this independence.

Fourth, venture capitalists always have an 'exit strategy' – a route to get their capital repaid. Venture philanthropists argue that they aim to help their organisations achieve financial self-sufficiency to release them from their commitments, but in the nonprofit situation this inevitably means replacing their funding with money from government, foundations or other donors.

To cap it all, some commentators argue that venture philanthropy is a spin off from the dotcom bubble that has now burst, and that there will not be further significant inflows of new money. There is already some evidence for this coming from existing venture philanthropy organisations, who reported difficulties finding new donors when the economy stopped growing in 2001.

The debate is best summed up by Eric Schwartz, founder of Citizen Schools. He says "venture philanthropy is too often cloaked in a blanket of for-profit superiority that lacks historical perspective and discounts what is most challenging about the nonprofit sector – the sector's focus on changing outcomes for the hardest-to-reach children and adults. However, most people agree with its substance – grant making that is long term, linked to performance and combined with strategic non-cash assistance – but many people object to the symbolism of venture philanthropy."

Reflections on five years of venture philanthropy implementation

The Roberts Enterprise Development Fund (REDF) was launched in 1997. Managing Director Melinda Tuan believes that five guiding principles have emerged as best practices in building productive partnerships with their portfolio of nonprofit organisations:

'**Clarity** – we sign a detailed memorandum of understanding that sets out REDF's expectations of the agency and the relationship, and what the nonprofit can expect from REDF. It is reviewed every year. Organisations appreciate the clarity of its contents and the fact that everything is documented

Communication – we conduct a semi-annual assessment (of each other) and hold a monthly venture committee meeting with each funded organisation involving REDF's managing director and business analyst and the nonprofit chief executive, chief finance officer and business manager. This increased communication is essential in building more productive working relationships.

Customisation – we tailor support to suit each organisation's requirements from a menu that includes hands-on assistance in planning, help with recruitment, networking, technology support and social outcomes assessment.

Collaboration – we build strong positive relationships where problems can be openly discussed and outcomes can be reviewed together rather than imposed by the funder.

Consistency – we avoid communicating inconsistent messages. This involves weekly portfolio review meetings with all REDF staff to discuss the status of organisations, the messages to be conveyed and who will convey them.'

Source: Melinda Tuan in *Alliance Magazine*[16]

Despite the criticisms, many believe that venture philanthropy will become a permanent feature of nonprofit funding. "It is here to stay" says Harvard's James Austin. "There will be unprecedented wealth transfer between generations over the coming years. Although its impact is limited at present, it is all part of the growing heterogeneity of social enterprise."

Virginia Hodgkinson, founding director of the Center for the Study of Voluntary Organizations and Service at Georgetown University, agrees. "It is not going to go away because there is a new breed of people who want a hands-on involvement in their philanthropy."

Some venture philanthropists recognise that they were insufficiently sensitive to the culture of the sector and did not acknowledge its achievements. Leading figure in the field and co-founder of the $32 million fund Venture Philanthropy Partners, Mario Morino, says "one of the budding venture philanthropist's mistakes is that we don't listen. Some of us impose our point of view on others instead of paying attention to what's going on around us".

There is an emerging view that venture philanthropy and high engagement funding were both given too much hype in the early stages of their development. The 2001 Annual Review prepared by Community Wealth Ventures now takes a more sanguine view 'A few years ago, the concepts of venture philanthropy and high engagement grantmaking were over-inflated with airy promises to transform philanthropy as we know it. Today we can see that their progress towards that promise is real but not yet revolutionary'.[13]

Yet high engagement funding and venture philanthropy have clearly had a major impact on the whole way people think about large gift philanthropy, and have provoked foundations to think about different approaches to grant making. According to Julie Rogers, President of the Meyer Foundation, "the challenge now is to widen the circle so that high engagement strategies define how philanthropy is done for years to come".

So the approach is here to stay. Those organisations that wish to seek this type of finance, and are willing to gear up to its requirements, will no doubt benefit, particularly when the economy returns to faster growth and more business people who make their fortunes then want to make a significant contribution to the community.

Summary

Take advantage of fundamental trends in finance sources

- Sources of finance are diversifying and now include programme related investments, venture philanthropy, community development finance institutions, loans, bonds and equity investments
- Traditional sources of finance have grown dramatically in real terms. Private contributions to nonprofit organisations have grown by 340% over the last 20 years and government funding has grown by 195%
- Changes in traditional sources of funding are likely to include:
  - greater concentration of wealth amongst a small number of donors
  - significant potential growth from bequests
  - further increases in non-cash donations.
- Commentators are beginning to conceive of a 'nonprofit capital market'. They see this market as being inefficient and needing reform.

Expect more demanding funders

- Funders are becoming much more involved with the organisations they finance, expecting clearer evidence of results and offering greater support
- Leading organisations are expecting to:
  - receive fewer, larger, more strategic grants
  - engage in more partnerships and provide greater accountability
  - share more learning across the sector.
- The characteristics of an effective funder include a coherent purpose, focus, knowledge of the field, a theory of change, strategic resource deployment, long-term commitment and active programme management.

Capitalise on new funding sources

- Leading organisations look to a range of different financial instruments to fund different types of capital and revenue requirements
- Programme related investment provides new capital funds to nonprofits and allows foundations to invest resources in their mission
- A new breed of high engagement funders is taking new approaches to philanthropy, combining funding with strategic coaching, practical support and tough accountability
- Although small in size and controversial, venture philanthropy has had a significant impact on the sector. Funders are offering a combination of multi-year funding, strategic coaching and assistance to build organisation capacity. They agree ambitious targets with funded organisations and have tough accountability requirements.

References

1 Murray Weitzman *et al.*, *The New Nonprofit Almanac and Desk Reference*, San Francisco, Jossey-Bass, 2002

2 Center on Philanthropy – Indiana University, *Giving USA 2002*, Indianapolis, AAFRC Trust for Philanthropy, 2002

3 William Ryan, *Nonprofit Capital – A Review of Problems and Strategies*, New York, Rockefeller Foundation, 2001 (download from www.rockfound.org)

4 Jed Emerson, *The US Nonprofit Capital Market* in *Social Purpose Enterprises and Venture Philanthropy in the New Millennium, Volume 2 Investor Perspectives*, San Francisco, The Roberts Foundation, 1999

5 John Havens and Paul Schervish, *Millionaires and the Millennium: New Estimates of the Forthcoming Wealth Transfer and the Prospects for a Golden Age of Philanthropy*, Boston, Boston College Social Welfare Research Institute, 1999 (download from www.bc.edu)

6 Lester Salamon, *America's Nonprofit Sector – A Primer*, New York, Foundation Center, 1999

7 John Havens and Paul Schervish, *Why the $41 Trillion Wealth Transfer Estimate is Still Valid*, Boston, Boston College Social Welfare Research Institute, 2003 (download from www.bc.edu)

8 Kevin Kearns, *Accountability and Government in Nonprofit Organizations: A Strategic Management Approach*, San Francisco, Jossey-Bass, 1996

9 Dennis Prager, *Raising the Value of Philanthropy*, Washington, Grantmakers In Health, 1999 (download from www.gih.org)

10 Loren Renz, *PRI Financing 1998–1999 Trends and Statistics*, Washington, The Foundation Centre, 2001 (download from www.fdncenter.org)

11 Jed Emerson, *Horse Manure and Grantmaking* in *Foundation News and Commentary*, Washington, May/June 2002 (download from www.foundationnews.org)

12 Christine Letts and William Ryan, *How High-Engagement Philanthropy Works*, Stanford CA, *Stanford Social Innovation Review*, Spring 2003

13 *Venture Philanthropy 2002*, Community Wealth Ventures, Venture Philanthropy Partners, 2002 (download from www.vppartners.org)

14 Nicole Etchart and Lee Davis, *Prophets for Non-profits?* in *Alliance Magazine*, London, Allavida, June 2002

15 Bruce Sievers, *If Pigs Had Wings: The Appeals and Limits of Venture Philanthropy*, Washington, Georgetown University, November 2001 (download from www.georgetown.edu)

16 Melinda Tuan, 'REDF –*The Evolution of a Venture Philanthropy Fund* in *Alliance Magazine*, London, Allavida, June 2002

6 Leading with integrity

Leadership is one of the most discussed and most documented aspects of management. The shelves of bookstores in the US burst with titles setting out a wide range of views on the topic. There are books written by leaders based on their own experience, books promoting particular approaches to leadership and many biographical books on business leaders that feed people's curiosity about how they make their organisations successful.

Leadership is viewed as immensely important in nonprofit organisations. A Brookings Institution survey of 250 researchers and providers of management assistance in the US highlighted leadership as the single most important ingredient of effective organisations. 'Leadership does appear to be the answer, but not the sparkly, charismatic leadership celebrated in glossy best-sellers. Rather it is a participatory, democratic leadership that draws upon strengths inside and outside the organisation.'[1]

One of the first people to promote ideas of leadership in the nonprofit sector was Peter Drucker. The second section of his book *Managing the Non-profit Organization*[2] was entitled 'Leadership is a foul-weather job'. He makes a number of pertinent points:

- The first task of the leader is to make sure that everybody sees the mission, hears it and lives it.
- In the nonprofit agency, mediocrity in leadership shows up almost immediately.
- The new leader of a nonprofit doesn't have much time to establish him or herself.

Throughout the 1990s the Drucker Foundation, now renamed the Leader to Leader Institute, did much to promote understanding of leadership and to offer training and practical support to nonprofit leaders.

The late John Gardner, founding Chair of Independent Sector, also recognised the importance of leadership in nonprofits. He wrote *On Leadership*[3], also published in 1990, in which he described what successful nonprofit leaders must do to instil confidence, morale and motivation in those who look to them for the future.

More recently, Burt Nanus and Stephen Dobbs wrote a *Leaders who Make a Difference* in response to 'the paucity of professional guidance available to leaders of nonprofit organisations'. They argued that leadership of nonprofits is different from leadership of business and government organisations. First, nonprofits have unpaid board members, many deliver their services through volunteers and most staff consider their salary secondary to the 'psychic income' they derive from working for a cause. 'Leading these kinds of people requires much more reliance on inspiration, passion, coaxing, persuasion and peer pressure than upon authority, financial incentives or fancy job titles.'

Second, 'success in nonprofit organisations is measured not in terms of profits and fulfilment of legislative intent, but in terms of social good. This is a more value-laden and less clearly defined criterion than these other organisations must meet, leaving considerable room for nonprofit leaders to exercise judgement, intuition and innovation'.

Finally, they argue that 'working with the board – some might say leading the board – is a much more critical part of the leader's job in nonprofits than in other types of organisation. The sheer number of people to be led is far larger in nonprofit organisations than in business or government agencies with similar-sized budgets'.[4]

Leadership is not just about the person at the top of the organisation, though the behaviour of that person clearly has a huge influence on the values and style of the organisation and its management. It is about the delivery of leadership in all parts of the organisation. Everyone in a position of authority has a responsibility to provide leadership for their area of work and to contribute to the wider leadership of their department, their division and the organisation as a whole.

This chapter

Chapter 6 focuses on what interviewees said about leadership of nonprofit organisations. It sets their views in the context of some of the current literature. The evidence shows that people in leadership positions learn to:

- be a leader
- mobilise around the mission
- focus people on results
- build a small focused team
- invest in leadership and management development.

6.1 Be a leader

Interviewees and the literature in the US stress the importance of leaders' behaviour.

Leaders have to embody the values of the organisation in what they do and how they do it. They have to be conscious of the need for complete congruence between the organisation's values and their own behaviour. Leaders are being watched all the time – and small differences between their deeply held values and the actions they take will be noticed. "Leaders are the embodiment of the mission and values in thinking, action and communication," according to Frances Hesselbein, Chairman of the Leader to Leader Institute. She recommends that leaders always think about what their legacy will be.

In her view, leaders need to understand 'how to be'. She describes this as having 'quality, character, mind-set, values, principles and courage'. Leaders who appreciate 'how to be' 'build dispersed and diverse leadership and hold forth the vision of the organisation's future in compelling ways that ignite the spark needed to build the inclusive enterprise'.[5]

Her view is echoed by Parker Palmer, author of *Let Your Life Speak*[6]. Interviewed in the *Leader to Leader* journal he said 'The best leaders work from a place of integrity in themselves, from their hearts. If they don't they can't inspire trustful relationships. In the absence of trust, organisations fall apart. It takes courage to lead from the heart because you're putting your own identity and integrity into the public arena. You're standing for things you believe in. You're professing values that are important to you – and in the public arena you will always draw slings and arrows for doing that. But you will have the best chance of creating something of true and lasting value'.[7]

Leaders have to deliver a number of roles. Nanus and Dobbs argue that leaders' attention needs to be focused in four directions:

'1 **Inside the organisation**, where the leader interacts with the board, staff and volunteers to inspire, encourage, enthuse, and empower them.
2 **Outside the organisation**, where the leader seeks assistance or support from donors, grantmakers, potential allies, the media or other leaders in the business or public sectors.
3 **On present operations**, where the leader is concerned about the quality of services to clients and the community, and also organisational structures, information systems and other aspects or organisational effectiveness.

4 **On future possibilities**, where the leader anticipates trends and developments that are likely to have important implications for the future direction of the organisation.'[4]

They argue that focusing attention in these four directions requires leaders of nonprofit organisations to deliver six essential roles:

1 **Visionary** – Leaders work with others to scan the realm of future possibilities, seeking clues to a more desirable destination. 'Great leaders have great visions and when they are widely shared they are the principal engines of organisational growth and progress.'

2 **Strategist** – Leaders are responsible for ensuring that organisations have strategies that position the organisation to be most effective in meeting present and future challenges. Leaders ensure that their organisations adopt strategies that hold the most promise of fulfilling the vision and achieving the greatest social good.

3 **Politician** – Leaders are 'super networkers' who champion the organisation's cause and use their contacts to further the organisation's mission.

4 **Fundraiser** – Leaders of nonprofits have an important role in raising funds from the public, foundations and corporations. The authors call this role campaigning, as the term 'campaigning for funds' is common in the US.

5 **Coach** – Leaders empower and inspire individuals and help them to learn, grow and realise their full potential.

6 **Change agent** – Leaders initiate change that positions the organisation for the future, introducing changes externally around the clients, the services offered and the means of financing them, and internally around the organisation's structures and processes.

The focus of leaders' attention and the roles they need to perform can be related in the following way:

The roles of nonprofit leaders

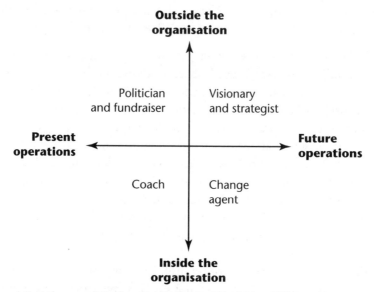

Source: Burt Nanus and Stephen Dobbs, *Leaders Who Make a Difference*[4]

Effective leaders recognise that they need to discharge all these roles all of the time. Being brilliant at one does not compensate for lack of skills in the other roles. Leaders are constantly juggling these different roles and taking actions that advance their agenda on each one.

In delivering these roles leaders have to gain the trust and respect of the people who are being led. A series of seminal studies asked managers from all sectors what values they looked for and admired in their superiors. The results consistently showed the same characteristics:

Characteristics of superior leaders

Characteristic	Percentage of managers selecting this characteristic
Honesty	83
Competence	67
Forward-looking qualities	62
Inspiration	58
Intelligence	43

Source: James Kouzes and Barry Posner, *The Leadership Challenge*[8]

The lowest rated characteristics were ambition, determination, self-control, loyalty and independence.[8]

Interviewees also stressed the importance of openness and honesty. "It is important to be up front with people," according to Michael Flood, Executive Director of Los Angeles Food Bank. "I strive to be both honest and ethical in all that I do." Buck Parker of Earth Justice, a $23 million national organisation that uses the legal system to protect the environment concurs, "you need to get to know people and build trust. I always try to be seen to be fair and to talk the truth".

RAISING AND RESOLVING CONFLICT AT THE LIGHTHOUSE

Anita Aaron is the Executive Director of The Lighthouse, the leading provider of services for visually impaired people in San Francisco. She believes that a key part of the executive director's role is to spot areas of conflict, bring them to the surface and ensure that they are resolved.

"People used to bring problems and differences of opinion to me and expect me to make judgements and take decisions," she said. "They also wanted closed door discussions about issues and other people. To begin with I acquiesced but I soon came to realise that my judgements were not always the best and that people were being encouraged to dump their problems on me."

"I now see my job as bringing these issues out into the open. Sometimes I get the relevant parties around the table and make them talk about the issue in front of each other. In other circumstances I send individuals or groups of people away to discuss the issue and come back to me with their preferred solution."

"I have taken this a step further and see my job as identifying potential areas of conflict and raising it with the relevant people. I had to learn how to have open and honest conversations with people who report to me. I may be less popular, but I believe that I am more respected."

"An important element of my job is conflict resolution, and the training I attended gave me the confidence to manage difficult conversations in a constructive way."

Being honest is not always as easy as it sounds. Leaders have information which they may not be able to share with everyone at the same time, for example plans for re-structuring staff, discussions about a potential contract or disciplinary matters. Leaders sometimes have preliminary thoughts that they wish to test on close colleagues without communicating more widely.

BEING A LEADER IN A CRISIS – THE STORY OF ELDERHOSTEL

In 1979 James Moses took on a short-term job with Elderhostel. At the time it had six employees. Today it provides extraordinary learning adventures for nearly 250,000 people aged 55 and over in over 100 countries every year.

Having worked for the organisation in many different positions for 23 years, James was given a challenge of a lifetime. The organisation had recently parted with its previous chief executive. The 2001 recession had led to a significant drop in bookings and the organisation faced a cash crisis. Staff had to be laid off and offices had to be closed. Staff morale was at an all time low. To cap all this, the tragedy of September 11th led to a further reduction in bookings as people stopped travelling.

James is a thoughtful man. He is not a management guru and admits to not being well versed in management literature. He works from his instinct and this is what he did when the organisation faced its crisis:

- He was encouraged by staff to apply for the chief executive post and when he was appointed he kept his previous vice president salary, despite pressure to take the chief executive salary
- He brought the staff together for a meeting to identify a few simple priorities to guide the organisation through the crisis (such as building lists of potential participants and being fiscally conservative)
- He bought everyone coffee and doughnuts from his own funds
- He expressed his passion for the cause
- He initiated a fortnightly newsletter to staff, which focused on business performance and included messages from clients for whom the organisation had made a big difference.

As a result of his actions, his senior staff decided not to take their annual salary rises. The atmosphere this created enabled him to make further budget cuts, but this time without layoffs. Taken together these actions were immensely important to staff.

Six months later the finances started to turn around. James consulted with each of his senior staff individually on what to do about salaries. He took a salary half way between his VP salary and the CEO's salary and his senior staff took their raises.

He saw one of his roles as working to develop other people's skills. He talked to people a lot and made sure they were clear what he wanted them to do. He used his ability to have difficult conversations. He took a questioning approach and believed people were honest when he was open.

So, whilst leaders should strive to be as open as possible, and people increasingly expect greater openness, in practice there are boundaries that need to be respected. However, using these to hide behind difficult decisions or conversations will damage the trust and respect that people have in their leaders. Michael Flood stressed, "You can't be a leader if you dislike conflict. People respect you if you have honest conversations and if their work is not good enough it is important to say so". He also emphasised the need to admit his own mistakes and encourage others to admit theirs.

6.2 Mobilise around the mission

Great leaders have a clear vision for the future of their organisation and a clear understanding of its mission. The terms 'vision' and 'mission' are defined in a number of different ways. A succinct definition comes from Nanus and Dobbs who describe vision as 'a realistic, credible, attractive and inspiring future for the organisation'. A vision does not show you how to get somewhere, but it does present a clear and exciting image of what the world might be like when you arrive. The mission is 'a brief delineation of the organisation's reason for being'.[4]

One of the more notable aspects of leading-edge US nonprofits is that their missions are pervasive. They are framed in the office entrance hall, they are on business cards, on the organisation's website, on screen savers, on directions for visitors, they are highlighted in all strategy and planning reports and they appear on documents the organisation publishes. Leaders ensure that they are omnipresent.

In these organisations the mission is also referred to frequently in conversation. It is alive, well understood and trips off people's tongues. According to John Bryson, author of the best-selling book on strategic planning, a clear and living mission creates 'a habit of focusing discussion on what is truly important'.[9] Thomas Holland noted in his research into board behaviour that 'In the middle of intense discussions on some complex issue before the group, it was not unusual for someone to remind the others of how their mission, core values and ethical responsibilities were key guideposts in these deliberations. In a variety of ways, members of these boards recognised that their board's actions were the embodiments of those values and their meetings the place where they could translate the mission and values into responsible decisions'.[10]

Missions are used by leaders to motivate people throughout the organisation. They are used along with strategies and plans to keep managers focused on the organisation's primary objectives.

Missions are also actively used in decision taking. Leaders encourage managers and board members to use the mission statement to inform strategic decisions. If there are major questions about strategic direction or about corporate priorities, the mission statement is the touch stone to which people refer. The first question Ray Considine, President of The Medical Foundation in Boston, always asks when considering a new initiative or a new contract bid is "how well does it fit with our mission?"

It is widely accepted that missions are more important in the nonprofit sector than in the for-profit sector. Mission is a nonprofit management idea that has much greater salience than in the business world. It is the *raison d'être* for the organisation. From a managerial perspective the mission has three main purposes:

1 It sets the boundaries on the organisation's work – the mission should answer the question 'What is provided and for whom?'.
2 It motivates staff and donors – the mission should 'carry the ideology of the organisation, to serve as a flag around which the organisation can rally'.
3 It assists in evaluating the impact of the organisation – the mission should be the starting point for measuring performance.

Organisations at the leading edge review their missions regularly to confirm that they are up-to-date, relevant and continue to encapsulate the organisation's purpose. This usually happens at the annual board strategic planning retreat. If the mission is clear, relevant and appropriate for current circumstances it will be confirmed. If not it will be adjusted.

Leaders who champion their mission will then seek more and more ways to promote it – on invoices, on contract documents, on e-mail signatures, in staff manuals and so on. It will remain central to the daily lives of everyone involved in the organisation.

Mission statements

Mission statements are short, precise and most critically are a central part of organisation life. They are real, used and regularly reviewed.

American Diabetes Association
'To prevent and cure diabetes and to improve the lives of all people affected by diabetes.'

The Nature Conservancy
'To preserve the plants, animals and natural communities that represent the diversity of life on Earth by protecting the lands and waters they need to survive.'

March of Dimes
'To improve the health of babies by preventing birth defects and infant mortality.'

Goodwill Industries of Southern California
'To enhance the quality of the lives of people who have disabilities and other vocational disadvantages by assisting them to become productive and self-sufficient through education, training and job opportunities.'

America's Second Harvest
'To feed hungry people by soliciting and distributing food and grocery products through a nationwide network of certified affiliate food banks and food-rescue programs and to educate the public about the nature of and solutions to the problem of hunger in America.'

Jewish Vocational Services
'To link employers and individuals together to achieve their employment goals by providing the skills necessary for success in today's workplace.'

Independent Sector
'To promote, strengthen and advance the nonprofit and philanthropic community to foster private initiative for the public good.'

The Alliance for Nonprofit Management
'To increase the effectiveness of individuals and organizations that help nonprofits build their power and impact.'

6.3 Focus people on results

Leaders have to manage strategy and its implementation. This is the central spine of management competence that is critical to high performance. Clarifying the mission, establishing top quality strategic and operational plans, creating teams to deliver the plans and establishing systems of accountability are widely seen as the indispensable elements of strong leadership. What these all boil down to is ensuring everyone at every level of the organisation understands their roles and priorities and is held accountable for their contribution to the achievement of the mission. These are the management arrangements that are absolutely essential to effective nonprofit organisations. They have to be implemented to the highest standard to provide a backbone onto which other managerial actions can be added.

Use planning as a focusing tool

When asked how they focus their organisations on achieving the mission, chief executives invariably said that the annual cycle of planning, budget setting and performance reviews were their most powerful management processes. "Strategic planning is the strongest lever I have on the organisation. It helps to clarify the vision and the goals. It enables us to focus on the things we can control," according to Donna Feingold, Executive Director of Toolworks, a San Francisco-based organisation that provides training and job opportunities for disabled people.

McKinsey Director Paul Jansen agreed: "The most powerful lever for management is getting the performance cycle going – setting goals, evaluating people against goals, linking this to compensation and next year's goals".

Clarifying objectives and holding people accountable for results does not mean putting people in a straitjacket. Circumstances do change, experience brings understanding of what works and what does not, and plans have to be modified. The characteristic of well-led organisations is that such changes are explicit and they clearly relate to agreed strategies and goals.

Strong leaders ensure that strategies are well integrated with implementable operational plans. "Tight linkage between the strategic plan and implementation is the key handle the CEO has for managing performance," according to Doug Barr, Chief Executive of Goodwill Industries of Southern California. "I ensure that people make their strategic plan commitments measurable and know that they will be held to account for their delivery." This view is echoed by other observers who believe that there is more progress to be made in tightening up the links between a realistic mission, robust strategies and clear action plans. In their view there is still too much sloppy thinking between these elements of management.

Strategic and operational plans in leading-edge organisations also demonstrate how the organisation capacity needed to support implementation will be built. "Strategising and good planning lead to increased focus but organisations tend to move straight from goals to programmes," according to Harvard's Christine Letts. "The 'business planning' stage is left out, and business planning is about developing organisation capacity to deliver the mission."

It is easy to create well-intentioned objectives. The critical leadership activity is to require managers to map out the essential steps required to achieve them – identifying the actions required and the obstacles that will have to be overcome. When this is done rigorously, "each departmental manager must know exactly what his or her department is trying to achieve," according to Michael Flood, Executive Director of the Los Angeles Foodbank. Furthermore, "the process must allow identification of areas where departments impact on each other for plans to be really robust".

Effective leaders ensure that plans are thoroughly scrutinised before being approved. In some organisations board sub-committees, such as the planning and performance review committee, will be involved in reviewing plans before they are submitted to the main board. In others the examination will happen at the annual board planning retreat and in some it will happen at both.

Well-managed organisations do not set their plans in stone. "Strategic plans needed to provide a clear structure, but the environment is increasingly volatile," says Mary Emmons of Los Angeles-based Children's Institute International, "so we also need capacity to be responsive to new opportunities as well". LA Foodbank works on a similar premise and leaves 15% of the available time for unanticipated activity.

Link plans to performance reviews

With robust plans in place, effective leaders ensure managers are held to account through a performance review process that connects plans with individual and corporate performance. Many organisations have a quarterly performance review cycle. Doug Barr of Goodwill Industries says, "I hold my staff clearly accountable for achieving plan targets and I expect them to hold their staff accountable, thus creating a clear hierarchy of accountability through the organisation". When individuals are held tightly to account for performance against plans, the organisation as a whole can be held to account initially by the chief executive and subsequently by the board.

Boards play an important role in establishing high expectations for the planning and performance cycle. Evidence for the increasing importance attached to evaluation comes from the number of boards that establish committees for planning and performance review. The main board in these organisations expects its planning and performance committees to oversee the planning process and continuously to improve reporting mechanisms so the full board has top-quality reports on the overall performance of the organisation.

In some cases the performance evaluation of the CEO is based on strategic plan achievements as reported to the board. "My evaluation is based on the Strategic Plan Monitoring Committee report," says Goodwill's Doug Barr.

Manage costs tightly

Managing for social results does not absolve leaders and managers from being held accountable for financial results as well. One of the characteristics of the nonprofit world noticed by people from the for-profit sector is that costs are not managed nearly as tightly as they are in the business world. "Private sector organizations in the same fields as nonprofits have a much better understanding of costs and whether expenditure is delivering value for money," according to Jeff Bradach of the Bridgespan Group – a nonprofit consulting firm linked to the global for-profit consultancy Bain and Company. "Understanding nonprofit's cost structure is increasingly important. In my view many nonprofits are managing with false books of account."

Leaders of some organisations have begun to treat departments as 'profit centres' and to hold managers accountable for the 'bottom line' that shows how the department performed, taking into acount both income and expenditure. These leaders ensure that managers are provided with financial reports that set out the income and expenditure streams associated with their departments. They expect managers to control both income and expenditure even if a significant proportion of income comes from 'corporate' funds held by the centre of the organisation. According to John Graham, CEO of the American Diabetes Association, "this concentrates people's minds on all the possible income raising opportunities they should be exploiting".

Leaders in these organisations also seek productivity improvements every year. The American Diabetes Association, for example, expects budget holders to find efficiency savings every year. 'Even if a department is experiencing double digit growth, we will expect infrastructure costs to rise by less than 3–4%.' This approach led the organisation to merge all phone and IT lines, saving a substantial sum every day.

USING THE BUDGET AS A LEADERSHIP TOOL AT THE WILDLIFE CONSERVATION SOCIETY

The Wildlife Conservation Society saves wildlife and wild lands through careful science, international conservation, education and the management of the world's largest system of urban wildlife parks, led by the flagship Bronx Zoo. With income of $125 million per annum and assets of over $500 million, managing costs can make a significant difference to performance.

President and CEO Steve Sanderson argues that the budget can be used as a key lever for change. He recommends six actions, which must be managed flexibly and collegially:

1 Link the budget explicitly to the mission by resourcing activities that contribute most to achieving the mission. Use unrestricted funds very strategically.
2 Require each part of the organisation to manage the net of its income and expenditure (i.e. its bottom line) even if it receives funding from the centre.
3 Expect managers to find cost savings each year, even if total income and expenditure are growing.
4 Incentivise departments that exceed their budget targets by allowing them to keep part of any 'surplus' that the department makes.
5 Penalise departments that do not meet budget targets by rolling over losses into the following year and expecting those departments to recover them.
6 Recognise that the enterprise should absorb any uncontrollable changes in income and expenditure but treat these as exceptional and be transparent about making such changes.

6.4 Build a small focused team

Leaders cannot deliver social results on their own. To fulfil their many roles they need a team, and for the chief executive the shape and composition of that team and its ability to perform at the highest level is critical to success.

The composition of the top team

Having a group of people who share the same mission, work together well, focus on corporate results and provide effective leadership is a major determinant of organisational effectiveness. A key decision for chief executives, therefore, is to determine the number of people who sit on this top team and which roles should be represented. With too few people there may not be sufficient diversity of thought. But having too many people runs the risk of the chief executive giving insufficient attention to external matters.

Chief executives state that somewhere between three and five direct reports is the ideal number in most circumstances. Most interviewees said that having more than five led them to become too internally focused. Anita Aaron, Executive Director of Lighthouse, established a team of eight people, but quickly realised it was a mistake. "I became a supervisor and could not provide the organisation with effective leadership. The structure drove me to be internally oriented. Even though I neglected external relationships, I was still not able to provide all the managers with sufficient support." She quickly reverted to a structure with four direct reports:

- programmes
- development (fundraising)
- finance
- administration.

A chief executive can hold only a few people tightly to account. The smaller the group the easier it is for the chief executive to have clear expectations and to be adequately supportive. John Graham, CEO of the American Diabetes Association, has three direct reports:

- chief scientific and medical officer
- chief of field operations
- chief operating officer.

All three attend and participate as equals in board meetings – creating a model that emulates the joint executive and non-executive board that is more common in the corporate sector.

Unicef USA has an even smaller team of two who report to CEO Charles Lyons:

- vice president marketing
- chief operating officer.

This group is supplemented by a wider operations committee that meets weekly or fortnightly and does not include the chief executive. "People like the arrangement because it gets faster decisions," according to Charles Lyons.

A small team at the top usually requires the appointment of a chief operating officer to take command of a range of functions. Chief operating officers are widespread. There are three models, the most common incorporating all 'back office' functions of finance, human relations, IT and property under one senior post. A variation on this excludes finance and puts all other back office functions under one person. The third and less common alternative puts all service delivery functions under one person. California-based Trust for Public Land has adopted this model with:

- chief operating officer
- chief finance officer
- development director
- marketing director.

The seven regional directors all report to the COO.

The position of COO is not an easy post to fill, particularly when the post is first created. Some interviewees reported difficulties finding suitable candidates and people with whom they could work effectively. A number recommended taking this critical step only when there is an internal candidate ideally suited for promotion to the position.

Skills to look for

Chief executives stressed that members of the top team must have strong management skills. Functional expertise is not sufficient at this level. "We look for people who have effective supervision skills, can work collaboratively, are good at holding people to account and who can establish realistic and measurable goals," says Amnesty

International's Deputy Executive Director, Curt Goering. "We do not appoint campaigners as managers unless they demonstrate clearly that they have management skills."

Good communication is of key importance, so regular meetings of this group are seen to be critical to success. Most top teams meet weekly, supplemented by regular retreats away from the office to address big issues. "Mutual respect and good communications are critical," according to Mike Flood, Executive Director of LA Foodbank. This is echoed by other chief executives who stress the importance of excellent relationships between members. "We encourage candid speaking and have regular dinners together," says Curt Goering, who interestingly also takes responsibility for running all senior team meetings.

Mary Emmons, CEO of Children's Institute International, expressed this view even more strongly: "The key is to have a senior team with an agency-wide perspective. To achieve that there has to be a high level of trust between members, to have great confidence in each other, an ability to share problems and to maintain strict confidentiality when required by the team".

Interviewees frequently spoke about leaders' skills in getting high performance from their teams. Doug Barr, Chief Executive of Goodwill Industries stressed the importance of "Ensuring that people feel challenged and that their successes are acknowledged". Roni Posner, Executive Director of The Alliance, saw her role as, "being the greatest cheer leader for every member of staff. I expect people to excel and I work with them to help them excel. My job is to provide staff with resources and to make people feel they are special".

Leaders stressed the need to see people's strengths but also to recognise that sometimes it is necessary to move them to jobs that better fit their skills and interests. "It is important to let people know if they are underperforming," according to Roni Posner. Doug Barr agrees, "If someone is struggling the first step is to get them support, for example from a national body or from consultants. I give people a number of chances but I also recognise the need to be decisive when the time comes to let someone go".

Reward performance

Leaders need to recognise and reward high performance of members of their teams. The most important reward for nonprofit managers is knowing that their organisation is achieving its mission and that they are able to make a significant contribution. Job satisfaction is usually much more significant than money.

Nevertheless, some organisations are devising systems to reward their more senior managers for effective performance. Performance-related pay is a tricky issue for nonprofits. There is public sensitvity over the idea of bonus payments, particularly if poor performance is rewarded, and there are some organisations that would never countenance the idea of performance pay.

Interviewees reported that there are two essential pre-requisites of a successful performance-related pay system. First, staff objectives must be really clear and measurable so that the system is fair and transparent. Second, there must be a high level of trust in the performance evaluation system and its results. Performance-related pay can work well only in organisations where it fits the culture and where other management processes are secure and well respected.

With these in place, a number of organisations are introducing performance-related pay. United Way of Los Angeles has bonus payments for all top managers. They are all evaluated on standard corporate criteria in addition to individual functional criteria. The evaluation is carried out by the personnel committee and payments do not exceed 10% of salary. President Joseph Haggerty says, "It keeps the senior team focused on the agreed corporate objectives".

Goodwill Industries of Southern California has performance-related pay for its top 150 managers. The chief executive's performance pay is linked directly to the achievement of agreed corporate strategic objectives. Performance pay for other managers has an element related to functional performance.

According to Paul Jansen of McKinsey, "It is not necessarily about the money, but the payment is the clearest communication a manager can give about a subordinate's performance".

However, whilst some organisations use financial incentives, others would never consider such a move. James Moses from Elderhostel is firmly against it. "Nonprofits have to challenge self interest. We have to express different underlying values from business and government and one way to do this is to make working for nonprofits distinctively different." Buck Parker of Earth Justice agrees, "We will never have bonus payments. It would conflict with our ethos and would be a headache to implement."

INCREASING PRODUCTIVITY AT CHILDREN'S INSTITUTE INTERNATIONAL

Children's Institute International (CII) is committed to the prevention, identification and treatment of all forms of child abuse and neglect. Based in Los Angeles, the $21 million-per-annum organisation employs teachers and social workers to provide training and therapy.

The extension of managed care packages for individuals supported by human service providers resulted in grant funding being replaced by 'fee for service' payments. CII had to start recording how professionals used their time. Management calculated that to remain viable, service delivery staff would have to charge for more than two-thirds of their time. A time recording system was introduced, and although there was considerable anxiety at the outset, it has now become an accepted way of working.

The bigger challenge was to ensure that everyone was achieving or exceeding their targets. Management introduced an incentive payment system known as CASH, which at the time made payments of $40 per hour for every chargeable hour that each member of staff delivered above their target of 68.5% of total time.

The approach did not sit comfortably with the culture of a nonprofit dedicated to meeting the needs of poor families. Much time was therefore invested in communicating with staff and listening to their concerns.

The system has proved to be remarkably successful.

- Financially the organisation has benefited because it charges its funders (mainly the county and the state) $120 for every extra hour delivered.
- It has given management much greater flexibility in delivering services. Instead of working elsewhere, staff now work overtime with CII to fill gaps in capacity caused by sickness, maternity leave and promotions.
- Good supervision was essential to ensure that quality was maintained. Supervisors also deliver services, but have lower targets. The strong culture of delivering the highest quality services and effective management of supervisors ensures that quality is maintained.
- The top management challenge changed. Rather than trying to persuade people to deliver chargeable hours for the agency, managers now work to remove any obstacles that made it difficult for staff to achieve and exceed their targets.
- People who delivered the highest quality work had the highest rates of extra chargeable time and the lowest 'no show' rates from their clients.

The next step for CII is to introduce a system of incentives for directors because the system now discourages people from seeking promotion.

6.5 Invest in leadership and management development

Leading organisations invest in leadership and management development and they are taking many different approaches to support people's growth. This development takes many forms, reflecting the fact that there is little evidence demonstrating which approaches are most effective.

A common starting point is a **360-degree review,** which helps people with leadership responsibilities to identify their development needs. Earth Justice, an organisation providing lawyers to fight key environmental campaigns, uses 360-degree reviews. "It was the best investment we ever made," said Executive Director Buck Parker, "and we use it as the basis for promotion decisions".

Role-specific training is used by Children's Institute International which identified three very different roles that key service delivery managers play:

- professional relationships with clients
- managerial relationships with staff
- effective handling of administration, contract and budgets.

They provide managers with training on the distinction between client relationships and staff relationships to help them perform their different roles with a different mindset. They also use a consultant to help individual managers improve their communication skills, and in particular to learn how to give difficult messages to their staff.

Many individuals attend the wide range of open and tailored **management training courses** on offer. There are over 90 universities and colleges providing courses in nonprofit management. "They are creating people who are skilled in the technical elements of managing nonprofits, such as fundraising, financial management and governance, though many are not creating people with vision who understand public policy and can provide organisations with leadership," according to Pablo Eisenberg of Georgetown University.

Some organisations use a **coaching methodology**. For example, Amnesty International gets experienced managers to coach the less experienced. It has an employee professional development programme based on staff identification of their needs. It also gives people sabbaticals to overcome the problem of burn out. It offers five months out after five years' service, provided people commit to returning for two years.

Most organisations have **training budgets** which managers can apply to for the required funding. Some go one step further and give people a personal financial allocation. Toolworks gives managers a personal training budget to attend accredited training courses. It grows from $300 per annum after two years service to $1,000 per annum after 10 years' service.

These training and development measures are supported by **regular meetings of all middle managers**. Many organisations have quarterly meetings of middle managers, some take place half yearly and some annually. When these meetings are carefully planned and well structured, they encourage communication across functions, keep people focused on corporate aims and provide further opportunities for supporting middle managers.

Chief executives' development was reported as taking a variety of forms. Some do attend leadership courses at institutions such as Harvard and the Center for Creative Leadership that are specifically for nonprofit leaders. Others attend business and public sector leadership development courses. "Some training is good," according to Audrey Alverado of the National Council of Nonprofit Associations. "The challenge is the application of the learning when you return to the office."

Some read extensively about leadership. "I read about the theory of leadership and study examples of excellent leadership and strive to apply the lessons in my work," says Linda Whitlock of Boys and Girls Clubs of Boston. "I also reflect a lot on my actions." Peter Shiras of Independent Sector stresses that, "Leaders need time to reflect and it is not easy to create that time in the maelstrom of daily activity".

Some use one or more coaches to support their reflecting, help them learn and develop their leadership skills. Linda Whitlock has a 'jedi council' of between five and seven people who she uses as a sounding board and consults on difficult issues.

Some network with other leaders in state, regional and national intermediary bodies. They share their issues and learn from each other.

Together these actions support leadership and management development throughout organisations. They strengthen management capacity and they reflect that individuals now expect continuous personal development. Strong leaders recognise that their organisation benefits from carefully chosen investments in individuals, and in their own development.

Summary

Be a leader
- Leaders embody the values of the organisation in what they do and how they do it
- Leaders need to focus their attention inside and outside the organisation and on present operations and future possibilities
- They deliver six roles: visionary, strategist, politician, fundraiser, coach and change agent
- Leaders have to gain the trust and respect of they people they lead
- Leaders have to be open and they have to have honest conversations.

Mobilise around the mission
- Great leaders have a clear vision for the future of their organisation
- Missions are used by leaders to motivate people
- Mission statements are short, precise and distinctive
- Leaders ensure missions are omnipresent, used and reviewed.

Focus people on results
- Planning and performance review are the most powerful lever leaders have to drive performance
- Leaders ensure that strategies, operational plans and individual work plans are tightly integrated
- Leaders ensure that plans are closely scrutinised before being approved
- Regular performance reviews are used to hold managers to account
- Boards enhance the quality of planning and performance review
- Leaders also hold managers accountable for costs and expect departments to be managed on 'bottom line' performance.

Build a small focused team
- Leaders create line reporting arrangements that enable them to lead
- The top team tends to have between three and five members
- Chief operating officer posts are increasingly prevalent
- Top teams meet regularly and hold regular retreats
- Trust, confidence and excellent communication are the hallmarks of an effective top team
- Some nonprofits use performance-related pay – others reject the idea.

Invest leadership and management development
- Leading organisations are taking many different approaches to leadership and management development
- Leading organisations get all their managers together regularly
- Leaders invest in their own development by attending courses, reading extensively, using coaches and networking with other leaders.

References

1 Paul Light, *Pathways to Nonprofit Excellence*, Washington, The Brookings Institution, 2002

2 Peter Drucker, *Managing the Non-Profit Organization*, Boston, Butterworth-Heinemann, 1990

3 John Gardner, *On Leadership*, Washington, Independent Sector, 1990

4 Burt Nanus and Stephen Dobbs, *Leaders Who Make a Difference*, San Francisco, Jossey-Bass, 1999

5 Frances Hesselbein, Marshall Goldsmith and Richard Beckhard (eds), *The Leader of the Future*, San Francisco, Jossey-Bass, 1996

6 Parker Palmer, *Let Your Life Speak*, San Francisco, Jossey-Bass, 1999

7 Parker Palmer, *Leadership and the Inner Journey*, interview in *Leader to Leader*, San Francisco, Jossey-Bass, Fall 2001

8 James Kouzes and Barry Posner, *The Leadership Challenge*, San Francisco, Jossey-Bass, 1987

9 John M. Bryson, *Strategic Planning for Public and Nonprofit Organizations*, San Francisco, Jossey-Bass, 1995

10 Thomas Holland, *Board Accountablilty* in *Nonprofit Management and Leadership*, San Francisco, Jossey-Bass, Summer 2002

11 Sharon M. Oster, *Strategic Management for Nonprofit Organisations*, New York, Oxford University Press, 1995

7 Strengthening governance

Demands on the boards of nonprofits in the US have grown dramatically over recent years and there is every expectation that the challenges will continue to increase in the future. Donors and the wider public expect boards to hold organisations to account for the quality and effectiveness of their work and the probity of the organisation. The high profile that the press now gives to the small number of scandals in the sector means that people's expectations are rising further.

Spectacular failures in the corporate sector have added to pressure for high performance. The downfall of Enron, World Com and Arthur Andersen has signalled to everyone that effective governance is important and these messages are trickling down to the nonprofit sector. They have reminded people that the boards of nonprofit organisations provide the public with trust and confidence and help to maintain organisations' reputations. These are all hard-won features that are secured primarily through effective governance.

The quality of governance of nonprofit organisations in the US has improved significantly over the last 15 years. Definitions of governance have been clarified, requirements of board members defined, induction for new members has been introduced and the need to manage the performance of the board itself has been established. Much of the momentum for these improvements originated from the establishment of BoardSource, the organisation that has set the standards for nonprofit governance and whose work has attracted worldwide interest.

A huge body of research and writing on nonprofit governance has been developed during this time. A recent review of governance research cited over 120 references to research on nonprofit governance[1] and there are more books on how to govern nonprofits than there are on the core task of managing them. Yet in a recent survey of chief executives, only 37% rated their boards as highly effective.[2] There is a widespread view that much work has to be done to further improve the governance arrangements of nonprofit organisations. 'All the evidence suggests that the interest in boards will continue to grow.'[1]

In a seminal 1996 article 'The New Work of the Nonprofit Board' Barbara Taylor and others argued that 'Nonprofit boards are often little more than a collection of high-powered people engaged in low level activities'. The authors suggested that 'Individual board members may not bring themselves fully to the task of governance, because board membership generally carries little personal accountability. And often the powerful individuals who make up the board are unpractised in working as members of a team'. They proposed that the new work of boards 'concerns itself with crucial, do-or-die issues central to the institution's success, is driven by results that are linked to defined timetables and has clear measures of success'.[3]

Boards in the US have a number of distinctive features. First, members are expected to make financial contributions. Research from BoardSource shows that almost half of board members have to pay for the privilege of joining, and more than half have to fundraise as well. According to Harvard Marketing Professor John Quelch, "Board members are left in no doubt about the amount they are personally expected to donate, and the most prestigious boards have the highest tariff".

Second, joining a board is an essential element of career development for people in all three sectors. People set goals for the types of boards they wish to join. Recruiters look at peoples' resumes and expect to see membership of boards of increasing prestige as their career progresses. When people have had insufficient nonprofit experience they may be advised to seek board positions to expand their horizons and develop new skills.

Third, people seeking positions on more influential boards are expected to have experience from lesser boards or to have contributed as a non-board member of a board committee. One chief executive of a comparatively small organisation said bluntly, "We want people with experience of governance so we don't accept first-time board members".

This chapter

Chapter 7 provides evidence from leading-edge organisations showing that they:

- ensure crystal clarity over the unique roles of the board
- structure the board around governance tasks
- take actions to enhance board performance
- deepen the chair/chief executive relationship
- continuously review the board's performance.

7.1 Ensure crystal clarity over the unique roles of the board

One of the enduring characteristics of nonprofit boards is that they are all different and there are no 'one-size-fits-all' solutions to improving board performance. According to The Urban Institute, 'boards are complex entities that defy sweeping generalisations. They are heterogeneous, subject to internal shifts and respond to multiple – and sometimes conflicting – influences'.[1] BoardSource's Marilyn Wyatt says, "There is no one model and flexibility is the key. Boards need to go through a process of discovery to find out what works best at their particular stage of development". Board development is therefore a never-ending process of discovery, because governance arrangements appropriate for one stage of an organisation's development will need to evolve to accommodate its next phase. Ideally the governance arrangements should anticipate organisations' future requirements.

The starting point for board development is the clarification of roles. Boards have many, and the trend is undoubtedly towards boards that focus sharply on their unique roles and discipline themselves to stick tightly to them. In the US the roles of the board are conceived of in terms of its accountability to different stakeholder groups. Leading boards recognise that funders, consumers, staff and the public all have legitimate interests in the organisation, that the board has to understand their views and consider them explicitly in their deliberations.

Whilst boards may be called upon to give judgement and wisdom on many matters, it is widely accepted that at the heart of good governance is high-standard delivery of the four essential functions of:

1 determining the organisation's mission, strategy and policies
2 appointing and overseeing the chief executive
3 monitoring the organisation's performance
4 managing governance processes.

Although the roles overlap with management, they are quite distinct. Some leading thinkers on governance believe that there should be a very strict division between the roles of governance and management. John Carver argues that 'the secret of new governance lies in policy-making' and that 'policy clarification is the central feature of board leadership'.[4] He developed the 'policy governance' model which proposes that boards should limit their work to the establishment of policies about:

- ends to be achieved
- means to achieve those ends
- the board/staff relationship
- the process of governance itself.

In his view, once the board has established policies in these areas, it should be strict in empowering management to deliver their implementation roles. Carver's books have been widely read and he has made many boards clarify the purpose and functions of governance. However, some leading thinkers argue that there are dangers in taking this distinction too far. Harvard's Bill Ryan argues that "Boards can become 'sealed off' if Policy Governance is applied too rigidly. The management/governance boundary needs to be clear, but there needs to be a degree of fluidity. Boards can become remote if they only consider strategic issues and feel they can't raise detail". Richard Chait, leading governance expert at Harvard School of Education agrees, "There is evidence that ruthless separation of 'means' and 'ends' is not helpful".

There is nevertheless widespread agreement that effective boards strive to maintain clarity about their roles, and continuously monitor their own performance to ensure that they are not inadvertently slipping into management's role. An analysis of interviews, consultations and meeting observations involving 169 board members identified practices that enhance board performance, the first of which was clear expectations. 'Some boards had developed explicit statements of expectations and responsibilities of the board as a whole as well as of its individual members. Nominating Committee members engaging in discussions with potential candidates said they drew upon these documents to explain what the board expected of its members and what context of mission, values and obligations underlay its work.'[5]

When the unique roles of the board have been defined, chairs have a critically important responsibility to ensure that boards stick to their roles and to call members to account when they transgress the boundary. 'The Chair needs to have the courage to correct, admonish and corral'.[6] Carver agrees: 'the chairperson bears a peculiar responsibility with respect to board process.... However, the entire board cannot avoid its share of responsibility. The existence of a chairperson does not relieve other board members from contributing to the integrity of the process'.[4] Chairs need to be continuously alert and to remind members hastily of the board's role when it slips outside the governance boundary.

Chief executives also play a crucial role in keeping boards focused on governance. When chief executives ask boards to advise on management issues or when they provide papers on management issues, the board inevitably slips into managerial tasks. When they focus their boards on governance issues, they are much more likely to stick to their proper roles.

Whilst leading boards maintain crystal clarity over their role, this is not the norm in much of the sector. 'Complacency about the board itself appears to be the norm and action the exception' reports Thomas Holland from his extensive studies. Bill Ryan agrees, "There is in many cases an accountability vacuum. Some boards exhibit dysfunctional politeness, when what they really need is to be equipped to challenge increasingly competent management. They should be asking the scary questions about performance and avoid being too courteous". Pablo Eisenberg, distinguished nonprofit sector commentator from Georgetown University, also concurs, "We need feisty boards, not rubber stamps".

Governance of Amnesty International USA

Amnesty is a membership organisation. It has a board of 18 people, each of whom can have a maximum of two three-year terms. All board members have job descriptions and there is an expectation of 'no unexcused absence' from board meetings.

The board has a nominations committee that interviews people interested in standing for election. Some people decide not to stand, having better understood the requirements Amnesty is seeking and the commitment that is required. As a safety valve, any member who is unsuccessful at the interview stage but still wishes to stand can do so by petitioning 100 members to support them as a candidate.

Board performance is reviewed regularly. After every meeting there is a questionnaire which includes an opportunity to comment on the performance of other members. The chair compiles comments and feeds back the results as one way of encouraging open discussion about board performance. The board also has an annual retreat with senior management and an external consultant to review performance jointly with board members.

7.2 Structure the board around governance tasks

Traditionally boards have structured their committees to mirror the organisation's functions such as services, finance, personnel and fundraising. This encourages boards to do management tasks. Leading organisations are now structuring their board committees around the key functions of governance and around the organisation's strategic priorities. They are delegating aspects of governance work to sub-groups that take particular responsibilities on behalf of the board. They keep committee structures lean by establishing a limited number of permanent committees and delegating all other governance work to task groups that disband when their job is done.

So, committees in leading organisations have very different functions from traditional governance structures. The titles of governance committees include:

- **Audit committee** – providing specialist recommendations to the board on financial controls.
- **Nominations committee** – taking responsibility for managing the board's skill and experience matrix and identifying talented and experienced people to stand for election to the board.
- **Governance committee** – taking responsibility for monitoring and enhancing the performance of the board and its committees. It oversees the performance review process and, when necessary recommends changes to governance structures and processes. It also takes responsibility for electoral and nominations processes.
- **Strategic planning and performance committee** – taking responsibility for managing the board's input into strategic planning. Some organisations link this with oversight of the organisation's performance management systems
- **Compensation committee** – taking responsibility for benchmarking and setting senior salaries.

Some boards have committees that are structured to reflect the organisation's strategic priorities. These are likely to be time limited, to focus on the achievement of one of the organisation's goals and to disband when the objective has been achieved. Given the special role board members of US nonprofits play in fundraising, most organisations will also have a permanent fundraising committee.

A significant challenge for many boards is balancing its decision-making role with its representation role. Doing both increases the size of the board and this inevitably changes its function. Boards have to consider whether particular stakeholders, such as people from regions of the country, from branches or chapters and from particular professions, gender and ethnic groups need to be represented. This is a significant issue in membership organisations and it can lead to demands for a large and potentially unwieldy board. A number of leading organisations are therefore separating the functions of governance and representation to accommodate the problem of having a board small enough to provide effective governance and yet large enough to allow representation of a wide range of views.

"Representation is a big issue because of the escalation of identity politics," according to Harvard's Richard Chait. "There is a growing demand for mechanisms that allow representatives to make an input to the board without being members of the board." Consequently, some boards have established one or more groups of representatives who advise the board. This enables key stakeholder groups to make their views known in a structured way, so the board can take them into account in decision taking. It also provides a channel for the board to communicate its views back to those stakeholder groups.

Larger boards are better suited to a broad policy-setting role and tend to debate the policy issues. Whilst some traditional nonprofits have large boards of 40 to 60 or even more members, some leading commentators argue that smaller boards provide more rigorous accountability. Some organisations with larger boards vest considerable responsibility for governance in a smaller executive committee, which is itself held accountable by a larger board.

Board size is also influenced by the mix of skills and expertise that the organisation believes it needs on its governing body. Boards of leading organisations have a 'skill matrix' which defines the skills and experience the board wants amongst its members. This provides criteria for seeking new members. In addition to financial and legal skills, boards also require people with a high level of professional expertise in the organisation's field of work.

Many boards also look for executives of other nonprofits who can bring experience from similar organisations. The *Nonprofit Governance Index* shows that whilst the majority of board members are employed by the private sector, almost a fifth are employed in the nonprofit sector.

Board members' employers

Employer	%
For-profit organisations	43
Nonprofit organisations	19
Self-employed	14
Retired	12
Government organisations	9
Other	4
	100%

Source: National Center for Nonprofit Boards, *The Nonprofit Governance Index* [2]

Because board members in the US are expected to make significant donations and to raise funds themselves, there is further pressure to maintain larger boards. Some organisations overcome this problem by having a separate board with responsibility for fundraising and giving it some power to influence how the funds it raises are spent.

Diversity is a significant aspect of board structure and particularly of board composition and there is a widely held view that a more diverse board is more likely to deliver effective governance than one which does not reflect the diversity of the communities in which the organisation works. Despite best intentions, this is not being achieved in practice.

Women are more likely to serve on the boards of smaller and less prestigious organisations and less likely to be found on the boards of hospitals, colleges and universities and policy-related organisations. They are more likely to serve on human service and cultural boards.[1] *The Nonprofit Governance Index* found that, although growing, minorities constitute only 15% of board members and that the majority of these were African Americans.[2] Foundation boards are even less racially diverse – 90% are white according to Council on Foundations research.[7] However, there is some evidence that minorities are better represented in less formal community organisations that are not captured in this research.

The Nonprofit Governance Index

BoardSource carries out regular surveys on the composition, structure, roles and practicalities of boards.

The most recent survey gathered data from over 1,300 chief executives, 200 board members and included 89 interviews. Although it is not a weighted national sample, it gives interesting insights into boards in the US.

In the 2000 survey the median size of boards was 17 people. Board members were predominantly male (57%), and aged between 40 and 59 years (64%). The majority of boards were self-perpetuating (66%) and most members served three-year terms (68%).

Almost half require members to make personal financial contributions (48%) and over one-third of respondents indicated that their entire board contributes annually. Half require board members to identify donors or solicit funds (52%) and to attend fundraising events (49%).

Boards spend most of their time on major policy questions (33%) and planning for the future (32%). Chief executives are most satisfied with board members' understanding of the organisation's mission and least satisfied with board members' understanding of the board's role and responsibilities.

Amongst board members surveyed:

- 69% identified policy making as the primary role of the board
- 44% said the board is an oversight body ensuring accountability
- 42% feel their boards are effective.

Factors citied as contributing to board effectiveness included strong relationships with the chief executive, highly active and committed board members and strong board member participation.

Source: National Center for Nonprofit Boards, *The Nonprofit Governance Index* [2]

7.3 Take actions to enhance board performance

Boards of leading organisations are striving to enhance their performance and they are adopting a wide range of measures to increase their effectiveness.

Evidence that an effective board contributes to strong organisations is also growing. However, measuring board effectiveness is fraught with difficulties. It is possible to ask board members and staff to rate effectiveness against agreed criteria for the performance of the board. It is harder to demonstrate a connection between board effectiveness and organisation effectiveness because that is dependent on so many other factors. There are consequently questions as to whether strong boards create strong organisations or whether it is just that strong organisations tend to have strong boards.

Thomas Holland asked boards to assess their own performance before and after board development initiatives and compared their results with those from boards that did not make such investments. Over a three-year period he demonstrated that the experimental group showed significant improvements in performance which were not evident in the comparison group. He concluded that 'focused and sustained efforts to improve board performance can realise measurable gains. Such efforts take long-term work by a board, they involve moving members out of familiar territories and comfortable habits and supporting their experimentation with new ways of doing business. Ongoing attention by a board to its performance leads to a culture of active responsibility for continuous improvement in the quality of its work and greater satisfaction among members. It enables the board to improve its leadership of the organisation and demonstrates to others inside and outside how the board expects value to be added to the organisation'.[8]

Enhance induction

Top quality induction for new members is recognised as a starting point for enhancing board performance. The BoardSource Index found that only 40% of new members receive formal orientation when joining the board. Some board members may require orientation on the role and function of the board and some may need support in developing their governance skills. Others may have governance skills but require orientation around the organisation's field of work and the services it offers.

Organisations that provide orientation are adopting a wide range of delivery methods including:

- a skills audit to determine what skills new members may need to develop
- pre-meetings before board meetings to brief new members
- appointing a mentor to guide new members during their first year
- board orientation workshops, when a number of new members join at the same time

- a board handbook containing all relevant background papers
- visits to see the organisation's work on the ground
- a review after six months to check how new members are feeling about their role and about the way the board works
- briefing on the board performance assessment process.

Keep the board focused on priorities

Board members' time is incredibly precious. A board meeting quarterly for a day adds up to 1,200–1,440 minutes per year. Twelve to fourteen minutes lost because someone raised a point of detail means 1% of the board's annual meeting time has been spent inappropriately.

Leading boards work hard to ensure that their time and energy is focused on the organisation's priorities. This starts from having a thorough understanding of the organisation's strategic plans and appreciating how these plans impact on the board's work. Thomas Holland's research found that on some boards members 'were more active participants in identifying the most important issues facing the organisation and setting priorities among them for the board's attention. These boards were careful to put in place procedures that would help them keep their time and attention focussed on their own goals and deal with attempts to divert energy onto other issues'. He cites one board that put its goals on a large poster that hung in the board meeting room so all eyes would be on the priorities at every meeting.

Richard Chait gets boards to ask themselves, "What are the three most important questions this board needs to address over the next 12 months?" Getting members to agree on the key questions starts to shape the high-level board agenda for the year. Having a discussion about the questions is a necessary pre-requisite to having board members engage with these issues.

Another way Chait gets boards to think about board performance is to ask, "What would be the gravest consequences of this board not operating for the next three years?" It focuses people's minds onto the non-substitutable functions that the board should carry out to the highest standards.

With a clear view of the essential functions of the board, members can discuss how the board's work should be organised to perform these tasks.

Encourage members to work as a team

Team working by the board is seen as critical for effective governance. It is a skill that requires continuous development. Boards need to work as a group, listening closely to each other, using each other's strengths and striving to find agreement. Chait has noted that 'the stronger the board members, the harder it is just to get them to meld into the group'.[9] So board members have to work to create a culture that is respectful and supportive, whilst also ensuring that the group delivers high quality governance.

Use many approaches to enhance performance

Interviewees described a wide range of approaches that enhance board performance.

They include:

- organising an education hour before each meeting
- holding a 'fireside chat' with the chief executive (this is particularly valuable for a preliminary rumination about an issue)
- encouraging members to attend industry conferences
- auditing individuals' skills and then offer training or coaching in areas where members need to enhance their skills
- arranging learning exchanges with comparable organisations, to share policy discussions and to compare methods of working
- ensuring that there is an annual board and senior management retreat to review performance and to shape future strategy
- giving members opportunities to improve their understanding of the organisation (site visits, specific tasks, shadowing meetings)
- developing a 'dashboard' of key indicators for improving board performance and reporting quarterly on progress
- asking experienced members to mentor new members
- inviting representatives of stakeholder groups to observe the board
- including stakeholder representatives in committee membership
- pairing board members with senior executives and giving them joint responsibility for representing different stakeholder views
- offering new chairs a coach to assist them in delivering this demanding role.

Ensure thorough preparation for board meetings

Board meetings are at the heart of good governance. The quality of the preparation by the chair and chief executive, the thought that goes into board papers and the development of an agenda that gets to the nub of the critical issues are all essential ingredients of effective meetings. Good performance here is very dependent on the senior management team and on the person responsible for board administration. Successful meetings are much more likely when:

- staff prepare well-argued papers that are circulated in sufficient time for members to ask questions of clarification before the meeting
- the agenda is carefully constructed and prioritised
- the chair and chief executive are clear about the outcomes they desire from each item on the meeting agendas.

ONE MEETING – TWO STYLES AT THE AMERICAN DIABETES ASSOCIATION

The American Diabetes Association (ADA) has a main board of 55 people that meets three times per year. It is supported by an executive committee of 10 people that meets six times per year. The main board is "the conscience of the organisation" according to CEO John Graham.

Board meetings last for four hours. The first two hours are spent discussing one major strategic issue, for example the Association's position on stem cell research. The setting is informal, the layout is cafeteria style, and the aim is to discuss all aspects of the issue and to begin the process of developing a consensus. The relevant committee will take the 'feel of the meeting' and work a draft policy statement on the issue.

The second two hours are formal and structured. The board moves into a different room with a board table and works through a tightly structured agenda with agreed times for each item. There are no committee reports – these are distributed beforehand and are not for discussion in the board meeting itself.

7.4 Deepen the chair/chief executive relationship

The relationship between the chair and the chief executive is a linchpin of a well-run organisation. The importance of managing this relationship was stressed by a number of interviewees, though, surprisingly, it is not an issue that is explored in the literature. When this relationship starts to break down, many aspects of good governance and management become increasingly difficult as conversations become more closed and positions more entrenched.

It is not easy to establish this relationship because these two people frequently do not select each other. They are chosen by different people and at different times. Chairs have to build a relationship with the incumbent chief executive when they are appointed and sometimes have to form a relationship with a new chief executive during their tenure. Frequently, chief executives will have a number of chairs during their term of office.

Chairs and chief executives of leading organisations invest time and effort in managing and strengthening this relationship. First, chairs and chief executives have an explicit discussion about their expectations of each other – covering both what they want and what they would find unacceptable. These expectations may even be written down for future reference and can provide the basis for an annual review of the relationship.

With clear expectations, both parties ensure that there is plenty of honest, fast and accurate communication, to minimise the opportunity for misunderstandings. Mary Pearl of Durrell Wildlife Fund says, "I talk to my Chair every Monday, almost with out fail". Roni Posner, Executive Director of the Alliance for Nonprofit Management, takes a similar approach: "I have a weekly phone call, I e-mail her regularly, I seek her guidance and I give her credit when it is due".

Extensive and open communication provides a foundation for developing a deeper and more trusting relationship. Both parties will increasingly find that they can confide more private thoughts with each other. Unformed ideas around possible future directions for the organisation, reflections on the performance of board members and senior managers, possible future management and committee structures and even their own personal futures become topics which can be discussed in confidence.

Creating this level of relationship ensures that neither surprises the other, or if they do so inadvertently, that there is sufficient trust and confidence to ensure that mistakes do not become big issues. It also enables both of them to convey respect for each other's roles to the board and to senior management.

Of course, chairs and chief executives do change, and when this happens the relationship building has to start all over again. And as no two relationships are the same, the existing partner has to adjust his or her approach and style to suit the new chair or chief executive.

7.5 Continuously review the board's performance

Leading boards in the US are overcoming the traditional reticence about discussing their own performance and finding that they can increase their effectiveness by putting performance firmly at the heart of their agenda.

Three elements of board performance are being reviewed:

1 assessment of meeting performance
2 assessments of the performance of the board as a group
3 individual performance assessments.

Review meeting performance

Leading boards review meeting performance, either orally or with anonymous written comments. These can cover the wide range of issues that make for high value meetings including:

- the quality of board papers
- the relevance of agenda items
- the clarity of the issues raised
- the balance of time for presentations and discussion
- the overall allocation of time to different issues
- the opportunities for everyone to participate
- the clarity of decisions taken
- the follow through of previous decisions
- the role of the chair.

In some cases written comments are analysed and reported back to the next meeting along with proposed actions to address problems raised. In this way performance review is established as a regular activity that is integrated with other board work and not a separate and one-off activity.

Evaluate the board's performance

Boards are increasingly establishing annual objectives for their own performance and reviewing their achievements against those goals. Self-assessment of board performance, often by a questionnaire, is common.

Thomas Holland's research on a large number of boards and members led him to suggest that boards should consider the following questions to enhance their performance.

- How is this group adding value to the organisation, beyond the contributions of staff and administration?
- Have we identified the most important issues facing this organisation?
- Are we spending time and energy on those key issues?
- Have we set clear priorities and then stuck with them in our meetings?
- What specific expectations do we have for ourselves individually as members of this board and of the group as a whole?
- Are the issues and questions coming before us clear, and do we have the right information for working on them?
- Have we listened to the concerns of those affected by our decisions and understood the impact of our work on them?
- What specific steps should we take to improve the performance of this board and increase the value we add to this organisation?
- What criteria or indicators would be appropriate for monitoring and demonstrating the improvements in our group's performance?
- How will we obtain and use such information to make further improvements in our work?

Source: Thomas Holland, *Nonprofit Management and Leadership*[5]

Whilst there are 'off-the-shelf' self-assessment packages, for example from BoardSource, experience suggests that each assessment needs to be tailored to suit each board's circumstances at that particular time. The core assessment issues will be the same, but each organisation has its own unique circumstances and idiosyncrasies that need to be incorporated into performance reviews.

There is growing evidence that boards tend to be less critical in self-assessments than they are in external assessments. "In a survey of 280 boards that did self evaluation, the overwhelming majority reported similar performance on all variables except relationships with the CEO. This suggests that there is a 'socially acceptable' performance level," according to Richard Chait.

Most boards would not accept self-evaluation as the only form of staff performance review, so to be consistent they should not accept it of themselves. "A self review may be a good starting point, but an external input allows boards to be more honest about performance," argues Richard Chait. External reviewers can also return after an agreed period and ask board members to report, openly, on progress. This gives the board improved programme life and vitality, and avoids the review becoming a bureaucratic process.

Evaluate individual performance

As well as reviewing the performance of the board as a whole, boards in some organisations review the performance of individual members. A pre-requisite for such reviews is that individuals were clear in the first place about what was expected of them and had a description of the role – sometimes cast in the form of a board member's job description. This task of reviewing individuals' performance is often delegated to the nominations or governance committee. These reviews are most common when someone's term of office is up for renewal, rather than being an annual event.

At this point the nominations committee will review the individual's performance on the board, their attendance record and their overall contribution. The chair of the nominations committee will ask members how they have found being a board member, whether they have any concerns and whether they are seeking promotion to a leadership position. This helps to build an open discussion about the future.

For example, Unicef USA has a nominations committee that established a set of performance criteria for board members. It evaluates their performance against these criteria at the end of their first term of office. If any member is deemed not to have made sufficient impact the chair of the committee will have a discussion about the board's expectations and their future involvement. At this point many people will agree to stand down, and they will be generously thanked for their efforts and allowed to move on with dignity.

One board asked its nominations committee to develop the leadership skills of all members after they came onto the board. That group was responsible for collecting individual assessments, discussing each member's self-assessment and plans for the coming year in the light of the full board's needs. The committee met with each member to offer suggestions about improving the quality of members' contributions and developing greater leadership skills. Examples included 'rotating committee assignments, serving as an understudy in another board role, attending a conference on a specific issue and talking with members of other boards to identify alternative approaches to a complex issue'.[5]

Develop performance review in stages

Board members often find it difficult to enter discussions about their own performance. They may be sceptical about the value of them, they may feel the board has more important priorities to address or they may feel threatened or insecure.

Reviewing meeting behaviour is the easiest starting place. With that in place the board can establish objectives for its own performance over the coming year. These objectives provide the basis for an annual review of the performance of the board as a whole. When members are comfortable with that, and when there are strong and trustworthy relationships between members (in particular between members and the chair), individual performance review can be considered.

Research suggests that when people do start working on board performance they are more comfortable talking about the board's roles and responsibilities, and its contribution to the organisation's strategy, than they are talking about teamwork and inter-personal relationships. 'Only as they began to experience more focussed, productive and satisfying meetings were some participants ready to revisit the interpersonal dimension.'[8]

As to what is next in governance, Chait sees the need for boards to move beyond their traditional controlling role. "They need to move beyond oversight to have a duty to provide the curiosity and creativity that can make a significant difference to organisation impact."

In the long term, the most critical tasks in enhancing the quality of governance are to:

- institutionalise the key processes for finding high calibre members
- provide training and development opportunities
- monitor board performance.

When these are an integral part of the way the board works, the conditions are right for top quality governance.

Summary

Ensure crystal clarity over the unique roles of the board

- Although the quality of governance has advanced significantly over the last 15 years, there are growing calls for further improvements
- There are no 'one-size-fits-all' solutions to enhancing board performance
- The key roles of the board are to:
  - determine the organisation's mission, strategy and policies
  - appoint and oversee the chief executive
  - monitor the organisation's performance
  - manage the governance process
- Boards of leading organisations explicitly define their unique governance role and monitor their performance to ensure that they remain focused on this role.

Structure the board around governance tasks

- Traditionally board structures mirrored staff structures. Leading boards are structuring committees according to governance tasks and according to the organisation's strategic priorities
- Governance committees take responsibility for audit, nominations, governance processes, strategic planning and performance review, and compensation
- A number of different approaches are used to balance decision-making functions with representation.

Take actions to enhance board performance

- Studies have shown that investment in board development leads to better board performance
- Actions boards are taking to improve their performance include:
  - enhanced induction
  - focusing time sharply on the organisation's priorities
  - explicitly agreeing key governance questions for the year ahead
  - a range of measures to encourage board members to engage in continuous development of their knowledge and skills.

Deepen the chair/chief executive relationship

- The relationship between the chair and chief executive is a linchpin of an effective nonprofit organisation. In leading organisations these two people invest time and effort in clarifying expectations of each other and communicating honestly, openly and fast
- Extra effort is required when there are changes in either position.

Continuously review the board's performance
- Leading-edge boards review meeting performance, the overall performance of the board and individual performance
- Establishing a performance review regime tends to start with meeting performance, develop into board performance reviews and finally engage with individual performance issues.

References

1 Francie Ostrower and Melissa Stone, *Governance Research: Trends, Gaps and Prospects for the Future*, Washington, The Urban Institute, 2001

2 National Center for Nonprofit Boards (now BoardSource), *The Nonprofit Governance Index*, Washington, 2000

3 Barbara Taylor *et al.*, *The New Work of the Nonprofit Board*, Boston, Harvard Business Review, September, 1996

4 John Carver, *Boards That Make a Difference*, San Francisco, Jossey-Bass, 1997

5 Thomas Holland, *Board Accountability* in *Nonprofit Management and Leadership*, San Francisco, Jossey-Bass, Summer 2002

6 Maureen Robinson, *Nonprofit Boards that Work*, New York, Wiley, 2001

7 Council on Foundations, *Foundation Management Series, 10th Edition, Vol. 2 Governing Boards*, Washington, Council on Foundations, 2002

8 Thomas Holland and Douglas Jackson, *Strengthening Board Performance* in *Nonprofit Management and Leadership*, San Francisco, Jossey-Bass, Winter 1998

9 Richard Chait *et al.*, *Improving the Performance of Governing Boards*, Phoenix, American Council on Education and the Oryx Press, 1996

8 Learning from each other

The aim of my journey to the US was to get an overview of the nonprofit sector and to see where there are opportunities for managers in the US and the UK to learn from each other's experience. This chapter therefore makes some comparisons between the nonprofit sectors in the two countries. It uses the research to identify areas where the UK could learn from the US, and my experience of the UK to suggest some areas where the US could learn from the UK.

The history of the two sectors provides a context for understanding the comparisons and the opportunities for learning. Charitable activity in the UK can be traced back to medieval times and earlier. However, the formal definition of charity is generally sourced in the 1601 Charitable Uses Act. This Act transferred to Britain's American colonies, so in both countries the early definition of charity had the same roots.

From that point, the development of nonprofit activity followed different paths. In Britain, charitable activity grew and diversified away from religious causes into education, child welfare and moral discipline. It was mostly associated with the urban middle classes and was sustained by civic pride and civic rivalry[1] The notion of charity in Britain is based on a deeply held assumption that people with resources should assist those with less. Today British people give proportionately more than Americans to international causes, use the word 'charity' to describe giving and talk about the 'voluntary sector'.

In the US a distinct nonprofit sector emerged only in the late nineteenth century and it was rooted in a tradition of cooperation and a mistrust of central authority.[2] Nonprofit organisations were created to solve community problems including infrastructure building and providing essential medical, educational and financial services. Americans give proportionately more than British people to local causes, they use the word 'philanthropy' to describe their giving and they talk about the 'nonprofit sector'.

Throughout history each country has adopted policies from the other. Until the twentieth century much of the learning that crossed the Atlantic was from the UK to the US.[3] The English 1601 Charitable Uses

Act provided an early definition of philanthropic activity. The idea of trusts (or foundations as they are called in the US) that use an independent group of people to oversee the distribution of funds, and the notion of the granting of tax relief to individuals and companies that donate money also originated in the UK.

In the twentieth century the UK attempted to import ideas that originated in the US including community foundations, payroll giving, contracting for the provision of public services, and more recently programme related investment and venture philanthropy. However, it is fair to say that none of these ideas has transferred easily into the UK culture or has been as successful as they are in the US.

The transfer of management and governance ideas from the US to the UK has been more significant and more successful than the adoption of different approaches to policy. Many of the great general management thinkers whose work determined how we conceive of management were American. Work by Frederick Taylor on scientific management, Abraham Maslow on the hierarchy of needs, Frederick Hertzberg on 'motivators' and 'hygiene' factors, Douglas MacGregor on 'theory x and y', Peter Drucker on management by objectives and Warren Bennis on leadership all emanated from the US.

It is not, however, a one way street and there is much that the US can learn from UK experience, particularly in the nonprofit field. The UK has a long history of government working in partnership with voluntary organisations and recently clear principles were established about the ways voluntary organisations and government should work together, known as the Compact. This now also has a monitoring regime to determine the extent to which the principles are being applied in practice. The UK has pioneered the involvement of users in many aspects of voluntary activity. Organisations 'for' disadvantaged people are increasingly frowned upon and organisations 'of' the same people are in the ascendancy.

Major events in the history of US nonprofit sector and UK voluntary sector

The US	The UK
	1793 Rose's Act encouraged formation of mutual aid societies
1844 Private nonprofit corporations placed under federal law	**1853** Charity Commission established to supervise charitable trusts exempt from income tax
	1869 Charity Organisation Society created to improve effectiveness of charities with scientific approach
1894 Congress supported tax exemptions for charitable, educational and religious organisations	**End of the 19th century** Income tax privileges extended to all charities
1900 First community foundation set up in Cleveland	**1905-09** The Royal Commission on the Poor Laws proposed larger governmental involvement
1907 The first open-ended foundation (The Sage Foundation) established	
1917 Charitable tax deductions for individuals	**1919** National Council for Social Service – umbrella organisation for charities – created (later called NCVO)
1936 Charitable tax deductions permitted for corporations	
1948 National Security Council and the Council of Economic Advisors – first governmental bodies with a planning function	**1948** Beveridge report Voluntary Action. Major social services taken under statutory provision. NHS took over charitable hospitals
1954 Establishment of Section 501 of the Internal Revenue Code recognising tax-exempt organisations	**1960** Charities Act enhanced powers of Charity Commission
1965 Establishment of Medicare and Medicaid	
1969 Tax Reform Act put foundations under federal oversight	**1978** Wolfenden Committee report emphasised necessity of voluntary/statutory partnership
1973–77 Filer Commission highlighted lack of knowledge about the sector	
1980 Independent Sector – umbrella body for the sector founded	**1992** Charities Act gave greater powers to Charity Commission, introduced a new accounting regime
1982 Verity Task Force – to stimulate higher levels of giving and voluntary effort	**1994** Gift Aid – individual charitable tax deduction for up to £250 introduced
	1996 Deakin proposed concordat between state and voluntary sector
	1998 Compact signed between government and voluntary sector
	2000 Limits on tax deductions for individual donations abolished
2001 CARE Act proposed support of faith-based organisations and charitable deduction for 'non-itemizers'	**2002** Cabinet Office review of Charity law and regulation – Private Action, Public Benefit

> ## *This chapter*
>
> The final chapter sets out how we can learn more from each other as we strive to:
>
> - recognise similarities and differences
> - build organisation capacity
> - manage performance
> - create strategic alliances
> - exploit changing patterns of funding
> - lead with integrity
> - strengthen governance
> - focus on the new agenda.
>
> The chapter ends with a summary of the key similarities and differences and some thoughts on sharing experience in the future.

8.1 Recognise similarities and differences

The UK and the US have much in common. We share the same language, though this is changing with the ascendancy of Spanish in the US and a variety of minority languages in the UK. We have a common and deeply held commitment to the principles of democracy, to liberalism and to capitalism within regulated boundaries. We share the 'special relationship' that established a bond between the two countries. We divide our economies into the three broadly similar categories of the business, government and nonprofit sectors. We share a largely similar understanding of charity and philanthropy and we have established similar taxation arrangements to encourage people and companies to make donations.

However, there are significant differences in the role of the state in the two countries and this in part defines the roles of the nonprofit sectors. In the UK the state has performed much wider roles in health, education, housing and social welfare, particularly since the Second World War. Indeed for part of that time the role of the voluntary sector was seen as an 'adjunct' to state provision.

That is now changing as the state is viewed in many areas as a funder and regulator of services that may be provided by either the public, private or nonprofit sectors. Consequently there has been huge growth in the provision of housing by the nonprofit sector as stock has been transferred to housing associations. A similar trend is taking place in social services, and is just beginning in Britain's much-cherished health service. As the state withdraws from service provision, opportunities for voluntary organisations are growing and the sector is developing characteristics that are increasingly similar to the American nonprofit sector.

Turning to nonprofit organisations themselves, both countries have similar definitions for organisations that :

- exist primarily for a social purpose, rather than having a profit-making objective
- are independent of the state, because they are governed by an independent group of people
- re-invest all their financial surpluses in the services they offer and the organisation itself.[4]

The nonprofit sectors responded in similar ways to moves by both governments to fund and regulate more public services and to provide less themselves. Here the US has a great deal more experience than the UK resulting from a long tradition of government contracting nonprofit organisations to deliver a wide range of services.[5] This has been given further impetus by the recent 're-inventing government' initiative.

Both countries carry out periodic reviews of their nonprofit sectors. The US had the Filer Commission and the Verity Task Force and the UK had the Wolfenden Committee and the Deakin Commission. Most recently the UK government has published *Private Action, Public Benefit* – a fundamental review of the legal and regulatory framework for charities and the broader nonprofit sector which proposed wide-ranging change including updating and expanding the list of charitable purposes, increasing the range of legal forms available to charities and social enterprises, developing greater accountability and transparency, and ensuring independent, open and proportionate regulation.[6]

There are also many similarities in the ways nonprofits organise and manage themselves. Both countries have a rich infrastructure of national, regional and local organisations, make similar distinctions between management and governance, have boards that govern in somewhat similar ways, struggle with the issues around encouraging effective representation and providing good governance, face tensions between consultation and decision making and are populated by people who have broadly similar values. The debate about 'core costs' in the UK is mirrored by a similar debate in the US about capitalisation and capacity building.

Language differences

Although the UK and the US have many similar concepts around nonprofit organisations, the language used is often different. The following are the most commonly used terms in the two countries, though there is not necessarily strict comparability between the concepts.

US	UK
Nonprofit sector	Voluntary sector
For-profit or private sector	Private sector
Corporation	Company
Philanthropy	Charity
Foundations	Trusts
Bequest	Legacy
Programmes	Services or activities
Constituent engagement	User involvement
Parent corporation	Group structure
Executive directors	Chief executives
Thrift store	Charity shop
Human services	Social services
Citizen participation	Voluntary work
Dues	Membership fees
Compensation	Remuneration

Different sizes

There are also many differences, the single biggest being size. The US has 5 times as many people, 6.7 times as much economic activity, income per head is 1.4 times as great and personal disposable income is 1.6 times larger than in the UK.[7]

Key statistical comparisons 2001

	US	UK
Population	285 million	60 million
Gross Domestic Product (GDP) at current Purchasing Power Parity (PPP)	£6,131 bn	£913 bn
Per capita GDP at current PPP	£22,250	£15,300
Disposable income per capita	£16,500	£10,000

Source: OECD, *OECD Main Economic Indicators* [7] converted at $1.6 = £1

Comparing the size of the nonprofit sectors is difficult because the definition of almost every dimension of size is different. Furthermore the data for the US is considerably less up to date than that for the UK. The figures set out in the table below should therefore be treated as indicative. They suggest that the sector in the US is somewhere between 10 and 20 times the size of the sector in the UK.

Comparisons of absolute size

US nonprofit sector	UK charities	Ratio
1,600,000 formally constituted organisations	140,000 general charities	11
	188,000 registered charities	8.5
£304 billion revenues (1998)	£16 billion gross income	19
10.9 million paid employees	563,000 paid employees	19
£141 billion volunteer time	£15 billion volunteer time	9

Sources: US – Murray Weitzman *et al.*, *The New Nonprofit Almanac and Desk Reference*[8] converted at $1.6 = £1; UK – The Strategy Unit, *Private Action, Public Benefit*[6] and Pauline Jas *et al.*, *The UK Voluntary Sector Almanac*[9]

Greater size allows the US sector to support a much stronger infrastructure of intermediary bodies (state and regional associations of nonprofits) and a much larger academic community. Greater size has also provided more funds for research on the issues and practices of governing and managing nonprofits.

The nonprofit sector in the US is not only larger in absolute terms, it also accounts for a greater percentage of economic activity.

Comparisons of relative size of nonprofit sectors

US	UK	Ratio
6.9% of GDP (1)	2.2% of GDP	3.1
7.8% of workforce (2)	2.2% of paid employment	3.5

(1) This figure from the Comparative Nonprofit Sector project is used to obtain a consistent comparison with the UK. It is 0.2% higher than the Independent Sector figure quoted in Chapter 1

(2) US figure is for non-agricultural workforce

Sources: US – Sokolowski in Lester Salamon and Wojciech Sokolowski, *Global Civil Society – Dimensions of the Nonprofit Sector*[10] ; UK – Kendal in ibid[10]

Different composition

In both countries the nonprofit sector consists of an extraordinary array of organisations that exist to help and entertain people and to protect the environment. Variety is an enduring characteristic of the sectors so it is not surprising that the mix of activities in each country is very different.

In the US, the sector is dominated by health services and the next largest recipient of income is education and research. Religion is central to life in the US and this is reflected in religious organisations accounting for 12% of the sector's income.

Neither health care nor education is present in a significant way in the UK's nonprofit sector because health is provided primarily by the National Health Service and further education is provided almost exclusively by the state. In the UK social services and medical research account for the largest proportions of income.

Distribution of income by sub-sector

US		UK	
Health services	49%	Social services	25%
Education/research	18%	Medical	21%
Religious organisations	12%	International	14%
Social and legal services	12%	Children and youth	10%
Civic, social and fraternal	3%	Religious organisations	9%
Arts and culture	2%	Heritage and environment	7%
Foundations	5%	Animals	5%
		Benevolent funds	4%
		Culture	3%
		Education	1%

Sources: US – Murray Weitzman *et al.*, *The New Nonprofit Almanac and Desk Reference*[8]; UK – based on the top 500 charities cited in Cathy Pharoah, *Charity Trends 2003*[11], and private correspondence with the author, the best available data at present

Different relationships with government

In the US, citizens have a right to form a nonprofit organisation. The major benefit of registering such organisations is exemption from paying corporation taxes and freedom to receive tax-exempt private and corporate donations. The primary federal regulatory body is therefore the Internal Revenue Service that grants this exemption and in return requires an annual submission of financial data (known as Form 990).

In England, charities have to demonstrate to the Charity Commission, a body that is semi-independent from government, that they have charitable objects and they also have to receive approval from the Inland Revenue. The Commission is the regulator of nonprofit organisations with charitable status and it can initiate inquiries into organisations' affairs. The arrangements are different in Scotland. Proposals have recently been made to re-define the fundamental definition of charity and to sharpen and enhance the role of the Commission. If approved, the definition will build on the four 'heads of charity' (the relief of poverty, the advancement of education, the advancement of religion and other purposes beneficial to the community) and require demonstration of the delivery of 'public benefit'.

In the past organisations in both countries have faced similar issues relating to the relationship between government and the nonprofit sector, including potential constraints on campaigning for policy and legislative change at the same time as receiving funds from government.

There is concern amongst many nonprofits in the US about engaging in advocacy when government is often on the receiving end of such campaigns. In 1995 representative Ernest Istook proposed legislation that would bar organisations that receive government funding from engaging in advocacy. Although the proposal has been defeated five times it has caused great concern about limits on advocacy. However, recent research on advocacy in human service organisations concluded that the extent of advocacy is more a function of the organisation's inclination, the commitment of its leaders, and its capacity to conduct research. It concluded that the threat of biting the hand that feeds the sector is more perceived than real.[12]

Relationships between the government and the voluntary sector have been the subject of much work in the UK following publication of the Deakin Commission report in 1996 highlighting the problems.[13] Since then the voluntary sector and the government have signed a Compact – a written understanding creating a framework for their relationship.

The Compact sets out undertakings by both government and the voluntary sector. The government undertook to:

- recognise the independence of the voluntary sector
- pay attention to the need for strategic funding and develop a code of good practice on government funding of the voluntary sector
- take account of effects of new policies on the voluntary sector; consult the sector on issues that are likely to affect it; take account of

those parts of the sector that represent women, minority groups and socially excluded people; and develop a code of good practice on consultation

- promote effective working relationships between government and the sector; review the operation of the Compact; and promote the adoption of the Compact by other public bodies.

The voluntary sector undertook to:

- maintain high standards in funding and accountability, respect and be accountable to the law, and develop quality standards
- ensure that service users, volunteers, members and supporters are informed and consulted about activities and policy positions
- promote effective working relationships with government; involve users in activities and services; and promote best practice and equality of opportunity.

Source: NCVO[14]

Codes of practice to support implementation of the Compact have been jointly developed on government funding, consultation and policy appraisal, black and minority ethnic groups and volunteering and community organisations. Local compacts mirror the national Compact, and are being drawn up in consultation between the voluntary sector at a local level and local councils and other local public bodies.

An annual meeting between ministers and leaders from the voluntary sector reviews the operation of the Compact. These arrangements are now being further strengthened following publication of the Treasury Cross Cutting Review on the role of the voluntary sector in delivering public services. Although implementation is patchy there is no doubt that this initiative has established a secure basis for the future relationship between government and the voluntary sector. This is one of the significant areas where the US could learn from UK experience.

One result of the partnership approach is that many of the recent programmes to address social issues have been developed and delivered jointly by government and the voluntary sector. Examples include the Sure Start programme for early education, the Neighbourhood Renewal Strategy, some of the programmes financed by the New Opportunities Fund and FutureBuilders, the £125 million government fund for strengthening voluntary sector infrastructure. Inevitably there have been some tensions but there have also been genuine attempts to involve the voluntary sector in policy formulation and service delivery.

Different tax regimes

Although donations to nonprofits and charities are tax deductible in both countries, the way they operate is fundamentally different. In the UK the majority of the benefit of tax deductions is given to the charity, whilst in the US the benefit goes to the individual making the donation. This echoes the different context in the two countries. In the US a much higher percentage of people file tax returns. For these people a charitable donation produces an immediate reduction in their tax payment. It also reflects a close link in the US between supporting community development and the promotion of self-interest.

In the UK, tax deduction for individuals was until recently restricted to people making four-year commitments and signing a witnessed covenant to make the payments. These restrictions have now been removed, but charities still reclaim the tax paid on donations. The benefit is seen to go to the charity, reflecting the more altruistic tradition of giving in the UK.

The value of tax exemptions in the US has been estimated to be over $17 billion (£11 billion). This compares with the value of tax relief on giving in the UK which is estimated to be worth £1.2 billion.[9] So US tax exemptions are worth nine times the value of UK tax relief.

Similar patterns of volunteering

The overall pattern of volunteering in the US and the UK is one of similarities, with some small but significant differences.

Comparisons of volunteering

	US	UK
Number of volunteers	110m	22m
% of the population volunteering	55%	48%
Average time given by volunteers	3.5 hours/ week	4 hours/ week
% women volunteering	61%	48%
% men volunteering	49%	48%
Main activities	Religion Education Youth development	Sport Education Social welfare

Sources: US – Murray Weitzman *et al., The New Nonprofit Almanac and Desk Reference*[8]; UK – Justin Davis Smith, The 1997 National Survey of Volunteering[15]

More Americans volunteer, but they give slightly less time than British volunteers. Americans give most time to religion whereas Britons give most time to sport. A higher percentage of women volunteer in the US, whereas a similar percentage of men and women volunteer in the UK.

Similar developments of social enterprise

In both countries new types of organisations are emerging which sit on the boundary of the nonprofit and for-profit sectors. These organisations have a social purpose but earn income from their activities, often employ disadvantaged people and operate as businesses rather than charities. Examples include furniture repair, janitorial services, bicycle shops and landscaping services.

In the UK the government has moved swiftly to propose the creation of a new legal form called the Community Interest Company (CIC). The assets of CICs will be locked into public benefit but they will not have access to the tax reliefs available to charities.

Summary of similarities and differences

In summary, whilst nonprofits in the two countries exist for similar reasons and have similar arrangements for their management and governance, there are great differences in their size, composition, their relationships with government and their tax regimes. The rest of this chapter looks at differences in management and governance practices, organised under the same headings as the previous chapters of the book. Each section ends with the author's reflection on the topic.

8.2 Capacity building

The term 'capacity building' has slightly different emphasis in the two countries. In the US the term tends to be used to refer primarily to building the strength of organisations and only secondarily to the idea of building the capacity of the sector as a whole. In the UK the emphasis is reversed, and there is much more talk about creating the institutional arrangements and infrastructure that enables the voluntary sector to deliver social results.

The key difference between capacity building in the US and the UK is that in the US efforts have been more systematic, more rigorous and better funded. In the US there is widespread recognition that lack of organisation capacity is a critical constraint on the potential impact of nonprofit organisations. Some organisations have successfully raised funds to invest in capacity building initiatives, are pursuing explicit strategies for increasing their capacity and endeavouring to measure the achievements of their capacity building work. As a result there is now a growing body of literature on capacity building, a national network of advice organisations and a number of funders that are committed to the principle.

In the UK there has been significant investment in strengthening organisations and in building the sector's infrastructure of intermediary organisations. Until recently, it has not been called capacity building and it has not commanded the same level of attention as the capacity building movement in the US. However, significant changes are now in the pipeline. Following a review by the Treasury, a fund of £93 million has been established to invest in a range of initiatives aimed at developing the capacity of the voluntary and community sector to deliver public services. In addition, the government has announced a £125 million fund called FutureBuilders as a one-off investment fund to equip the sector for the future.

In both countries the elements of organisation capacity that are perceived to be important are almost identical. Common components include strategic and business planning, fundraising, governance and marketing. Tools to assess capacity translate well across the Atlantic and there is a great deal to be learned from each other about what works best in this sphere.

The scale of nonprofit organisations is a topic of much more debate in the US than in the UK. The proponents of larger scale in the US make a strong case for larger organisations that give managers and staff jobs with clearer boundaries, and spend less through not duplicating the costs of governance and core management functions. They are challenged by those who argue that many of the major social changes, such as the end of slavery, women's emancipation and environmental protection, resulted from campaigns by a large number of smaller organisations that networked together to achieve social justice. People holding the latter view suggest that the seeds of the next social changes may be growing in grass-roots organisations across the country rather than in the organisations at the top of the nonprofit league table.

In my experience the challenge for all organisations that set out to build their capacity is to distinguish between essential organisation capacity and useless bureaucracy. Managers can go through the process

Comparing capacity and bureaucracy

Essential capacity	Useless bureaucracy
A **mission** that is sharp, realistic and widely used	Much debated missions that are not sufficiently specific, over-ambitious and seldom used
Boards and committees that add high value at every meeting	Boards that consume time and effort and cost more than they contribute
Strategic plans that are precise, prioritised and tightly linked to operational plans	Strategic plans that are too long, not well prioritised and unrealistically ambitious
Managers and staff having a limited number of objectives organised into an integrated hierachy from organisation goals to individuals' objectives	Managers and staff having many objectives that are not tightly linked across the whole organisation
Directors and managers who delegate and empower staff	Directors who slip into doing managers' jobs and managers who slip into doing staff jobs
Directors and managers who use supervision to hold people to account for meeting their commitments, who coach their staff and expect them to learn from experience	Supervision not related to objectives and not viewed as a learning opportunity
Performance reports that lead to decisions and new priorities	Performance reports that do not result in action
Short, well-planned **meetings** with clear objectives, effective leadership that draws on everyone's perspectives and deliver specified outcomes	Long, poorly planned meetings that are unfocused and skirt around the real issues because people do not speak openly
Training and professional development directly linked to the organisation's objectives	General training linked to individuals' interests
Personal appraisals that are well prepared, give honest feedback and lead to action	Appraisals that are polite, not supportive and do not address poor performance
Timely **financial management information** that relates directly to people's responsibilities and the resources that they control, and is laid out to focus people on the key numbers	Management accounts that are full of numbers which people do not understand and which include resources that they do not control

of developing a particular aspect of capacity but it may not make the desired difference to performance. Rigorous, systematic and dedicated commitment to developing each aspect is crucial to embedding new capacity into an organisation's culture.

The key point to learn is that it takes time, effort and funding to create strong organisations with the clout to make a significant impact on social issues. Investment is the major consideration. Organisations that under-invest in their capacity are not preparing themselves for the future. They are short-changing their successors and they are not contributing to the creation of a strong social infrastructure that has the capacity to address the pressing social issues faced by both countries.

8.3 Performance management

The need for better performance information

There are increasingly strong calls for organisations in the US and the UK to report on what they have achieved. Most observers on both sides of the Atlantic believe that these demands will rise, particularly in the US.

The most notable difference between the two countries is that much more information about nonprofit performance is available in the US than in the UK, most of it on the web. There are a number of charity watchdog organisations that evaluate nonprofit organisation performance. There is information about whether organisations conform to pre-determined criteria, such as those promoted by Better Business Bureau. There is the annual financial return information published by Guidestar. The web also allows organisations to provide information on their mission and their programmes. There is the Arco listing of the 100 best organisations to work for and the Worth list of America's 100 best charities that provides factual and financial information to donors, including details of administrative and fundraising costs.

Major US charity watchdog groups

	American Institute of Philanthropy	Better Business Bureau Wise Giving Alliance	Charity Navigator	Wall Watchers' Ministry Watch
Year started	1993	2001	2002	2000
Budget	$350,000	$1.3 million	$500,000	$500,000
Employees	4 full time	10 full time	9 full time	4 full time; 1 part time
Sources of income	Individual donors, foundations and corporations	Individual donors, Council of Better Business Bureaus, foundations and corporations	A single donor, John P. Dugan, chairman of PDI, a pharmaceutical sales company (Saddle River, N.J.)	A single donor, Howard Leonard, CEO of Stewardship Partners Investment Counsel (Matthews, N.C.)
Rating system	A+ to F	Judged on 23 standards	0 to 4 stars	1 to 5 stars
Nonprofit groups evaluated	450	559	1,750	475
Basis for evaluations	Forms 990, annual reports, audited financial statements	Forms 990, annual reports, audited financial statements fundraising materials, bylaws, conflict-of-interest policies, other materials	Forms 990	Forms 990, audited financial statements
Address www.	charitywatch.org	give.org	charitynavigator. org	ministrywatch. com

Source: *Chronicle of Philanthropy* [16]

Better Business Bureau Reports

Here are Better Business Bureau (BBB) reports on an organisation that conforms to its standards and an anonymised one that does not:

American Diabetes Association 'Meets all standards.'

Dreams Foundation 'Does not meet the following standards:

(1) that the soliciting organization's financial statements present adequate information to serve as a basis for informed decisions, including expenses reported in categories corresponding to the descriptions of major programs and activities contained in informational materials, and a detailed schedule of expenses by natural classification, presenting the natural expenses incurred for each major program and supporting activity;

(2) that a reasonable percentage (at least 50 percent) of total income from all sources be applied to programs and activities directly related to the purposes for which the organization exists;

(3) that a reasonable percentage (at least 50 percent) of public contributions be applied to the programs and activities described in solicitations, in accordance with donor expectations; and

(4) that solicitations in conjunction with the sale of goods, services, or admissions identify at the point of solicitation the actual or anticipated portion of the sale or admission price to benefit the charitable organization or cause.

As of August 2002, the organization had not provided complete information about its solicitations, informational materials, and fund-raising practices. Therefore, the alliance is unable to determine if Dreams Foundation meets three additional standards.'

Another notable difference is in the annual reports from organisations in the US and UK. In the UK annual reports tend to be more lively, presented in many different formats and leading-edge organisations are striving to report on their outputs and the impact they have achieved in addition to reporting on financial performance. The 'Impact Report' published by the Royal National Institute for Deaf People sets out the aims, achievements and future plans for each area of its work. It also highlights how unrestricted voluntary income was allocated to different activity areas and it has established a standard for others to follow.

Debates about performance

Despite these differences, there are many similarities in the debates about nonprofit performance in the two countries. Although there is demand for information, and an expanding body of experience, observers in the US and the UK are acutely aware that measuring and monitoring the performance of nonprofit organisations is at an early stage of development. Organisations that deliver a range of services face particular difficulties, as the measures used for different services are generally not additive. Lobbying organisations face the challenge that campaign successes can seldom be ascribed to the work of one organisation.

There are also people on both sides of the Atlantic who argue that performance metrics will never describe the activities of nonprofit organisations and that searching for them and collecting the resulting data will not yield managerially valuable information. The champions of performance management retort that performance measures may not be as good a proxy for performance as organisations might like, but that having some measures is better than judging performance without measures.

A further criticism of performance measurement in both countries is that it can be expensive, particularly when new data is required. Measures such as Social Return on Investment require significant investment and some argue that this is not a good use of resources.

Organisations in the US and the UK are striving to find ways of boiling down reports on their overall achievements to a manageable set of data. They are also attempting to find ways to report on the health of their organisations as well as its financial performance. Concepts such as the balanced scorecard and the corporate dashboard have been applied in both countries.

In my view performance management will become an increasingly important part of management and governance, but more development work is required to enable organisations to understand the essential elements of their own performance. The notion of a balanced scorecard of different metrics is appropriate, but the idea has been lifted from the corporate sector and nonprofit performance has been squeezed into categories that are more appropriate for profit-seeking organisations. Application of the scorecard therefore needs to be much more highly tailored to nonprofit circumstances, with organisations selecting both the overall categories of data to assemble, and the individual performance metrics that pinpoint their achievements and the health of their organisations.

In both countries growing public expectations for performance information mean that those organisations which start to make progress now will have an advantage over those that wait until they are pressurised by external forces to improve their performance monitoring and reporting.

8.4 Strategic alliances

From time to time in both the US and the UK there are calls for more mergers between nonprofit organisations. Proponents of mergers argue that there are far too many organisations chasing the same funds and delivering similar services. Opponents point out that organisations often come from different value bases and provide different services, so the real opportunities for mergers are fewer that might appear to be the case. Experience on both sides of the Atlantic is that independence is a much cherished attribute for people working in the sector. Managers, staff and board members therefore often view potential mergers as a threat to their autonomy, and as a result mergers are rare in both countries.

Despite this, there is a body of evidence to suggest that the nonprofit sector as a whole could achieve more if its resources were not dissipated amongst a large number of organisations. Consequently, there is growing discussion in the US and the UK about the potential for a range of strategic alliances that do not involve complete mergers.

In the US the case for greater collaboration has been well made[17] and the range of options for strategic alliances is well documented ([18] and [19]). Strategic Solutions has been established as a small centre dedicated to advancing knowledge and understanding of the options for strategic alliances and how to implement them.

In the UK housing associations have made much progress in this area through the formation of group structures. Larger associations have joined with one or more smaller associations and organised themselves into a parent board and a series of subsidiary boards. The roles of the parent board include agreeing group strategy and identifying the subsidiaries needed to achieve the strategy. They also agree the strategy of the subsidiaries and monitor their performance. They allow them varying degrees of freedom in how they achieve their strategy.

Recent research into group structures in housing associations in the UK shows that:

■ group structures are well established and there is little evidence of groups reverting to unitary organisations

- groups can improve the tax efficiency of most members
- some associations like to focus both managerial and board expertise through a system of subsidiary companies that enable boards and managers to concentrate their efforts on specific activities or geographic areas
- where a small association does not wish to lose its identity but is under pressure to change, joining a group can seem a better solution than a merger
- there is no clear link between membership of a group and improvement in management costs or performance.

Source: Audit Commission, *Group Dynamics*[20]

In my opinion, strategic alliances and mergers have the potential to enhance significantly the impact of the sector. In many situations organisations can combine resources and capabilities to achieve more than they could realise separately. However, they have to be developed by organisations that are themselves secure and well managed and their instigators have to recognise that there are additional management challenges in creating and managing successful alliances.

8.5 Funding

It is not easy to get a clear picture of the differences between the overall funding structure of the nonprofit sectors in the US and the UK because the data is collected in different categories, reflecting the different histories of the sectors. Furthermore income data for the UK can be more rigorously separated into sources of income (e.g. the general public, government, business and investments) and types of transaction (e.g. earned income, voluntary income and returns on investments). Some US data conflates sources and transaction types. So, while it is possible to see some significant similarities and some differences between the two countries, the following conclusions should be treated with some caution.

Different balance of income sources

The largest source of income to nonprofits in the US is membership dues, fees and charges which together account for 38% of income. This category is broadly equivalent to earned income from the general public in the UK, which accounts for only 15% of total income. So earned income from the public in the US is more than double earned income in the UK.

The second largest source of income to US nonprofits is government grants and contracts. These represent a slightly larger proportion of income than in the UK. However the US figure excludes some fees that are paid or reimbursed by government, such as Medicaid and Medicare payments. Total income from government would be larger if these fees were included. The US sector is therefore more dependent on government income than the UK sector.

The percentage of income from private contributions is broadly similar, with the UK sector slightly more dependent on the general public. The UK sector is, however, more dependent on foundations.

In the UK, investment income accounts for twice as much income as in the US and, somewhat surprisingly, the UK sector earns a significantly higher percentage of its income from the business sector.

Sources of income

US independent sector		UK general charities	
Dues, fees and charges	38%	Earned income from the general public	15%
Government grants and contracts	31%	Government	29%
Private contributions	17%	Voluntary funding from general public	20%
Private contributions from foundations	2%	Voluntary organisations (mainly foundations)	9%
Investments, interest and dividends	11%	Investment income	23%
Corporations	1%	Business sector	5%
Totals	100%		100%

Sources: US – Murray Weitzman *et al., The New Nonprofit Almanac and Desk Reference*[8]; UK – NCVO[21]

Overall, the sources of income are significantly different, reflecting the different contexts of the two countries and the different roles, services and activities of the organisations within the sectors.

Different patterns of private funding

The US is a richer country than the UK, on average Americans have more disposable income than British people and they are much more generous than the British. In the US the average household gave $754 (£471) to nonprofit organisations in 1998,[22] whereas in the UK the average annual donations from a contributing household was £83.[23] US households are therefore about 5.6 times more generous than UK households. This is reflected in figures for giving as a proportion in individual income. In the US donations from individuals have consistently accounted for around 2% of Gross National Product since 1986.[24] UK giving is estimated as being 0.77% of Gross Domestic Product.[25]

Recipients of giving in the two countries differ markedly. Gifts to religious organisations account for 44% of donated funds in the US but only 16% of donated funds in the UK. Furthermore, in the US there has always been a strong tradition of alumni giving to universities – and this has only recently begun to develop in the UK.

There are significant differences in the reasons why Americans and British people make donations. In the US giving is heavily interlaced with self-interest. People give to organisations that provide them with services. In the US 'Self-interested motivations are not only acceptable, but are socially approved'.[26] Americans also tend to give and volunteer for the same organisations whereas the British tend to volunteer and give to different organisations.

The motives for giving are quite different in the UK. 'Giving is seen largely as a private decision, and peripheral to both social identity and civic responsibility. For the British, moral motivation is deeply rooted in collective duty, a concept that would be quite foreign to Americans, just as enlightened self-interest does not translate across the Atlantic in the other direction'.[26]

The methods of giving also differ significantly. In the US the majority of people make their donations at the end of the year when they complete their tax returns. This explains the importance of the annual appeals that many nonprofits organise. Payroll giving is much more significant in the US, but despite promotional efforts, has not become as significant in the UK. Donations in the UK are still dominated by spontaneous giving which is estimated to account for around 80% of gifts, though there are indications that this percentage is falling.[27]

Yet another difference is the growing role of non-cash donations in the US (such as cars and food) that now account for 28% of all charitable contributions. Again the tax system may explain some of the difference, as people who have itemised tax returns can claim deductions for non-cash contributions in their annual tax return.

American generosity is also evident in business. In the US corporations gave 1.2% of pre-tax profits in 2000,[24] whereas in the UK companies only gave 0.2% of pre-tax profits.[26]

Similar concerns about government funding

The nonprofit sectors in both countries are dependent on government funding, and increasingly this takes the form of contract funding. Nonprofits in the US have a long history of pursuing their missions supported in part by government funding. However, there are widespread concerns that government funding sometimes finances low quality services and that it inevitably places considerable administrative burdens on organisations. One seasoned observer speaks of 'complex regulations, complicated reporting requirements and injurious financial terms'.[12]

More debate about funding

There is more debate in the US about new sources of funding and the capital structure of nonprofit organisations.

Venture philanthropy began in the US five years before it travelled across the Atlantic to the UK. Together with high engagement funding, it has had an impact on grant making out of all proportion to the value of its funding. It has influenced debates about the relationship between funders and funded organisations. The jury may be out on whether strong support combined with tough accountability is a formula for long-term success, but there is no doubt about the impact of venture philanthropy on the way people think about this crucial relationship.

There are growing calls for US foundations to increase their payout rates, particularly at present when income from a number of sources is no longer growing at previous rates, and in some cases is falling. Foundations are required to pay out a sum equivalent to at least 5% of their capital each year, but this figure is often treated as a maximum as well as a minimum. Foundations now have $1 trillion in investment assets and there are growing calls for more of this funding to be used to address today's pressing social problems.[28]

In the US the question about how foundations invest their funds and the role of programme related investments has led to small but significant capital investments in nonprofit organisations. The debate about the role of trusts in the UK is only just beginning, assisted by the publication of *From Charity to Creativity – Philanthropic Foundations in the 21st Century.*[29]

Together these changes in the types of funding and the nature of relationships have led to the beginning of a debate about the 'social capital market' in the US. Early discussion suggests that this is an inefficient market, characterised by poor information flows about what works and what does not work. There are propositions that the sector as a whole could have greater impact if this market could be made more effective.

Little thought has been given to the efficiency of the market for funding in the UK. A brief glance at the lists of funders in recipients' annual reports suggests that many organisations are chasing many funders for comparatively small amounts of funding. This implies significant potential for a major review which might lead to funders giving fewer, larger grants and consequently expecting much tighter accountability.

Finally, increasing thought is being given in the US to the capital structure of nonprofit organisations. Whilst not a new subject, it is one that is now being more widely discussed.[30] Most nonprofit organisations have few borrowings compared to their assets (they are not highly geared in the technical jargon) and many use donors' funds for capital investments when borrowing might be a more appropriate form of finance.

My overall impression is that people in the nonprofit sector in both countries tend to focus most of their energy on services and campaigns and very little on financial structures. The private sector puts greater effort into ensuring that different financial instruments are used for different purposes, and the nonprofit sectors could benefit from their more sophisticated approaches to managing the capital structure of their organisations.

8.6 Lead with integrity

In both the US and the UK there is growing discussion about leadership, the role that it plays in creating successful nonprofit organisations and in particular the leadership role of the chief executive. A key challenge for chief executives in both countries is to keep a large number of balls in the air at the same time. On both sides of the Atlantic, chief executives talk about the challenge of:

- building and maintaining a rich network of external relationships and keeping a close eye on changes in the external environment
- keeping a really tight grip on every stage of the planning and performance cycle
- keeping the quality of the board and its work at the highest level
- raising the funds, and maintaining personal relationships with key funders

- building the senior team, investing in personal relationships and supporting members of the team
- demonstrating a personal commitment to all strategic alliances
- taking actions that lead to catalytic change (speaking, writing etc.).

This is a hugely challenging job, and one that has to be done in consultation with a wide range of stakeholders, all of whom have legitimate interest in the organisation.

To free up time to deliver these roles, an increasing number of organisations in the US are appointing people to the role of chief operating officer. Although this role is defined in a number of different ways, its primary purpose is to reduce the demands on the chief executive. Like all structural arrangements, it is critically dependent on good personal relationships. However, its popularity in larger organisations in the US implies that it can often relieve the pressure on chief executives and enable them to discharge their leadership roles more effectively.

The size of the sector in the US has enabled it to provide greater support to leaders. There is a body of literature devoted specifically to the leadership of nonprofit organisations and there are organisations devoted to nonprofit leadership, most notably the Leader to Leader Institute. Some nonprofit management education includes courses on leadership and there is strong evidence that managers want better leadership development. In a survey of the leading public policy and administration schools, graduates reported that leadership was the second most important skill in helping them to succeed in their jobs. However, whilst 76% rated leadership as very important, only 39% said that their schools had been very helpful in teaching that skill.[31]

In the UK various initiatives to develop leadership skills for the voluntary sector are being promoted and could usefully draw on US experience.

In my view, the challenge of the chief executive job in managing complex organisations with multifaceted relationships with external stakeholders cannot be underestimated. Better training and stronger support are required to make this role more do-able and enjoyable, and to attract and retain people willing to take on this demanding job.

8.7 Strengthen governance

Ten years ago there was no doubt that the US was ahead of the UK in driving the modernisation of nonprofit governance. The establishment of BoardSource, their publications and their annual conference that attracts people from around the globe, was a driving force that created a new agenda for governance.

Today, the differences are much less. In the UK the relentless drive to improve corporate governance, the influence of BoardSource, and the energy of the NCVO Trustee and Governance team and other bodies over many years led to significant improvements in governance, which have in turn spread to quasi-governmental bodies and the housing sector.

There are many similarities between US and UK boards. In terms of size, the median US board has 17 members and average size is 19 members – both numbers being constant over the last five years. In the UK the average board has 9 members – a figure that has grown from 7 in 1994. However this average masks significant differences. Average board size varies from 8.7 for charities with income of less than £10,000 per year to 21 for those with income over £10 million per year. The average size is reported to be converging, with smaller organisations increasing the size of their boards and larger organisations reducing the number of board members.[32]

The representation of women is similar in the US (43%) and in the UK (45%). However, in the US women serve more often on the boards of smaller organisations than larger ones. They are also better represented on arts, health, human services and educational organisation boards. Men serve more often on larger boards and are better represented on management support, United Ways and environmental organisation boards.[33]

Overall, minorities in both the US and the UK are under-represented on boards. In the US minorities make up 28% of the population, but only take 15% of the seats on boards. African Americans are better represented than other groups, accounting for 9% of board positions and 12 % of the population.[33] In the UK 3.3% of board members are black, compared to 2.3% of the population, and 1.4% are Asian compared to 4% of the population.[32]

The most significant difference is that US board members are generally expected to contribute financially themselves and to raise funds from other donors. This means that members have a financial stake in the organisation and are therefore likely to take a close interest in how the organisation spends its funds and what it achieves. Being a donor also makes it easier to ask other people to give, because there is a sense in which new donors are entrusting their funds to the board member in the knowledge that he or she will provide close oversight over the organisation's affairs.

A noteworthy difference is in board members' employment. In the US 57% of board members are employed by for-profit organisations or are self-employed. That means the majority of boards are made up of people from a business background. A further 19% are employed in the nonprofit sector. Although no comparable data is available for the UK, people with a business background are often a small minority on UK boards.

A final difference in governance is the widespread use of nominations committees to oversee recruitment and induction to US boards, and increasingly to take responsibility for advising the chair on individual board member performance. Governance committees, that oversee all governance matters including board performance, are also more prevalent in the US.

My overall impression is that over recent years board effectiveness has increased significantly in both countries. However, the journey from governance that was comparatively amateurish to skilled governance that reflects the needs of organisations and the wider demands of the community will take time. In both countries there is a long way to go before the majority of boards and board members deliver governance of the highest standards and add maximum value to their organisations.

8.8 Focus on the new agenda

The origin of this research project was a desire to understand what managers and board members of medium-sized and larger organisations in the UK could learn from experience in the US. So the best place to end might be to summarise my findings.

My over-riding experience in carrying out the research for this book is that the similarities between our nonprofit sectors are far greater than the differences. Our two countries have a common language, commitment to democracy, liberalism and capitalism. We have nonprofit organisations that exist for broadly similar reasons and they have similar governance and management arrangements. It would therefore be surprising if there was not a great deal we could learn from each other.

However, whilst our nonprofit sectors are based on similar values, there are distinct differences of ethos. In the UK there is greater emphasis on voluntarism or 'meeting the needs of strangers' as one report characterised the voluntary sector.[34] There is greater emphasis on involving users in every aspect of nonprofit activity, including representation to government, service delivery, campaigning, staffing and governing organisations.

In the US there is greater emphasis on efficiency and effectiveness. Americans have a much stronger culture of commitment to management. Management training is much more widespread and the language of management pervades the way people think and speak. Management is more often derided in the UK and more widely accepted in the US.

However, the forces that shape the context in which the nonprofit sector operates are driving the two sectors to become increasingly similar. In both countries:

- the public sector is withdrawing from providing services and focusing on funding and regulating them
- profit-seeking firms are being attracted into providing services that were previously the preserve of the public and nonprofit sectors
- social enterprise is emerging as a new way of tackling social problems and it straddles the traditional boundaries between the private and nonprofit sectors
- new forms of funding and financial instruments are emerging and opening opportunities for organisations to structure their finances in different ways.

These and other changes point to the challenges managers and board members will face over coming years. In summary, when I stand back from the work I have undertaken over the last two years, I conclude that managers and board members will need to:

Invest in building strong organisations that have the skills, experience and capacity to have a significant impact on the social issues they exist to address. They need to recognise the potential for step changes in organisation performance and not assume that the status quo is sufficient.

Know what organisations are achieving so they can learn much more from experience and orient every aspect of management to what works and to delivering results. They need to understand the key drivers of performance and ensure that everyone in and around the organisation is focused on successful outcomes. They also need to provide greater accountability to funders, other stakeholders and the wider public.

Work strategically with other organisations to maximise the potential to be unleashed by combining the resources of different organisations. They need to seek out alliances and put their organisation's mission ahead of its autonomy and independence.

Diversify their funding to exploit a range of new sources of finance and therefore obtain greater leverage from existing funding. They need to create a much better fit between activities and investments, and the sources of funding used to pay for them.

Provide leadership at every level to get the best from their organisation's people. They need to recognise that most staff feel they are not well managed, that the key aspects of top quality management are well known and that people will increasingly expect them to be applied.

Enhance the quality of governance through sharper understanding of the unique roles of the board and through higher standards for board members in delivering those roles effectively. They need to use every tool available to improve their own performance.

Finally, how can the two countries best learn more from each other?

1 People throughout both countries could make greater use of the web. There is now a wealth of material available electronically and free of charge. Many sites have been referenced in this book. Reports and other materials can be downloaded and used to stimulate new thinking and to draw on each other's experience.
2 There is a growing literature on managing and governing nonprofit organisations in both countries and a much larger quantity of material in the US. Most can be purchased electronically and delivered within days. Like surfing the web, reading about experience from other countries can often stimulate more ideas and thoughts than exploring material from one's own country.
3 There are opportunities for people to recruit and seek employment across the Atlantic, particularly if it is for a time-limited period. Multinational companies have gained a great deal from moving executives across national boundaries and there is much to be gained from nonprofit executives making similar moves, albeit across organisation boundaries rather than within organisations.
4 Much could be gained from recruiting board members across national boundaries. Some organisations have already taken this step. People from other environments bring new ideas and fresh thinking – an important element of an effective board.

5 There are great opportunities for organising exchanges and shadowing experiences so that managers can learn from their counterparts. Exchanges bring great benefits both to the organisations involved and to the individuals, who learn to see similar issues in a different context and can be re-energised by the experience.

I hope that this book has laid some foundations for greater learning from each other. As I said in the introduction, I see it as 'work in progress' and welcome comment and criticism in the spirit of two great countries gaining a deeper understanding of each other's nonprofit sectors.

Summary

Recognise similarities and differences
- Similarities between the nonprofit sectors in the US and the UK include the values that underpin nonprofit activity, the definition of the nonprofit sector, the infrastructure of intermediary organisations and many management and governance practices
- Differences include the size of the sectors, their composition, their relationships with government and the tax regimes.

Capacity building
- In the US more attention has been given to building the capacity of individual organisations. In the UK more attention has been given to sector infrastructure
- The issue of organisation 'scale' is more widely discussed in the US
- Both countries would benefit form a better understanding of the difference between organisation 'muscle' and organisation 'fat'.

Performance management
- The legitimacy of organisations in both countries will depend on better performance information
- The challenges of creating measures of performance are recognised in both countries
- The US has more experience of moving from debates about performance measures to introducing organisation-wide performance management systems.

Strategic alliances
- Early evidence from both countries suggests that more could be achieved by organisations working in strategic alliances.

Exploit changing patterns of funding

- US organisations earn more income from fees and UK organisations are more dependent on income from investments and business
- American households give more than five times as much as British households to charity. People in the two countries give for different reasons and by different means
- The two countries share similar concerns about government funding
- There is more debate in the US about the 'social capital market' and the capital structure of nonprofit organisations.

Lead with integrity

- The role of the chief executive is similarly demanding in both countries. Organisations in the US more frequently appoint a chief operating officer to reduce the pressure on the chief executive.

Strengthen governance

- Boards in the US are larger, include more people from business and more people who work in the nonprofit sector. Nominations committees are more common
- Minorities are under-represented on boards in both countries.

Focus on the new agenda

- There are many similarities between the UK voluntary sector and the US nonprofit sector and many opportunities to learn from each other
- The UK voluntary sector places greater emphasis on voluntarism and involving users in policy making and service delivery
- The US nonprofit sector emphasises efficiency and effectiveness and has a stronger commitment to management
- The new agenda is concerned with building strong organisations, knowing what they are achieving, working strategically with other organisations, diversifying funding, providing leadership and enhancing governance
- The forces that shape the context for both sectors are driving them to become increasingly similar
- The web, literature, visits, exchanges and membership of each other's boards and staff will provide greater opportunities for learning from each other.

References

1 Justin Davis Smith, *The Voluntary Tradition – Philanthropy and Self Help in Britain 1500–1945* in *An Introduction to the Voluntary Sector*, London, Routledge, 1995

2 Lester Salamon, *Defining the Nonprofit Sector: A Cross-National Analysis*, Manchester and New York, Manchester University Press, 1997

3 Stephen Block, *A History of the Discipline* in *The Nature of the Nonprofit Sector*, Boulder, CO, Westview Press, 2001

4 Mike Hudson, *Managing Without Profit*, London, Directory of Social Change, 2002

5 Richard Gutch, *Contracting Lessons from the US*, London, National Council for Voluntary Organisations, 1992

6 The Strategy Unit, *Private Action, Public Benefit*, London, Cabinet Office, 2002

7 OECD, *OECD Main Economic Indicators*, 2003

8 Murray Weitzman *et al.*, *The New Nonprofit Almanac and Desk Reference*, San Francisco, Jossey-Bass, 2002

9 Pauline Jas *et al.*, *The UK Voluntary Sector Almanac*, London, National Council for Voluntary Organisations, 2002

10 Lester Salamon and Wojciech Sokolowski, *Global Civil Society – Dimensions of the Nonprofit Sector*, Baltimore, MD, Johns Hopkins Comparative Nonprofit Sector Project, 1999

11 Cathy Pharoah *et al.*, *Charity Trends 2003*, London, Caritas Data, 2003

12 William Ryan, *Government Funding of Nonprofit Human Service Organizations – A Review of Challenges and Opportunities*, not yet published

13 Nicholas Deakin, *Meeting the Challenge of Change: Voluntary Action into the 21st Century*, London, National Council for Voluntary Organisations, 1996

14 NCVO, 2003 National Council for Voluntary Organisations website, www.ncvo-vol.org.uk

15 Justin Davis Smith, *The 1997 National Survey of Volunteering*, London, The National Centre for Volunteering, 1998

16 Ian Wilhelm, *Charity Under Scrutiny* in *Chronicle of Philanthropy*, Washington, 28 November 2002

17 James Austin, *The Collaboration Challenge*, San Francisco, Jossey-Bass, 2000

18 Jane Arsenault, *Forging Nonprofit Alliances*, San Francisco, Jossey-Bass, 1998

19 David La Piana, *The Nonprofit Mergers Workbook*, Saint Paul, Amherst Wilder Foundation, 2000

20 Audit Commission, *Group Dynamics*, London, Audit Commission and Housing Corporation, 2001

21 NCVO, 2002 National Council for Voluntary Organisations website, www.ncvo-vol.org.uk

22 Susan Saxon Harold, *Giving and Volunteering in the United States*, Washington, Independent Sector, 1999

23 Dennis Down, *Family Spending – A Report on the 1999–2000 Family Expenditure Survey*, London, Office for National Statistics, 2000

24 Centre on Philanthropy – Indiana University, *Giving USA 2002*, Indianapolis, AAFRC Trust for Philanthropy, 2002

25 Lester Salamon *et al.*, *The Emerging Sector – A Statistical Supplement*, Baltimore, Johns Hopkins Institute for Policy Studies, 1996

26 Karen Wright, *Generosity Versus Altruism: Philanthropy and Charity in the US and the UK*, London, London School of Economics Centre for Civil Society, 2002

27 National Council for Voluntary Organisations, *Charitable Giving – The Tide has Turned*, in *NCVO Research Quarterly*, London, June 2001

28 Paul Jansen and David Katz, *For Nonprofits, Time is Money* in *The McKinsey Quarterly*, Number 1, 2002 (download from www.mckinseyquarterly.com)

29 Helmut Anheier and Diana Leat, *From Charity to Creativity – Philanthropic Foundations in the 21st Century*, Stroud, Comedia, 2002

30 Clara Miller, *Hidden in Plain Sight: Understanding Nonprofit Capital Structure* in *The Nonprofit Quarterly*, Boston, Spring 2003

31 Paul Light, *The New Public Service*, Washington, Brookings Institution, 1999

32 Chris Cornforth, *Recent Trends in Charity Governance and Trusteeship*, Milton Keynes, Open University Business School, 2001

33 National Centre for Nonprofit Boards (now BoardSource), *The Nonprofit Governance Index*, Washington, 2000

34 Ken Young, *Meeting the Needs of Strangers*, London, Gresham College, 1991

Appendix 1

Highlights from the McKinsey Capacity Assessment Grid

Following extensive research into capacity building, management consultants McKinsey & Company developed a tool for nonprofits to assess their organisation capacity.* The tool is structured to follow the elements of organisation capacity described in Chapter 2. They are:

- aspirations
- strategy
- organisational skills
- human resources
- systems and infrastructure
- organisational structure
- culture.

The tool identifies 58 categories of organisation capacity. Each category has four levels of performance which organisations can use to assess their own performance. They are:

1 clear need for increased capacity
2 basic level of capacity in place
3 moderate level of capacity in place
4 high level of capacity in place.

The full grid is available on the web at www.vppartners.org

The top level of capacity in each of the 58 categories is repeated here to demonstrate the performance standards that leading organisations are striving to attain.

---

* McKinsey & Company, Inc., Effective Capacity Building in Nonprofit Organizations, Reston, VA, prepared for Venture Philanthropy Partners, 2001 (download from www.vppartners.org).

'I ASPIRATIONS

Mission Clear expression of organisation's reason for existence which describes an enduring reality that reflects its values and purpose; broadly held within organisation and frequently referred to

Vision clarity Clear, specific, and compelling understanding of what organisation aspires to become or achieve; broadly held within organisation and consistently used to direct actions and set priorities

Vision – boldness Vision reflects an inspiring view of future and is demanding but achievable.

II STRATEGY

Overarching goals Vision translated into clear, bold set of (up to three) goals that organisation aims to achieve, specified by concrete to measure success for each criterion, and by well-defined time frames for attaining goals; goals are broadly known within organisation and consistently used to direct actions and set priorities

Overall strategy Organisation has clear, coherent medium to long term strategy that is both actionable and linked to overall mission, vision, and overarching goals; strategy is broadly known and consistently helps drive behaviour at all levels of organisation

Goals/performance targets Limited set of quantified, genuinely demanding performance targets in all areas; targets are tightly linked to aspirations and strategy, output/outcome-focused, have annual milestones, and are long-term nature; staff consistently adopts targets and works diligently to achieve them

Program relevance and integration All programs and services well defined and fully aligned with mission and goals; program offering are clearly linked to one another and to overall strategy; synergies across programs are captured

Program growth and replication Frequent assessment of possibility of scaling up existing programs and when judged appropriate, action always taken; efficiently and effectively; able to grow existing programs to meet needs of potential service recipients

New program development Continual assessment of gaps in ability of existing programs to meet recipient needs and adjustment always made; ability to create new, truly innovative programs to meet the needs of potential service recipients; continuous pipeline of new ideas

Funding model Highly diversified funding across multiple source types; organisation insulated from potential market instabilities (e.g. fully developed endowment) and/or has developed sustainable revenue-generating activities; other nonprofits try to imitate organisation's fund-raising activities and strategies.

III ORGANISATIONAL SKILLS
Performance management

Performance measurement Well-developed comprehensive, integrated system (e.g. balanced scorecard) used for measuring organisation's performance and progress on continual basis, including social, financial, and organisational impact of program and activities; small number of clear, measurable, and meaningful key performance indicators; social impact measured based on longitudinal studies with control groups, and performed or supervised by third-party experts

Performance analysis and program adjustments Comprehensive internal and external benchmarking part of the culture and used by staff in target-setting and daily operations; high awareness of how all activities rate against internal and external best-in-class benchmarks; systematic practice of making adjustments and improvements on basis of benchmarking

Planning

Monitoring of landscape Extensive knowledge of players and alternative models in program area; refined ability and systematic tendency to adapt behaviour based on understanding

Strategic planning Ability to develop and refine concrete, realistic and detailed strategic plan; critical mass of internal expertise in strategic planning, or efficient use of external, sustainable, highly qualified resources; strategic planning exercise carried out regularly; strategic plan used extensively to guide management decisions

Financial planning/budgeting Very solid financial plans, continuously updated; budget integrated into full operations; as strategic tool, it develops from process that incorporates and reflects organisational needs and objectives; well-understood divisional (program or geographical) budgets within overall central budget; performance-to-budget closely and regularly monitored

Operational planning Organisation develops and refines concrete, realistic, and detailed operational plan; has critical mass of internal expertise in operational planning, or efficiently uses external, sustainable, highly qualified resources; operational planning exercise carried out regularly; operational plan tightly linked to strategic planning activities and systematically used to direct operations

Human resources planning Organisation is able to develop and refine concrete, realistic, and detailed HR plan; has critical mass of internal expertise in HR planning (via trained, dedicated HR manager), or efficiently uses external, sustainable, highly qualified resources; HR planning exercise carried out regularly; HR plan tightly linked to strategic planning activities and systematically used to direct HR activities.

Fund-raising and revenue generation

Fund-raising Highly developed internal fund-raising skills and expertise in all funding source types to cover all regular needs; access to external expertise for additional extraordinary needs

Revenue generation Significant internal revenue-generation; experienced and skilled in areas such as cause-related marketing, fee-for-services and retailing; revenue-generating activities support, but don't distract from focus on creating social impact.

External relationship building and management

Partnerships and alliances development and nurturing Built, leveraged, and maintained strong, high-impact, relationships with variety of relevant parties (local, state, and federal government entities as well as for-profit, other nonprofit, and community agencies); relationships deeply anchored in stable, long-term, mutually beneficial collaboration

Local community presence and involvement Organisation widely known within larger community, and perceived as actively engaged with and extremely responsive to it; many members of the larger community (including many prominent members) actively and constructively involved in organisation (e.g., board, fund-raising)

Other organisational skills

Public relations and marketing Organisation fully aware of power of PR/marketing activities, and continually and actively engages in them; broad pool of nonprofit PR/marketing expertise and experience within organisation or efficient use made of external, sustainable, highly qualified resources

Influencing of policy-making Organisation pro-actively and reactively influences policy-making, in a highly effective manner, on state and national levels; always ready for and often called on to participate in substantive policy discussion and at times initiates discussions

Management of legal and liability matters Well-developed, effective, and efficient internal legal infrastructure for day-to-day legal work; additional access to general and specialized external expertise to cover peaks and extraordinary cases; continuous legal risk management and regular adjustment of insurance

Organisational processes use and development Robust, lean, and well-designed set of processes (e.g., decision making, planning, reviews) in place in all areas to ensure effective and efficient functioning of organisation; processes are widely known, used and accepted, and are key to ensuring full impact of organisation; continual monitoring and assessment of processes, and systematic improvement made.

IV HUMAN RESOURCES

Staffing levels Positions within and peripheral to organisation (e.g., staff, volunteers, board, senior management) are all fully staffed (no vacancies); no turnover or attendance problems

Board – composition and commitment Membership with broad variety of fields of practice and expertise, and drawn from the full spectrum of constituencies (nonprofit, academia, corporate, government, etc.); includes functional and program content-related expertise, as well as high-profile names; high willingness and proven track record of investing in learning about the organisation and addressing its issues; outstanding commitment to the organisation's success, mission and vision; meet in person regularly, good attendance, frequent meetings of focused subcommittees

Board – involvement and support Provide strong direction, support, and accountability to programmatic leadership and engaged as a strategic resource; communication between board and leadership reflects mutual respect, appreciation for roles and responsibilities, shared commitment and valuing of collective wisdom.

CEO/executive director and/or senior management team

Passion and vision Contagiously energetic and highly committed; lives the organisation's vision; compellingly articulates path to achieving vision that enables others to see where they are going

Impact orientation Guides organisation to succeed simultaneously in dual mission of social impact and optimal financial efficiency; constantly seeks and finds new opportunities to improve impact; anticipates possible problems; has sense of urgency about upcoming challenges; communicates compelling need for change that creates drive; aligns entire organisation to support change effort

People and organisational leadership/effectiveness Constantly establishing successful, win-win relationships with others, both within and outside the organisation; delivers consistent, positive and reinforcing messages to motivate people; able to let others make decisions and take charge; finds or creates special opportunities to promote people's development

Personal and interpersonal effectiveness Is viewed as outstanding "people person"; uses diversity of communication styles, including exceptional charisma, to inspire others and achieve impact; continually self-aware, actively works to better oneself; outstanding track record of learning and personal development

Analytical and strategic thinking Has keen and exceptional ability to synthesize complexity; makes informed decisions in ambiguous, uncertain situations; develops strategic alternatives and identifies associated rewards, risks, and actions to lower risks

Financial judgment Has exceptional financial judgment; has keen, almost intuitive sense for financial implications of decisions

Experience and standing Highly experienced in nonprofit management; many instinctive capabilities from other field(s) (e.g., for-profit, academia); exceptional evidence of social entrepreneur-like qualities; possesses a comprehensive and deep understanding of the sector; recognized nationally as a leader/shaper in particular sector

Management team and staff – dependence on CEO/executive director Reliance but not dependence on CEO/executive director; smooth transition to new leader could be expected; fund-raising and operations likely to continue without major problems; senior management team can fill in during transition time; several members of management team could potentially take on CEO/ED role

Senior management team Team highly experienced in nonprofit or for-profit management; drawn from full spectrum of constituencies (nonprofit, academia, corporate, government, etc.); outstanding capabilities and track record from other fields; outstanding track record of learning and personal development; contagiously energetic and committed

Staff extraordinarily diverse backgrounds and experiences, and bring broad range of skills; most staff are highly capable in multiple roles, committed both to mission/strategy and continuous learning; most are eager and able to take on special projects and collaborate across divisional lines; staff are frequent source of ideas and momentum for improvement and innovation

Volunteers Extremely capable set of individuals, bring complementary skills to organisation; reliable, loyal, highly committed to organisation's success and to "making things happen"; often go beyond call of duty; able to work in a way that serves organisation well, including ability to work easily with wide range of staff and play core roles without special supervision; volunteers managed very well and significantly contribute to overall success of organisation.

V SYSTEMS AND INFRASTRUCTURE
Systems

Planning systems Regular planning complemented by ad hoc planning when needed; clear, formal systems for data collection in all relevant areas; data used systematically to support planning effort and improve it

Decision-making framework Clear, formal lines/systems for decision making that involve as broad participation as practical and appropriate along with dissemination/interpretation of decision

Financial operations management Robust systems and controls in place governing all financial operations and their integration with budgeting, decision making, and organisational objectives/strategic goals; cash flow actively managed

Human resources management – management recruiting, development and retention Well-planned process to recruit, develop and retain key managers; CEO/executive director takes active interest in managerial development; individually tailored development plans for brightest stars; relevant and regular internal and external training, job rotation, coaching/feedback, and consistent performance appraisal are institutionalised; proven willingness to ensure high-quality job occupancy; well-connected to potential sources of new talent

Human resources management – general staff recruiting, development, and retention Management actively interested in general staff development; well-thought out and targeted development plans for key employees/positions; frequent, relevant training, job rotation, coaching/feedback and consistent performance appraisal institutionalised; proven willingness to ensure high quality job occupancy; continuous, proactive initiatives to identify new talent

Human resources management – incentives Well-designed, clear, and well-accepted incentive system; includes competitive salary (partly performance-based), attractive career development options, opportunities for leadership and entrepreneurship; system effective in motivating staff to over deliver in their job

Knowledge management Well-designed, user-friendly, comprehensive systems to capture, document, and disseminate knowledge internally in all relevant areas; all staff is aware of systems, knowledgeable in their use and makes frequent use of them.

Infrastructure

Physical infrastructure – buildings and office space Physical infrastructure well tailored to organisation's current and anticipated future needs; well-designed and thought out to enhance organisation's efficiency and effectiveness (e.g. especially favourable locations for clients and employees, plentiful team office space encourages teamwork, layout increases critical interactions among staff)

Technological infrastructure – telephone/fax Sophisticated and reliable telephone and fax facilities accessible by all staff (in office and at frontline), includes around-the-clock, individual voice mail; supplemented by additional facilities (e.g. pagers, cell phones) for selected staff; effective and essential in increasing effectiveness and efficiency

Technological infrastructure – computers, applications, network, and e-mail State-of-the-art, fully networked computing hardware with comprehensive range of up-to-date software applications; all staff has individual computer access and e-mail; accessible by frontline program deliverers as well as entire staff; used regularly by staff; effective and essential in increasing staff efficiency

Technological infrastructure – Web site Sophisticated, comprehensive and interactive Web site, regularly maintained and kept up to date on latest area and organisation developments; praised for its user-friendliness and depth of information; includes links to related organisations and useful resources on topic addressed by organisation

Technological infrastructure – databases and management reporting systems Sophisticated, comprehensive electronic database and management reporting systems exist for tracking clients, staff, volunteers, program outcomes and financial information; widely used and essential in increasing information sharing and efficiency.

VI ORGANISATIONAL STRUCTURE

Board governance Legal board, advisory board and managers work well together from clear roles; board fully understands and fulfills fiduciary duties; size of board set for maximum effectiveness with rigorous nomination process; board actively defines performance targets and holds CEO/ED fully accountable; board empowered and prepared to hire or fire CEO/ED if necessary; board periodically evaluated

Organisational design Roles and responsibilities of all organisational entities (e.g. headquarters, regional and local entities) are formalised, clear and complement each other; organisation chart is complete and reflects current reality

Interfunctional coordination Constant and seamless integration between different programs and organisational units with few coordination issues; relationships are dictated by organisational needs (rather than hierarchy or politics)

Individual job design All roles have associated dedicated positions; all individuals have clearly defined core roles which must be achieved and an area of discretion where they can show initiative and try to make a difference; core roles are defined in terms of end-products and services rather than activities; individuals have the ability to define their own activities and are empowered to continuously re-examine their jobs.

VII CULTURE

Performance as shared value All employees are systematically hired, rewarded and promoted for their collective contribution to social, financial and organisational impact; day-to-day processes and decision making are embedded in comprehensive performance thinking; performance is constantly referred to

Other shared beliefs and values Common set of basic beliefs and values (e.g. social, religious) exists and is widely shared within the organisation; provides members sense of identity and clear direction for behaviour; beliefs embodied by leader but nevertheless timeless and stable across leadership changes; beliefs clearly support overall purpose of the organisation and are consistently harnessed to produce impact

Shares references and practices Common set of references and practices exist within the organisation, which may include: traditions,
rituals, unwritten rules, stories, heroes or role models, symbols,
language, dress; are truly shared and adopted by all members of the
organisation; actively designed and used to clearly support overall
purpose of the organisation and to drive performance.'

Other nonprofit materials published by McKinsey & Company can be
found at www.mckinsey.com/practices/nonprofit

Appendix 2
People interviewed

A total of 65 people were given structured face-to-face interviews in the US for this research. The sample included:

- 23 nonprofit organisations
- 10 intermediary bodies
- 9 university departments
- 4 consulting firms.

Organisation	City	Name	Job title
Nonprofit organisations			
American Diabetes Association	Washington	John Graham	CEO
Amnesty International USA	New York	Curt Goering	Senior Deputy Executive Director
Big Brothers/Big Sisters	New York	Bill Tyman	Executive Director
Boys & Girls Club of Boston	Boston	Linda Whitlock	President & CEO
Children's Institute International	Los Angeles	Mary Emmons	President & CEO
Earthjustice	San Francisco	Buck Parker	Executive Director
Elderhostel	Boston	James Moses	Senior Vice President
Goodwill Industries of Southern California	Los Angeles	Doug Barr	President & CEO
Jewish Vocational Service	San Francisco	Abby Snay	Executive Director
KIPP Schools	San Francisco	Mike Feinberg	Co-Founder & CEO
Lighthouse for the Blind & Visually Impaired	San Francisco	Anita Aaron	Executive Director
Los Angeles Regional Foodbank	Los Angeles	Michael Flood	Executive Director
The Medical Foundation	Boston	Ray Considine	Executive Director
National Urban League	New York	Hugh Price	President
Origin	New York	Jeffrey Jablow	President & CEO
Toolworks	San Francisco	Donna Feingold	Executive Director
Trust for Public Land	San Francisco	Ralph Benson	Senior Vice President
US fund for UNICEF	New York	Charles Lyons	President

Organisation	City	Name	Job title
Nonprofit organisations contd			
Volunteers of America	Washington	Charles Gould	National President
Wildlife Conservation Society	New York	Steven Sanderson	President & CEO
Wildlife Trust	New York	Mary Pearl	Executive Director
YWCA	New York	Margaret Tyndall	CEO
Intermediary organisations			
Alliance for Non Profit Management	Washington	Roni Posner	Executive Director
Aspen Institute	Washington	Alan Abramson	Director – Non Profit Sector & Philanthropy
BoardSource	Washington	Marilyn Wyatt	Director of Consulting & Training for Europe & Asia
BoardSource	Washington	Outi Flynn	Consultant
Center for Non Profit Management	Los Angeles	Peter Manzo	Executive Director – General Counsel
CompassPoint	San Francisco	Jan Masaoka	Executive Director
Council on Foundations	Washington	Dorothy Ridings	President
Council on Foundations	Washington	Char Mollison	Vice President – Constituency Services
Council on Foundations	Washington	Joanne Scanlon	Senior Vice President – Professional Development
Foundation Center	New York	Sarah Engelhardt	President

Organisation	City	Name	Job title
Foundation Center	New York	Loren Renz	Vice President for Research
Independent Sector	Washington	Peter Shiras	Interim President & CEO
Leader to Leader Institute	New York	Frances Hesselbein	Chairman of the Board
National Council of Non Profit Associations	Washington	Audrey Alvarado	Executive Director
National Council of Non Profit Associations	Washington	Lora Pollari-Welbes	Director of Member Relations & Services
Urban Institute – Center on Non Profits and Philanthropy	Washington	Elizabeth Boris	Director
Urban Institute – Center on Non Profits and Philanthropy	Washington	Francie Ostrower	Senior Research Associate
Funders			
Ford Foundation	New York	Mike Edwards	Director, Governance & Civil Society
Meyer Foundation	Washington	Mary Ann Holohean	Director – Non Profit Sector Advancement Fund
New Profit Inc	Boston	Kelly Fitzsimmons	Managing Partner & Co-Founder
New Schools Venture Fund	San Francisco	Kim Smith	Co-Founder & CEO
The Roberts Enterprise Development Fund	San Francisco	Melinda Tuan	Managing Director
United Way of Greater Los Angeles	Los Angeles	Joseph Haggerty	President

Organisation	City	Name	Job title
Universities			
The Center for Social Innovation – Stanford Business School	San Francisco	Jed Emerson	Lecturer
Center for the Study of Voluntary Organizations and Service – Georgetown University	Washington	Pablo Eisenberg	Senior Fellow
Center for the Study of Voluntary Organizations and Service – Georgetown University	Washington	Virginia Hodgkinson	Professor
Harvard Business School	Boston	John Quelch	Senior Associate Dean
Harvard Business School	Boston	James Austin	Chair – Initiative on Social Enterprise
Harvard Business School	Boston	Allen Grossman	Professor of Management Practice
Harvard Business School	Boston	Jane Wei-Skillern	Visiting Assistant Professor – Social Enterprise Group
Harvard Graduate School of Education	Boston	Richard Chait	Professor of Higher Education
Hauser Center for Non Profit Organizations – Harvard University	Boston	Christine Letts	Associate Director
Hauser Center for Non Profit Organizations – Harvard University	Boston	Bill Ryan	Research Fellow
Institute for Non Profit Organization Management – University of San Francisco	San Francisco	Michael Cortes	Director

Organisation	City	Name	Job title
Johns Hopkins University	Boston	Stefan Toepler	Associate Research Scientist
New School University	New York	Rikki Abzug	Assistant Professor Non Profit Management
New School University	New York	Dennis Derryck	Professor of Professional Practice
Consulting firms			
Bridgespan Group	Boston	Jeff Bradach	Co-Founder & Managing Partner
Human Interaction Research Institute	Los Angeles	Tom Backer	President
La Piana Associates	San Francisco	David La Piana	Principal
McKinsey & Company	Boston	Stephanie Lowell	Manager Non Profit Practice
McKinsey & Company	San Francisco	Paul Jansen	Director
McKinsey & Company	Washington	Les Silverman	Director

Appendix 3
Steering Group members

This project was overseen by a Steering Group of practitioners, academics and consultants with extensive experience of nonprofit organisations. Its members were:

Name	Job title	Organisation
Richard Gutch (Chair)	Director, England	Community Fund
Helmut Anheier	Centennial Professor	London School of Economics
Ian Bruce	Director General	Royal National Institute for the Blind
	Professor	City University Business School
Helen Cameron	Visiting Fellow	London School of Economics
David Carrington	Independent Consultant	
Stuart Etherington	Chief Executive	National Council for Voluntary Organisations
David Green	Director General	British Council
Joel Joffe	Chair	The Giving Campaign
Natalia Leshchenko	Researcher	Centre for Civil Society, London School of Economics
Melinda Letts	Chairwoman	Long-term Medical Conditions Alliance
Mary Marsh	Chief Executive	National Society for the Prevention of Cruelty to Children
Robert Napier	Chief Executive	World Wide Fund for Nature
Rob Paton	Professor of Social Enterprise	Open University
Geraldine Peacock	Chief Executive	Guide Dogs for the Blind
Chris Staples	Community Services Director	Zurich Financial Services
Tina Tietjen	Chair	Women's Royal Voluntary Service

Appendix 4
The best reading

This appendix picks out some of the best books and reports on the nonprofit sector and the management and governance of nonprofit organisations in the USA. I chose them because I found them interesting, authoritative and informative books that I believe will stand the test of time and be relevant for many years to come.

The nonprofit sector in America

The New Nonprofit Almanac and Desk Reference, Murray Weitzman *et al.*, Independent Sector, 2002

This is the reference book for statistics on the sector, packed with figures, charts and a clear commentary. It covers the place of the independent sector in the national economy, employment trends, private giving trends and financial trends in each of the main parts of the sector. It also takes a detailed look at reporting public charities.

www.independentsector.org

America's Nonprofit Sector, Lester Salamon, The Foundation Center, 1999

This is a wide-ranging guide to the sector, giving an overview of why it exists, the scope and structure of the sector, the context in relation to business and government and an analysis of recent trends. It has a detailed analysis of each of the main sub-sectors (health, education, social services, arts, culture and recreation, advocacy, legal services and international aid, and religion). It ends with an interesting glimpse into the future.

www.fdncenter.org

Nonprofit Nation – A New Look at the Third America, Michael O'Neil, Jossey-Bass, 2002

This is a great book if you really want a thorough understanding of the nonprofit sector and each of its sub-sectors. In its second edition, it describes the development and current issues in great detail. It is packed with quantitative analysis and is also a great read. It is written by a Professor who has tracked the sector for many years and really understands what the figures mean and how they affect the critical issues facing the sector.

www.josseybass.com

The State of Nonprofit America, Lester Salamon (ed.), Brookings Institution, 2002

This authoritative and comprehensive assessment of the sector by leading authors reports on each part of the nonprofit sector and the five major challenges facing the sector. It includes an excellent introductory overview by Lester Salamon.

www.brookings.edu

The Nature of the Nonprofit Sector, J. Stevens Ott (ed.), Westview, 2001

This is a fascinating collection of the best writing about the sector starting with Andrew Carnegie's 1889 essay 'The Gospel of Wealth' and including 35 other chapters on the history and sociology of the nonprofit sector, its distinctive contribution to society and economic, organisational and political theories of the sector, ending with challenges facing the sector.

www.westviewpress.com

Capacity building

Effective Capacity Building in Nonprofit Organizations, McKinsey and Company, Venture Philanthropy Partners, 2001

This first-rate report sets out the seven elements of nonprofit capacity, based on 13 case studies. It reports on why capacity building is important and why nonprofit organisations tend to ignore it. The authors develop a capacity framework and it includes a self-assessment tool for organisations to rate their own capacity. Download:

www.vppartners.org

High Performance Nonprofit Organizations, Christine Letts, William Ryan and Allen Grossman, Wiley, 1999

This ground-breaking book makes a powerful case for capacity building and through comparisons with private sector organisations, sets out areas where nonprofits could make greatest improvements to their performance; quality processes, product development, benchmarking and human resources. Written by three of the leading thinkers from Harvard University, it is an inspirational read.

www.wiley.com

Pathways to Nonprofit Excellence, Paul Light, The Brookings Institution, 2002

This book reports on a pioneering project to seek the views of 250 leading thinkers and 250 executive directors of leading nonprofits on the characteristics of effective organisations. Paul Light heads Brookings' Pathways to Nonprofit Excellence project and is driving new thinking in this field. The book includes the full answers to the original questionnaires and his lively commentary on the results.

www.brook.edu

Making Nonprofits Work – A Report on the Tides of Nonprofit Management Reform, Paul Light, The Brookings Institution, 2000

Drawing on confidential interviews with leaders of nonprofit management reform and other sources, Light examines four popular philosophies being advocated for nonprofit management reform. He cautions leaders to recognise the limits of the reform models and to limit reform energy to a handful of priorities.

www.brook.edu

Performance management

Outcome Measurement in Nonprofit Organizations, Elaine Morley, Elisa Vinson and Harry Harty, Independent Sector, 2001

In the absence of a good book on performance management, this report is the most succinct and valuable summary of the state of the art. Harry Harty is a known guru in this area, having previously worked on the United Way measures project. The report looks at current practices in the types of information collected, data collection procedures, analysing outcome information, and reporting and use of outcome information. It also has recommendations for future development of outcome measurement.

Summary from www.IndependentSector.org

Outcome Measurement: Showing Results in the Nonprofit Sector, Margaret Plantz *et al.*, in *New Directions for Evaluation,* Jossey-Bass, reproduced by United Way, 1999

This report is from United Way's Outcome Measurement Resource Network. It summarises the history of performance measurement in the nonprofit health and human services sectors and defines key concepts. It describes the lessons learned about the value of outcome measurement, about effective implementation, about the role of funders and about using outcome measures in resource allocation decisions. It also sets out the challenges for the future.

www.unitedway.org

Strategic alliances

Forging Nonprofit Alliances, Jane Arsenault, Jossey-Bass, 1998

Jane Arsenault is an experienced consultant who has been involved in many strategic alliances and mergers. This comprehensive guide is based on her practical experience with a wide range of strategic alliances. The main body of the book describes the many options for strategic alliances, when they are best used, the authority and control relationships, the integration of mission, values and culture, the risks and the management issues.

www.josseybass.com

The Collaboration Challenge, James Austin, Jossey-Bass, 2000

James Austin is Chairman of the Initiative on Social Enterprise at Harvard Business School. This excellent book demonstrates how nonprofit organisations and business create strategic alliances that benefit both. Packed with case studies, the book sets out how to identify opportunities, ensure strategic fit, generate value for both parties and manage the relationship. It ends with guidelines for collaborating successfully.

www.josseybass.com

The Nonprofit Mergers Workbook, David La Piana, Amherst Wilder Foundation, 2000

Subtitled 'The Leaders Guide to Considering, Negotiating and Executing a Merger', this thoughtful and practical book covers the options for structuring a merger, the pre-requisites for a successful merger, the assessment of potential partners, anticipating difficulties and roadblocks, negotiating stages and strategies and implementation. It includes a useful section on advice for consultants facilitating mergers.

www.wilder.org

Nonprofit funding

Nonprofit Capital – A Review of Problems and Strategies, William Ryan, Rockefeller Foundation, 2001

This is the reference for anyone wanting to understand the latest thinking on financing the capital requirements of nonprofit organisations. Written by one of the leading researchers who really understands the sector, it defines the need for different types of nonprofit capital. It sets out a series of proposals for reforming the nonprofit capital market and for reforms that funders and nonprofit organisations themselves could introduce. It finishes with a section on expanding access to private capital markets.

www.rockfound.org

Venture Philanthropy 2002, Community Wealth Ventures, Venture Philanthropy Partners, 2002

This is the third annual survey of organisations involved in venture philanthropy and high-engagement grantmaking. As well as a series of articles on the hot topics in the field by leader practitioners, the report sets out an overview of the field and details of most of the organisations operating this type of funding. It is a great read for anyone interested in venture philanthropy.

www.vppartners.org

Leadership and management

Leaders Who Make a Difference, Burt Nanus and Stephen Dobbs, Jossey-Bass, 1999

This book is specifically about the leadership of nonprofit organisations, establishes the key roles leaders have to discharge as visionaries, strategists, politicians, campaigners, coaches and change agents. Each role is illustrated with a pertinent case study, making the book essential reading for current and potential leaders.

www.josseybass.com

Understanding Nonprofit Organizations, J. Steven Ott (ed.), Boulder, Westview Press, 2001

This is a compendium of the best articles about the management of nonprofit organisations. It contains articles by many of the leading academics in the field written during the 1990s. They are more useful in understanding the history and context of nonprofit management. The articles cover governance, the legal framework, leadership, strategic planning, fundraising, entrepreneurship, contracts, budgets, managing volunteers, accountability and international organisations.

www.westviewpress.com

Governance

Boards that Make a Difference, John Carver, Jossey-Bass, 1997

Now in its second edition, this book sets out Carver's Policy Governance model. It describes itself as 'the world's most published and provocative authority on effective board design'. It covers his approach to board job design, board/staff relationships, the chief executive role and performance monitoring. Although seen as extreme by some, it applies rigour and makes readers think through what roles the board should deliver.

www.josseybass.com

Nonprofit Boards that Work – The End of One-Size-Fits All Governance, Maureen Robinson, Wiley, 2001

Maureen Robinson is better placed than many to write a book on governance, having been Director of Education at BoardSource for eight years. The book encourages boards to look at the particulars of their own organisation before determining the best approach to governance. It discusses the structure and substance of board work, board culture, the executive director/board partnership and the way individual members should discharge their roles.

www.wiley.com

Improving the Performance of Governing Boards, Richard Chait *et al.*, Oryx Press, 1996

Although derived from working mainly with education institutions, the three authors have between them huge experience of nonprofit boards. Their first book established the basic competencies required of boards and much more besides. This book, based on extensive research and practical experience, addresses the topics of effective trusteeship, board development, board cohesion, trustee education and the improvement of board processes. It also discusses effective ways of responding to the resistance some trustees exhibit towards board development.

Index